# Treating Alcohol Dependence

TREATMENT MANUALS FOR PRACTITIONERS
David H. Barlow, *Editor*


TREATING ALCOHOL DEPENDENCE
A COPING SKILLS TRAINING GUIDE
Peter M. Monti, David B. Abrams,
Ronald M. Kadden, and Ned L. Cooney

SELF-MANAGEMENT FOR ADOLESCENTS
A SKILLS-TRAINING PROGRAM
MANAGING EVERYDAY PROBLEMS
Thomas A. Brigham

PSYCHOLOGICAL TREATMENT OF PANIC
David H. Barlow and Jerome A. Cerny

# Treating Alcohol Dependence
## A Coping Skills Training Guide

PETER M. MONTI
Brown University and VA Medical Center, Providence

DAVID B. ABRAMS
Brown University and The Miriam Hospital, Providence

RONALD M. KADDEN
University of Connecticut School of Medicine, Farmington

NED L. COONEY
VA Medical Center and University of Connecticut School of
Medicine, Farmington

*Editor's Note by* David H. Barlow

*Foreword by* G. Alan Marlatt

THE GUILFORD PRESS
New York   London

© 1989 The Guilford Press
A Division of Guilford Publications, Inc.
72 Spring Street, New York, NY 10012

Printed in the United States of America

Last digit is print number: 9 8 7 6 5 4

**Library of Congress Cataloging-in-Publication Data**

Monti, Peter M.
    Treating alcohol dependence: A coping skills training guide / Peter M.
Monti, David B. Abrams, Ronald M. Kadden, Ned L. Cooney.
        p. cm.—(Treatment manuals for practitioners)
    Bibliography: p.
    Includes index.
    ISBN 0-89862-204-2     ISBN 0-89862-215-8 (soft)
    1. Alcoholism—Treatment.   2. Alcoholics—Rehabilitation.   3. Life
skills.   4. Adjustment (Psychology) I. Abrams, David B.   II. Kadden, Ronald M.
III. Cooney, Ned L.   IV. Title   V. Series
    [DNLM:  1. Adaptation, Psychological.   2. Alcoholism—
rehabilitation.   3. Interpersonal Relations.   4. Social Adjustment.
WM 274 M791c]
RC565.M634   1989
616.86'1—dc19
DNLM/DLC
for Library of Congress                                                88-36838
                                                                            CIP

## A Poison Tree

*I was angry with my friend:*
*I told my wrath, my wrath did end.*
*I was angry with my foe:*
*I told it not, my wrath did grow.*

*And I water'd it in fears,*
*Night & morning with my tears;*
*And I sunned it with smiles,*
*And with soft deceitful wiles.*

*And it grew both day and night,*
*Till it bore an apple bright;*
*And my foe beheld it shine,*
*And he knew that it was mine,*

*And into my garden stole*
*When the night had veil'd the pole:*
*In the morning glad I see*
*My foe outstretch'd beneath the tree.*

—WILLIAM BLAKE

# Editor's Note

This book presents the highly successful Brown University/ Providence VA treatment program for addictive behaviors. Originated with problem drinkers, a wealth of evidence has now been amassed supporting the effectiveness of this program with patients with alcohol abuse and dependence. As the authors point out, the principles presented in specific step-by-step detail in the book could be applied to a variety of other addictive behaviors with minimal adaptation.

Emanating from the tradition of skills training, this book recognizes the biological contribution to alcoholism and addictive behavior in general and incorporates this thinking into this highly successful program. A total of 28 sessions administered in either an inpatient or outpatient setting, as well as in either an individual or group format, are presented in such a way that the therapist can rearrange these sessions to fit any particular setting. Finally, presented for the first time in this manual are clinical procedures based on the recently established evidence for "cue reactivity" in the addictive behaviors which describes an involuntary but overwhelmingly strong physiological craving that seems to form the basis for the addiction. Any therapist treating problem drinkers or other individuals with addictive behavior would want to be familiar with this treatment program.

David H. Barlow
*Series Editor*

# Foreword

Research conducted on the effectiveness of various treatment approaches for alcohol dependence has shown mixed results. Surveys of the treatment outcome literature often conclude that no single treatment method, from chemical aversion to spiritual conversion, has been found to be more effective than any other approach. Such findings have led researchers and treatment professionals alike to search for commonalities in the "stages of change" that alcohol-dependent individuals pass through on the road to recovery. Studies have been conducted, for example, to compare those who are successful in response to treatment (treatment "survivors") with those who have relapsed, regardless of the treatment modality employed. Others have examined the "natural history" of overcoming alcohol dependency by assessing people who have overcome this problem on their own, without the benefit of treatment.

The overall pattern of results based on these research studies provides support for the skills training approach outlined in the present book. One such research finding shows that what happens to the patient after treatment has been completed has a greater influence in determining outcome than what happens during the treatment phase itself. Post-treatment factors such as the patient's social relationships, social support, employment environment, stress levels, and associated coping skills appear to play critical roles in recovery. As a result, treatment programs that fail to address these important post-treatment factors may be lacking the "essential ingredients" associated with successful outcomes. Many traditional programs primarily focus on motivational issues (e.g., information on adverse effects of excessive drinking and on alcoholism as a disease determined by biological factors)—in other words, they tell the patient WHY not to drink, but they often fail to provide necessary skills to show patients HOW not to drink. Although motivation is important in the recovery process, treatment goals must be coupled with training as the means required to attain one's goals. The present volume provides these means in the form of effective coping skills.

Readers who are unfamiliar with the cognitive and behavioral skills training approach to alcohol dependence may be surprised to find that these methods can be used in support of an abstinence goal. Many popular accounts have equated behavioral approaches with a controlled drinking goal. While it is true that controlled drinking methods have been pursued by some advocates of the behavioral approach, others have argued that these same methods can be applied in abstinence programs. In this case, coping skills can be acquired to prevent relapse and/or to intervene in the relapse process. Many of the skills outlined in the present volume are consistent with principles of relapse prevention. Research on the determinants of relapse has consistently shown that coping with high-risk situations associated with relapse (e.g., temptations associated with urges to drink) is an essential aspect of successful recovery. Some individuals who successfully maintain abstinence demonstrate effective coping even in the absence of formal skills training. Most, however, will benefit from a programmatic attempt to acquire and practice adaptive coping. In this sense, skills training helps accelerate the natural course of recovery.

The authors of this book represent a well-established and seasoned group of researchers/clinicians in the field of skills training. They have demonstrated in their writings and empirical studies that a skills-training approach is effective with a variety of clinical problems other than alcohol dependence. Skills-training has been applied by the authors to such diverse problems as smoking and psychiatric disorders with considerable success. This approach shows great promise in the treatment of alcohol dependence and other addictive behaviors.

This book is the first detailed training manual for skills training with alcohol-dependent individuals. I am impressed with the breadth and depth of the information presented on skills training and how to apply it in various clinical settings. The skills training material is broken into two main sections: Interpersonal skills (Chapter 2) and Intrapersonal skills (Chapter 3). Interpersonal skills include instructions in communication training, assertion, giving and receiving criticism, drink-refusal skills, and enhancing social support networks. Intrapersonal skills include cognitive coping with maladaptive thoughts, relaxation training, anger management, problem-solving, and planning for emergency situations associated with relapse risk. Skills in both the interpersonal and intrapersonal domains are important, since studies have shown that many relapses occur in both interpersonal (e.g., social pressure) and intrapersonal (e.g., negative emotional states) situations. Each skill is presented in detail, complete with step-by-step instructions. We are fortunate, therefore, in having access to a complete and comprehensive handbook of skills training methods in the form of this book.

The book itself offers more than just a detailed "how to" manual of skills training. It also provides us with a comprehensive literature review and theoretical rationale for this approach to treatment (Chapter 1), and it gives readers valuable assistance in implementing such programs in a variety of treatment settings, from inpatient to outpatient, and from group to individual therapy (Chapter 4). Finally, the authors have given us an updated account of the effectiveness of skills-training programs in the treatment of alcohol dependence, and have outlined directions for future clinical and research studies (Chapter 5).

The successful treatment of alcohol dependence remains an important challenge for society. According to some authorities, alcohol dependence is characterized by a "loss of control" and an inability to abstain from drinking. Yet those with alcohol problems can acquire skills to cope more effectively and thereby reduce the risk of relapse. The materials outlined in this book go a long way towards meeting this goal.

G. Alan Marlatt, PhD
Addictive Behaviors Research Center
University of Washington

# Acknowledgments

The authors wish to thank many individuals for their work that has contributed to this book. The initial drafts of some of the sessions that constitute Chapter 2 were taken from the first author's (P. M.) earlier social skills treatment manuals, which were developed in collaboration with Drs. James Curran, Donald Corriveau, William Norman, Toy Caldwell-Colbert, and Steven Hayes. Among the students who participated in the revisions of these sessions were Sue Hagerman and Gail Beck. Some of the materials for Chapter 3 were originally developed by David Abrams and Peter Monti for a relapse prevention program in collaboration with Drs. Roger Pinto, Richard Brown, and John Elder. Thanks go to all of these individuals.

A more recent generation of manuals, specifically written and/or revised for our work with alcoholics, was prepared by Dr. Jody Binkoff during her tenure working with Peter Monti and David Abrams at Brown University. While Jody's work is most apparent in Chapters 2 and 3, her contribution to this book goes far beyond these. In her role as coordinator of the research project that refined and evaluated our coping skills training program for alcoholics, Jody contributed immeasurably to our thinking, writing, and clinical work.

We also thank those authors of clinical handbooks and other manuals whose ideas and techniques were sometimes adapted for our work with alcoholics. We have attempted to acknowledge these contributions in the text.

We are grateful to the many students and therapists who made use of these materials in our clinical trials and who provided us with much valuable feedback.

The work of Peter Monti and David Abrams was supported, in part, by a Veterans Administration Merit Review Grant, by National Heart, Lung and Blood Institute Grant No. 5-R01-HL32318, and by National Cancer Institute Grant No. 5-R01-CA38309. The work of

Ronald Kadden and Ned Cooney was supported by National Institute of Alcohol Abuse and Alcoholism Grant No. 5-P5D-AA03510 and by the Alcohol Research Center at the University of Connecticut. We also wish to thank Lori Kessler, Elyes Moore, and Deborah Talamini for their patience and hard work in preparing the manuscript.

Finally, it is with love and appreciation that we dedicate this book to Sylvia Monti, Marion Wachtenheim, Renana Kadden, and Judith Lifshitz Cooney.

# Contents

# 1

## Introduction and Theoretical Rationale

### Introduction and Outline for This Book

We have been guided in our work over the past 10 years by an emerging cognitive–social learning perspective on alcohol use and abuse. This model, in combination with our earlier work on social competence and psychiatric disorder (Curran & Monti, 1982; Monti, Corriveau, & Curran, 1982; Monti, Curran, Corriveau, DeLancey, & Hagerman, 1980), has resulted in the development of a comprehensive coping skills treatment program, which forms the core of this book. The central tenet of the coping skills approach to treatment is that through a variety of learning techniques (behavioral rehearsal, modeling, cognitive restructuring, didactic instruction), individuals and their social networks can be taught to use alternative methods of coping with the demands of living without using maladaptive addictive substances such as alcohol.

The skills that constitute the core of this handbook were designed for clients diagnosed according to the revised third edition of the *Diagnostic and Statistical Manual of Mental Disorders* (DSM-III-R; American Psychiatric Association, 1987) as alcohol-dependent. However, clients diagnosed as alcohol abusers or individuals with less severe drinking problems can also benefit from the skill components presented in this book. Furthermore, given the assumption that addictive behavior is related to difficulties in coping, the skills training offered here may also be effective in the treatment of other drug abuse problems. Thus, we have found that our approach is very appropriate for the increasing numbers of alcoholics who also abuse other substances, such as cocaine, marijuana, and sedative drugs. Regardless of a client's diagnosis, the orientation of the treatment program in this book is abstinence from all substances of abuse. The consensus at the present time is that abstinence is the treatment goal of choice for clients diagnosed as alcohol- or drug-dependent (Nathan, 1986).

The application of a general coping skills training approach to the treatment of alcohol dependence has grown out of several treatment programs that were, in part, based on the principles of social learning theory (SLT). In an early program, Miller and Mastria (1977) developed a handbook that focused on "problems in living." Another behavioral treatment program has more recently been described by McCrady, Dean, Dubreuil, and Swanson (1985). A major focus of that program is on functional analysis of the relationships between and among antecedents, behaviors, and consequences. Although the McCrady et al. (1985) treatment program is well described in their chapter, the limitations of presentation in the context of a single chapter preclude as detailed a presentation as that offered in the present book. We believe that there is a need for a clinical handbook that describes, in considerable detail, a well-integrated program of behavioral group therapy for alcoholism.

In this first chapter, we review the historical roots of the coping skills approach to alcoholism and lay out the rationale for the coping skills training program. Although much of this first chapter takes the form of a selective review of the pertinent research literature, we have attempted to integrate examples from our clinical experience.

Chapters 2, 3, and 4 represent the core of our program, which has been developed and empirically tested in both inpatient and outpatient alcohol treatment settings. This core is interwoven with clinical examples and anecdotes. The final chapter considers treatment outcome and other data on the effectiveness of skills training approaches, as well as challenges for future work.

## Historical Roots of the Coping Skills
## Approach to Alcoholism

The techniques, principles, and approaches to alcohol dependence outlined in this book are derived in part from an emerging model that construes addictive behavior as a habitual, maladaptive way of coping with stress. Major life events; everyday hassles; family, work, and community concerns; and individual lifestyle are all instances of the "stressors" that must be resolved. The resultant strain placed on an individual is also influenced by biological/genetic vulnerability to stressors, by behavioral deficits or excesses that are a result of an individual's social learning history, and by acute situational demands. Thus, the interaction of biopsychosocial factors is crucial to understanding the reasons for abuse (see Abrams, 1983).

"Stress" may be defined as an "adaptational relationship" (Marlatt, 1985b) between an individual and a situational demand (stressor). Accordingly, the conceptual framework adopted in this book views stress as resulting from an imbalance between environmental demands and an individual's resources (Shiffman & Wills, 1985; Wills & Shiffman, 1985). "Coping" is an attempt to meet the demand in a way that restores balance or equilibrium. If the individual does not have adequate coping skills in his/her repertoire to meet the demand, then alcohol may be used as an attempt to restore equilibrium (to cope). An "adaptive orientation" (Alexander & Hadaway, 1982; Marlatt, 1985b) views addiction within a comprehensive biopsychosocial framework as an attempt to adapt to stress.

According to Moos (1985), an "adaptive orientation" to addiction has historical roots based on: (1) stress and coping theory (based on studies of adaptation to life crises and transitions, e.g., Lazarus & Folkman, 1985); (2) psychoanalytic theory and ego psychology (based on Freud's notions of ego defense mechanisms and unconscious conflicts); (3) evolutionary theory and behavior modification (stemming from Darwin's evolutionary perspective on adaptation and more recently on classical and operant conditioning); and (4) life cycle perspectives (e.g., Erikson's [1963] stages). Beyond these historical roots, Marlatt (1985b) places additional emphasis on both SLT (Bandura, 1977) and cognitive–behavioral therapy (e.g., Meichenbaum, 1977; Wilson & O'Leary, 1980). The content and process material outlined in this book are derived from an evolving SLT model of alcohol use and abuse that assumes an "adaptive orientation." (The reader unfamiliar with cognitive–behavioral theory and treatment is referred to O'Leary & Wilson, 1975, for a general presentation of techniques and outcome.)

SLT acknowledges the role of biological and genetic factors in alcohol dependence. Although it is true that alcoholism runs in families, SLT holds that this phenomenon can best be understood by considering the interaction between genetic influences and psychosocial factors (Abrams & Wilson, 1986; MacAndrew & Edgerton, 1969). It has become increasingly clear that there is a genetic predisposition for alcoholism. This fact is based on several sources of evidence, including (1) studies of adoptees, in which sons of alcoholic fathers who were adopted were compared to similarly adopted sons of nonalcoholic fathers, and were found to be four times more likely to become alcoholic (Goodwin, 1977); and (2) studies of alcoholics with half-siblings, which showed that the half-siblings who were also alcoholic were three times more likely to have a natural parent who was alcoholic than the siblings who were nonalcoholic (Schuckit, Goodwin, & Winokur, 1972). Clearly, these and other studies support a genetic influence in the development of alcoholism in males. However, there is also support in these studies showing that "sociocultural influences are critically important in the majority of genetically predisposed individuals, suggest[ing] that changes in behavior and social attitudes by and toward individuals at high risk can alter both the course and prevalence of alcohol abuse and alcoholism" (National Institute on Alcohol Abuse and Alcoholism, 1983, p. 19). Thus, it is possible that a genetic vulnerability interacts with psychosocial factors, resulting in coping skills deficits that require a skills training approach for remediation.

The SLT model is derived from the principles of experimental, social, and cognitive psychology. It has also been referred to as the "addictive behavior model" of alcohol use (Marlatt & Gordon, 1985). The major assumption is that clients can take responsibility for learning new behaviors and can learn to better manage their genetic and social learning vulnerabilities. It is of interest to note that the shift from a disease model, or from a focus on pathology identification, to skills training has also been identified as the "deficit-to-competence movement" (Brickman et al., 1982; Meichenbaum, Butler, & Gruson, 1981; Pentz, 1985). Although an understanding of etiology and aspects of current pathology is useful for diagnosis and treatment, those factors that maintain alcoholism, and the coping skills that must be mastered to overcome them, can be independent of the factors involved in etiology.

## Social Learning Theory of Alcohol Consumption: Early Formulations

In an early formulation of SLT, Bandura (1969) stated that "alcoholics are people who have acquired, through differential reinforcement and modeling experiences, alcohol consumption as a widely generalized dominant response to aversive stimulation" (p. 536). Central to Bandura's theory is the assumption that consuming alcohol has negatively reinforcing effects (i.e., further drinking becomes more likely because it has been associated with an apparent reduction of stress). Alcohol use is then generalized to other aversive conditions and is reinforced by what is perceived as a reduction of tension (see Cappell & Greeley, 1987, for a detailed coverage of tension reduction theory). After prolonged and excessive alcohol use, physical dependence and avoidance of withdrawal are also thought to maintain consumption.

Unlike earlier theories of alcohol use, Bandura's (1969) theory implies that all drinking behavior, from moderation to abuse, is governed by the same principles. Drinking behaviors vary as a function of settings and time, but there is no fixed gradation through stages of alcoholism, as suggested by Jellinek (1960). Likewise, there are no fixed personality factors (e.g., "alcoholic personality"; Miller, 1978).

SLT goes beyond the notion that learning occurs exclusively through conditioning processes. According to Bandura (1977), SLT emphasizes cognitive mediational factors in the explanation of learning and behavior. The theory postulates that an individual's expectations about alcohol's effects will influence his/her behavior when intoxicated. SLT suggests that drinking is acquired and maintained by reinforcement, modeling, conditioned responding, expectations about alcohol's effects, and physical dependence.

A broad-spectrum behavioral approach to treatment has been in existence since at least the mid-1960s. Lazarus (1965) proposed an approach to problem drinking that included (1) medical attention to alcohol-related physical problems; (2) conditioning to modify or eliminate abusive drinking; (3) behavioral assessment to identify specific stimulus antecedents of anxiety that trigger drinking; (4) assertiveness training to equip the client to respond more appropriately to interpersonal stressful situations; (5) behavioral rehearsal to develop more effective interpersonal coping skills; (6) counterconditioning of anxiety responses; and (7) marital therapy to help the client's spouse modify his/her role in maintaining the problem drinking.

## Social Learning Theory of Alcohol Consumption: Central Principles

Since its beginnings, SLT has generated much basic and clinical research on alcohol and its abuse (Wilson, in press). A recent comprehensive review (Abrams & Niaura, 1987) of this research has identified a set of principles that form a comprehensive version of an SLT of alcohol use and dependence. Since the core of this book reflects the application of many of these principles, we shall review them and provide selected examples here.

One principle of SLT embodies the developmental notion that learning to drink occurs as part of growing up in a particular culture in which the social influences of family and peers shape the behaviors, beliefs, and expectancies of young people concerning alcohol. Youthful drinking is influenced by the modeling of alcohol consumption; the creation of specific expectations of the benefits of drinking via media portrayals of sexual prowess, power, and success; and by social reinforcement from peer groups.

In support of this principle of cultural transmission is the fact that the attitudes and behaviors of parents regarding alcohol appear to be among the best predictors of adolescent drinking (Barnes, 1977; O'Leary, O'Leary, & Donovan, 1976). Indeed, we have frequently observed examples of children who associate their parents' relaxation time with drinking. Just as the family dog may be conditioned to fetch a newspaper as Dad sits down in his comfortable chair after a hard day at work, the children may be taught to go automatically for a cold beer to help Daddy relax. We are convinced that such scenarios occur in both alcoholic and nonalcoholic households, and increasingly with mothers as well as fathers. However, the relationship to parental behavior is complex. Conflicting parental attitudes toward alcohol are related to excessive youthful drinking (Jackson & Connor, 1953), and the children of abstainers who have fixed and extreme attitudes toward temperance are at increased risk for developing problems (Wittman, 1939).

Marlatt and his associates have studied the effects of peer modeling on drinking for more than a decade. In an early report, Caudill and Marlatt (1975), studying heavy-drinking college students, showed that those who were exposed to a heavy-drinking model drank more than those exposed to either a light-drinking model or no model at all. Other studies have shown that modeling effects are influenced by gender and drinking history (Lied & Marlatt, 1979), by the nature of the interaction between drinking partners (Collins, Parks, & Marlatt, 1985), and by the setting in which drinking occurs (Strickler, Dobbs, & Maxwell, 1979). The overall results of the modeling phenomenon are robust (Abrams & Niaura, 1987).

Modeling techniques are used therapeutically in the coping skills training program described in this book. As each new skill is introduced, the therapists demonstrate the performance of the skill. Other potential sources of modeling influences are group members themselves, as well as relatives (when relatives are included in treatment groups).

An important effect of both parental and peer modeling may be the development of internalized expectancies for alcohol effects. Indeed, Biddle, Bank, and Marlin (1980) suggest that modeled behaviors get translated into expectancies, which are more important direct determinants of drinking than modeling itself. The phenomena of alcohol-related expectancies and their effect on drinking have been studied extensively (Marlatt & Rohsenow, 1980; Wilson, 1978; Wilson, Perold, & Abrams, 1981) and form another principle of SLT.

Brown, Goldman, Inn, and Anderson (1980) developed an Alcohol Expectancy Questionnaire that has been administered to a variety of populations. The results of studies done with this questionnaire show that adolescents' expectancies of positive alcohol effects predate their actual experiences with drinking. In addition, the more heavily a person drinks, the more reinforcing qualities he/she expects alcohol to provide, with alcoholics expecting the most reinforcement (see review by Christiansen & Brown, 1985). Rohsenow (1983), using a modification and extension of the scale to distinguish between beliefs about the effects of alcohol on oneself and beliefs about its effects on people in general, found that heavy drinkers most strongly expected to obtain social/physical pleasure and decreased social inhibition from alcohol, and least expected alcohol to enhance their own aggression or sexual pleasure. All drinkers studied expected to become impaired and careless after drinking, but heavier drinkers also expected many positive alcohol effects. Interestingly, we have recently found that alcohol expectancy effects do not predict relapse following our treatment program (Rohsenow, Monti, Binkoff, Zwick, & Abrams, 1988), whereas Brown (1985) did find that expectancy predicted relapse. Clearly, there is much yet to be learned about the role of alcohol expectancies in the treatment of alcoholism. (See Monti, Rohsenow, Abrams, & Binkoff, 1988, for further consideration of alcohol expectancy effects.)

Although it is likely that alcohol-related expectancies are first inculcated by parents and peers, other cultural agents such as the media are likely to have an influence as well. For example, a child who sees his/her parents reach for a martini or two to ease the stress of a hard day at work, or to enhance their ability to socialize at a party, is likely to have these notions reinforced and generalized when watching alcohol-related scenes on television. Peers may serve as additional models for using alcohol to reduce tension, and may further reinforce its use to enhance social pleasure. The adolescent who never learns ways to modulate anxiety without alcohol may come to rely increasingly upon alcohol to decrease stress in more and more situations, thus increasing the risk for developing alcoholism.

Although the steps from bringing Daddy a beer to learning to relax only when drinking may be numerous and may span many years, it is not difficult to imagine the stages of this process.

Interestingly, our clinical work suggests that many adult children of alcoholics claim that they have chosen substances other than alcohol (e.g., marijuana, cocaine) because they did not wish to become alcoholics. Thus, it seems that individuals may have imitated the substance abuse behavior of their parent(s), but have been more directly influenced by the behavior of their peers and situational factors (e.g., availability) when choosing a particular substance.

Reinforcement is another central principle of SLT. Alcohol use is strongly influenced by positive reinforcement (e.g., feelings of euphoria or getting "high"; Wills & Shiffman, 1985) or by the expectation of positive reinforcement (Marlatt, 1985b). Alcohol enhances cutaneous and gastric blood flow, and thereby results in a feeling of warmth (Grunberg & Baum, 1985). It may be that some maturing adolesents never learn alternative ways to experience positive feelings and sensations, and thus alcohol use develops to serve this need. Social reinforcement, whether through increased conviviality, gaining the attention of others, or release from responsibilities, is another important potential source of reinforcement for drinking behavior. Negative reinforcement (the strengthening of behavior by termination or avoidance of unpleasant experiences) may also be a potent factor in developing or maintaining drinking problems, through reduction of tension or negative moods, relief from pain, or release from social inhibitions. Clearly, both the positive and the negative reinforcing aspects of alcohol consumption should be considered when assessing clients and planning their treatment.

A fourth principle involves the role of environmental stimuli, which either may elicit drinking by means of a Pavlovian conditioning mechanism, or may set the occasion for the operant behavior of drinking. A two-factor conditioning model of alcoholic drinking (Kadden, Pomerleau, & Meyer, 1984) combines Pavlovian and operant mechanisms: Stimuli that are frequently paired with alcohol ingestion or withdrawal eventually become capable of eliciting physiological responses, which in turn serve as discriminative stimuli that occasion operant drinking behavior. This two-factor model may help to account for the perseverative nature of alcoholic behavior by virtue of its inclusion of involuntary elicited responding, which often occurs without awareness on the part of the individual. Studies in our laboratories have begun to elucidate some of the parameters of the conditioning process (e.g., Abrams, Monti, Carey, Pinto, & Jacobus, 1988; Cooney, Baker, Pomerleau, & Josephy, 1984; Monti et al.,

1987; Pomerleau, Fertig, Baker, & Cooney, 1983) and its effect on the drink refusal skills of alcoholics (Binkoff et al., 1988).

The clinical response to these conditioning phenomena may involve the identification and rearrangement of environmental drinking cues (Miller & Mastria, 1977). Clients are advised to avoid certain situations that are determined to be high in risk; to avoid former drinking companions; and to develop alternative activities for high-risk times of the day that are incompatible with drinking. Doing these things may require considerable rearrangement of schedules or activities, but this is critical in the early stages of recovery. Clients are also taught behavioral and cognitive skills for coping with stimuli that elicit cravings and/or drinking. Eventually, clients may be gradually reintroduced to former high-risk situations, but the situational cues then become associated with nondrinking activities.

The conditioning model carries the implication that extinction, by repeated presentations of alcohol-related conditioned stimuli in the absence of alcohol consumption, will reduce the effectiveness of the stimuli to elicit drinking behavior. Although we have employed extinction procedures clinically (Cooney, Baker, & Pomerleau, 1983), they have not as yet been adequately validated and thus have not been included in this handbook. The interested reader is referred to Niaura et al. (1988) for a conceptual overview and further treatment implications of the cue reactivity phenomenon.

In addition to social learning history and contextual cues, SLT emphasizes the importance of current experience and other cognitive and emotional factors. Abrams and Niaura (1987) refer to the immediate cognitive and environmental determinants of drinking as "proximal determinants" and include among them antecedents such as the environmental setting, the individual's repertoire of general and drinking-relevant coping and problem-solving skills (e.g., drink refusal skills), beliefs and expectations, and the current cognitive–emotional physiological state of the individual.

Cognitive factors other than expectancies also play a central role in Bandura's theory, and they are thought to modulate all person–environment interactions. Whether or not a person drinks in a particular situation is determined by the principle of self-efficacy and outcome expectations. "Self-efficacy," an individual's sense that he/she can cope successfully in a particular situation, is another SLT principle relevant to alcohol consumption. A person's confidence that he/she can cope in a specific situation, and his/her estimation of the chances of succeeding, will determine the selection of coping behaviors. Clinically, clients must develop *strong* and *realistic* confidence that they can cope with life's demands without having to drink.

Realistic confidence develops gradually over time, and it is necessary actually to engage in coping behavior in the natural environment to enhance one's sense of mastery. Often alcoholics in the early phases of treatment have very high confidence that they will "never drink again." This is usually treated with some skepticism by experienced alcohol counselors; these alcoholics are usually unrealistic or overly confident individuals who have not yet experienced how difficult it is to stay sober. Gradual exposure to more and more difficult situations, and successful avoidance of drinking in these situations, helps one to develop a realistic sense of confidence in one's control over drinking. Graduated practice is therefore emphasized, both in actual treatment sessions and between treatment sessions.

By way of summarizing the foregoing principles, consider the following example: Imagine a person in a high state of distress because of a recent marital argument and pressure at work. The individual attends a party where the expectations are to relax and enjoy. Several of his/her friends are already drinking and having a good time (modeling influences). Coping will be determined by the individual's general and specific coping skills and self-efficacy expectations. Self-efficacy percepts will be influenced by the individual's current stress level and history of coping in similar situations. The individual's expectations about the short- and long-term effects of drinking on behavior will also be important. That is, the individual may emphasize the immediate positive outcome expectations of the effects of alcohol (e.g., relaxation and euphoria), while ignoring the longer-term negative consequences (e.g., hangover, depression, accidents). If drinking is initiated, various actual reinforcing effects of alcohol may come into play. In sum, a combination of social learning, situational, cognitive, and biological/psychophysiological factors will interact with one another. This interaction will result in self-efficacy expectations leading to behavior that can vary from abstinence and finding alternatives to drinking on the one hand, to drinking to excess on the other. We feel it is important that both clients and therapists understand and attend to these multiple factors in determining clients' vulnerabilities that will require treatment.

## Rationale for Coping Skills Training

Most of the treatment material presented in this book is derived from the general principles of SLT, and a major emphasis has been placed on skills training per se. Thus it may be useful to consider, in some detail, the rationale for these skills training procedures. In the broader context of an SLT of alcohol abuse, we view coping skills deficits as a major predisposing individual risk factor. Skill deficits interact with situational demands and genetic vulnerability, and may undermine an individual's ability to cope effectively. We shall attempt to show here that coping skills deficits are related to the development and maintenance of problem drinking, as well as to recovery and the potential for relapse.

There are at least two major categories of factors that can increase the risk of alcohol abuse, or of relapse after abstinence. These are *inter*personal factors, such as social supports, marital and family relationships, and work relationships; and *intra*personal factors, such as cognitions, perceptions, expectations, and mood, and the skills to manage these. In the following sections, we shall present the rationale for our focusing on these two major elements in our treatment program.

## Interpersonal Considerations

A major thesis of our treatment program is that social skills deficits may restrict alternatives of actions in a social situation, minimize an individual's control over the situation, and decrease the individual's access to desired resources (Bandura, 1969). In addition, such deficits may prevent the individual from obtaining social and emotional support from others that may be necessary to maintain abstinence. Social skills deficits may also increase intrapersonal risk factors—for example, by producing increased anxiety or tension in social encounters. Situations have been conceptualized as "high in risk for drinking" if the individual does not possess adequate skills for coping with the situation at hand, and if drinking has been learned as a response providing at least short-term relief (Marlatt & Gordon, 1985). If social skills deficits are chronic over the course of psychosocial development, the individual's potential for abusive drinking may increase (cf. Monti, Abrams, Binkoff, & Zwick, 1986).

It is important to note that, for some individuals, social anxiety may mediate the relationship between social skills deficits and alcohol abuse. An individual may have the required skills in his/her behavioral repertoire, but may not be able to execute them because of debilitating anxiety. Here the social skills deficit would be viewed as secondary (Trower, Yardley, Bryant, & Shaw, 1978), in contrast to the primary skills deficit discussed previously. Although it is important to consider the nature of the observed skills deficit when considering assessment and treatment (Bandura, 1977), repeated practice in high-risk social encounters is likely both to improve social skills and to reduce social anxiety. Thus, anxiety may be reduced without focusing on it specifically.

The following section considers the role of developmental factors in social skills deficits.

## DEVELOPMENTAL STUDIES

In an extensive review, O'Leary et al. (1976) examined the empirical evidence supporting the notion that prealcoholics can be considered deficient in social skills. They cite evidence showing that parents of problem drinkers are frequently heavy drinkers or problem drinkers themselves (Robins, Bates, & O'Neal, 1962; Rosenberg, 1969), and that the parents tend to show approval of their children's drinking. As Bandura (1969) points out, in familial situations where alcohol consumption is modeled across a variety of circumstances and as a means of coping with stress, children are likely to learn a similar pattern of drinking. It may be that some children of problem drinkers learn that heavy drinking is necessary for adequate coping in interpersonal situations. These children may never learn appropriate social skills that could be utilized effectively in the absence of alcohol.

Several studies focusing on adolescent and college-age problem drinkers are pertinent to the formulation of O'Leary et al. (1976). Jones (1968) showed that, during high school, prealcoholic boys were judged to be less productive, less socially perceptive, less calm, and more sensitive to criticism. Similarly, Braucht, Brakarsh, Follingstad, and Berry (1973) found that adolescents who drank heavily were overly aggressive, impulsive, and generally deficient in personal controls. These findings have been extended by Asher and Renshaw (1984), who found that children and adolescents at risk for alcohol abuse were likely to have poor social skills, and by Cadoret, O'Gorman, Troughton, and Heywood (1985), who found that symptoms characteristic of an antisocial personality were related to development of later alcoholism. Finally, the recent work of Jessor (1984) suggests that problem drinking in adolescents co-occurs with other problem behavior that may be considered antisocial (e.g., delinquency and precocious sexuality).

Regardless of the nature or the cause of the problems found in some children of alcoholics (e.g., conduct disorder, attention deficit disorder), if the behavioral repertoire suggests deficiencies in skills, then remedial skills training is indicated. Thus, Tarter and Edwards

(1986), after reviewing the biobehavioral determinants of the behavioral disturbances of children "at risk" as well as the behavioral "risk" factors for alcoholism, suggest that "social skills training would be expected to enhance treatment success" (p. 356).

Excessive drinking in adolescence and adulthood also seems to coincide with difficult peer relationships. Lentz (1941) reported that heavy-drinking young adults had few extracurricular activities and more interpersonal maladjustment. Similarly, Kalin (1972) found that college-age problem drinkers were more "antisocially assertive" and were less involved in long-term relationships. Other data cited by O'Leary et al. (1976) include the findings that alcoholics were more often single, separated, or divorced (Koller & Castanos, 1969; Rosenberg, 1969) and showed decreased levels of social competence (Levine & Zigler, 1973). O'Leary et al. (1976) conclude that problem drinkers find it increasingly difficult to establish and maintain social relationships expected of individuals, and that their social behavior is inadequately or only partially learned, rather than learned and then forgotten. They speculate that "with prealcoholics there is a two-fold process involved which prevents the acquisition of more appropriate social responses and which serves to maintain an inadequate and maladaptive response repertoire" (p. 115). In support of this observation, Braucht et al. (1973) showed that adolescent problem drinkers select heavy drinkers for friends, thereby making it less likely that they will learn more appropriate social behavior from their peers.

The link between deficits in social competence and abusive drinking has been extended to include the abuse of other drugs, such as nicotine (Abrams et al., 1987) and the opioid peptides (Kolko, Sirota, Monti, & Paolino, 1985; Monti et al., 1986). Indeed, correlational studies have shown that cigarette smoking in early adolescents is related to inadequate social skills, such as inability to refuse cigarette offers (McAlister, Perry, & Maccoby, 1979).

In summary, there is growing support for the notion that socialization deficits may predispose an individual to abusive drinking or other substance abuse. In a vulnerable adolescent, these deficits may in part predispose the adolescent toward becoming involved with peers who themselves provide a poor source of peer models for normal socialization. Involvement with a heavy-drinking subculture further exacerbates maladaptive adjustment, including abusive drinking. In adolescents who became severely addicted, important developmental milestones may never be achieved. Alcohol use may serve to maintain pre-existing socialization deficits or may prevent the learning of more appropriate social skills as development continues. Next, we will briefly consider selected assessment and analogue studies that further link social skills and alcohol abuse.

ASSESSMENT AND ANALOGUE STUDIES

Sturgis, Best, and Calhoun (1977) demonstrated a link between assertiveness and problem drinking in a study in which they compared problem drinkers to a college student control group. In a follow-up study, Sturgis, Calhoun, and Best (1979) found that among problem drinkers, two groups could be identified: (1) passive, less assertive individuals who reported that they drank in order to facilitate social interaction; and (2) highly assertive individuals who reported drinking to change their sensations and to reduce boredom.

Hamilton and Maisto (1979) studied problem drinkers and a matched group of nonproblem drinkers on self-report and behavioral tests of assertiveness and discomfort. Results showed that although there were no differences between groups on assertiveness, problem drinkers reported more discomfort in situations that required assertiveness.

In a rather extensive study, Miller and Eisler (1977) examined two groups of psychiatric patients, one with drinking problems and one without, on self-report and role-play measures of assertiveness and drinking. Both patient groups showed equal deficits on the role-play measure of assertiveness. Interestingly, the problem drinkers perceived themselves as being more assertive and consumed more alcohol.

Given the implication of skills deficits in alcoholics, an important theme in the skills assessment research has been more precise identification of the exact nature of such deficits (Monti et al., 1986). Whereas earlier studies focused on the general social skills of alcoholics (e.g., Monti, Corriveau, & Zwick, 1981), more recent work has sought to identify specific alcohol-related skill deficits. Twentyman et al. (1982) used a 50-item audiotaped role-play test to compare problem drinkers and a control sample. Items represented two categories of specific skills (drink refusal, and frustrating interpersonal situations requiring assertiveness) and three categories of general skills (other types of refusals, expression of positive sentiment, and response to positive sentiment). Overall, problem drinkers gave shorter responses, and their responses contained fewer speech dysfluencies. However, their responses were generally worse than those of the controls on a subset of the drink refusal items. There were no between-group deficiencies on general skills.

We have recently developed a role-play measure of social skills in alcohol-relevant situations. The situations include five interpersonal situations (in which a confederate participates in a role play with the subject) and five intrapersonal situations (in which the subject is instructed to respond to a situation that does not involve the presence of another individual). The 10 situations comprise a behavioral instrument called the Alcohol-Specific Role-Play Test (ASRPT). The situations represent categories of drinking situations that were derived from a behavior-analytic study of alcoholics' drinking situations (Monti, Zwick, Binkoff, Abrams, & Nirenberg, 1984). This type of situational analysis should be clinically relevant, because it was derived empirically from actual drinking situations elicited from a sample of alcoholics. In a recent study of general and alcohol-relevant skills deficits of alcoholics (Abrams et al., in press), this instrument was tested along with a standardized behavioral measure of general social skill (the Simulated Social Interaction Test; Monti, Wallander, Ahern, Abrams, & Munroe, 1983). When compared to a control group, alcoholics were found to be less skillful on the ASRPT. There were no differences between groups on measures of general social skills. The ASRPT has also been used to evaluate (see Chapter 5) the interpersonal and intrapersonal coping skills techniques presented in the core of this book.

In addition to the above-described studies on the assessment of assertion and other social skills, several experimental analogue studies have suggested that, as social stress increases, alcohol consumption increases as well. Higgins and Marlatt (1975) have found this to be true in social drinking populations, and Miller, Hersen, Eisler, and Hilsman (1974) found that problem drinkers tended to consume more alcohol than moderate drinkers in an analogue situation. Furthermore, heavy drinkers who were given the means to cope effectively with an anxiety-provoking situation consumed less alcohol than did those for whom there is no means of coping (Marlatt, Kosturn, & Lang, 1975). When taken together, these studies suggest that a combination of a stressful situation with an inability to cope effectively can lead to an increase in alcohol consumption.

## Intrapersonal Considerations

### EXPERIMENTAL STUDIES AND THEIR IMPLICATIONS

Just as several lines of evidence have implicated interpersonal factors in alcohol abuse, there is reason to believe that intrapersonal factors play a significant role as well. Consistent with the "adaptational" model outlined above, abusive drinking may serve as a means of coping with negative affect. According to the tension reduction hypothesis, alcohol is reinforcing because it reduces tension, and individuals consume alcohol to obtain this effect. Although experimental studies have not always supported this hypothesis (Cappell & Greeley, 1987), it is undoubtedly valid under certain circumstances (e.g., with a relatively low dose of alcohol) and in certain individuals (e.g., Sher, 1987; Sher & Levenson, 1982).

Even if alcohol does not always reduce tension or stress, many people believe that it will. Laboratory research on expectancy indicates that cognitions and expectations about the effects of alcohol on behavior must be carefully assessed and targeted for modification during treatment. For example, cognitive restructuring exercises might help a client to replace thoughts about drinking as the "only" method to calm down after a fight. Alternative thoughts can be substituted, such as "My wife doesn't really hate me as a person; she was just mad at me for being late and not telling her ahead of time." Other coping behaviors could also be substituted, such as deep breathing or going for a brisk walk. Training in altering expectations and cognitions, as well as other intrapersonal coping methods, may reduce the likelihood of drinking after the next marital conflict.

Alcoholics tend to focus on the positive, immediate effects of drinking and to ignore or minimize the longer-term negative or destructive consequences of drinking. This is all the more likely in a high-risk situation, where proximal determinants have their strongest effect (Cooney, Gillespie, Baker, & Kaplan, 1987). Thoughts about the positive effects of drinking enable alcoholics to rationalize their decision to drink, since the short-term "pros" of drinking usually appear to outweigh the long-term "cons" of drinking. Treatment must specifically alter alcoholics' cognitive structures so that the "cons" of drinking begin to outweigh the "pros" *prior* to actual consumption. This creates more balanced, realistic expectations, and reduces the chances of a lapse or binge. Cognitive exercises such as covert rehearsal, imagery, and thought stopping, as well as the use of concrete reminders (e.g., index cards that list the negative consequences of drinking), can all help to bring these negative consequences into sharp focus *prior to* an actual drinking episode. Alcoholics are taught to catch themselves thinking about the positive consequences of drinking ("One little drink will help me relax at this party") and substitute a more balanced viewpoint for decision making ("Stop! Remember that the last time I got drunk, I punched someone out and landed in jail overnight. Perhaps I should try to relax another way by finding someone to talk to about last night's baseball game").

The next section considers developmental factors that may influence the perception of control in alcoholics.

DEVELOPMENTAL STUDIES

One of the strongest findings from developmental studies in support of the importance of intrapersonal factors in alcohol abuse is the evidence pointing to disturbed behavioral regulation. Tarter, Alterman, and Edwards (1985), in a thorough review of the psychological and neurological literature, found that males who are vulnerable to alcoholism have been "tentatively demonstrated" to have disturbance in intrapersonal aspects of functioning, such as cognition, emotion, motivation, and arousal regulation. Tarter and Edwards (1986) conclude, after reviewing the available limited evidence, that an association exists among impulsivity, high activity, attentional problems, and adolescent alcohol abuse. The notion that some individuals consume alcohol because of a relative lack of perceived personal control is consistent with these studies.

Based on research studying the tension reduction hypothesis and the tentative implications from the studies cited above, it is likely that interventions that teach skills to enhance cognitive control over behavior will be useful for alcoholics. Tarter and Edwards (1986) argue that relaxation training should be effective in treating the emotional lability and anxiety that have been reported in some studies to antedate alcoholism, and Klajner, Hartman, and Sobell (1984) also present a rationale for the use of relaxation training for substance abusers. The latter authors conclude that "there is some evidence that relaxation training techniques can produce an increase in the individual's perceived sense of control, and that they may be of benefit in subsequent coping with natural stressors" (p. 46). In Chapter 3, we will describe other techniques for coping with intrapersonal stress.

## Studying Relapse and Broader-Based Conceptual Models

In addition to using SLT to guide choice of treatment procedures, one can also consider the process of relapsing to alcohol abuse in the context of SLT. Because this topic has been considered more thoroughly elsewhere (Abrams, Niaura, Carey, Monti, & Binkoff, 1986; Brownell, Marlatt, Lichtenstein, & Wilson, 1986; Marlatt & Gordon, 1985; Monti, Rohsenow, et al., 1988), here we shall briefly consider several assessment studies that implicate coping skills deficits. Investigations of relapse precipitants have discovered that situations posing a high risk for relapse to alcohol abuse include interpersonal anger and frustration, social pressure, intrapersonal negative emotional states, and stimulus-elicited craving (Marlatt & Gordon, 1980). This analysis suggests that to prevent relapse, comprehensive treatment strategies may need to focus both on developing social skills to cope with interpersonal stressors and on cognitive–behavioral mood management skills to cope with negative affective states.

In addition, Rosenberg (1983) showed that nonrelapsed alcoholics responded to problem situations more assertively, and with more effective drink refusal, than those alcoholics who relapsed. In her studies concerning the precipitants of relapse, Litman and colleagues (Litman, Eiser, Rawson, & Oppenheim, 1979; Litman, Stapleton, Oppenheim, Peleg, & Jackson, 1983) have shown that an alcoholic's ability to cope with the posttreatment environment is an important factor in maintaining sobriety. Jones and Lanyon (1981), studying a group of alcoholics 1 year following treatment, found a significant relationship between posttreatment drinking and clients' ability to cope with stimuli that could trigger drinking. Finally, Rist and Watzl (1983) found that those alcoholics who relapsed within 3 months after treatment evaluated situations involving social pressure to drink as more difficult to deal with and more uncomfortable than did abstainers, despite the fact that the groups did not differ in self-rated assertiveness in non-alcohol-related situations. Results of these studies have been interpreted as suggesting the need for social skills training programs for alcoholics.

Many of the studies reviewed above have led researchers to focus on the processes of relapse and on broad-based conceptual models of addiction that are consistent with the "adaptive orientation" model adopted in this book. For example, Cronkite and Moos (1980) have formulated a model that considers the domains of extratreatment factors (e.g., family, work settings, and stressful events) along with patient and treatment factors. Indeed, these researchers have found that the inclusion of extratreatment factors more than doubles the explained variance in treatment outcome, leading them to suggest that treatment may be more effective when oriented toward ongoing life circumstances. Abrams (1983) has proposed a triple-response-mode model of factors that initiate and maintain problem drinking. Emphasis is placed on psychosocial stressors, cognitive factors, and physiological arousal mechanisms. The implication of these models is that environmental factors, especially stress and social networks (including the family, the workplace, and friendships), should be considered as a means of improving treatment. Coping skills training can be used to enhance the social support for sobriety and to substitute more healthy alternatives for managing the stresses at work and with family and friends.

There is a consistent body of empirical and clinical evidence for the role played by specific intrapersonal and interpersonal high-risk situations and their related coping skills deficits in alcoholism. An individual's social learning history sets the stage for, and interacts with, proximal situational determinants. Cognitive factors such as learned expectations and self-efficacy percepts mediate the successful use of coping behaviors. Direct practice, role playing, and the fine-tuning of new coping skills in the natural environment are thought to be the best ways to enhance self-efficacy and treatment outcome. Thus the central goals of this clinical handbook are derived directly from the current state of the art in SLT and behavioral clinical practice. Treatment outcome studies are reviewed in the final chapter of this book, along with potential future directions.

The next two chapters present our SLT-based interpersonal and intrapersonal coping skills group treatment program for alcoholics.

# 2

## Coping Skills Training: Part I. Interpersonal Skills

### General Introduction

This chapter and the next provide session-by-session instructions for therapists who wish to apply a coping skills training approach to the treatment of alcohol dependence. The goals and the methods for each element of the training program are described through the detailed instructions provided to therapists. These two chapters describe the content of each treatment session. However, there are some additional session instructions in Chapter 4. We thus proceed with the major content of the sessions in Chapters 2 and 3, to be followed by structural and process considerations in Chapter 4.

The skills training modules presented in this chapter follow a behavioral approach to interpersonal, or communication, skills training. (In this chapter, the terms "communication skills" and "interpersonal skills" are used interchangeably.) Communication skills are important for the rehabilitation of alcoholics for at least two reasons: (1) They can enhance coping with high-risk situations that commonly precipitate relapse, including both interpersonal difficulties and intrapersonal discomfort, such as anger or depression; and (2) they provide a means of obtaining social support that is critical to the maintenance of sobriety. Clients who began heavy drinking during early adolescence may never have adequately developed or strengthened these skills; these alcoholics will need considerable practice and feedback. Clients whose abusive drinking began after their adolescent years may never have applied these skills appropriately, or previously adequate skills may have fallen into disuse as the clients became increasingly isolated with increases in drinking, or these skills may have become distorted as social interactions became increasingly defensive and argumentative with increases in drinking. For some, therefore, this skills training will contain much that is new; for many others, it will provide needed review and correction. In our clinical experience with this program, we have found that virtually all clients have found it useful.

The treatment manual that follows has been implemented by cotherapy teams of psychologists, physicians, nurses, psychology interns, and/or alcoholism counselors. The treatment has been delivered in group format, and groups have usually ranged in size from 8 to 15 clients. Although group treatment has proven very useful for the addictive disorders, such treatment must be balanced with appropriate attention to the individual needs of each client. Effective treatment can only be provided by balancing the delivery of content material with adequate attention to process issues. This point is further discussed in Chapter 4.

The topics for each session are presented in this chapter in order of increasing difficulty and complexity. The actual sequences in which we have presented them clinically, and the rationales for those sequences, are presented in Chapter 4. Although clinicians may feel free to try other sequences to suit their program needs, types of clients, and so forth, it is recommended that the considerations of program sequence that are discussed in Chapter 4 be reviewed before deciding upon new arrangements of the topics.

The program elements are presented, in this chapter and the next, in the form of a handbook. Each program element is intended to be self-explanatory to practicing clinicians, with ample rationale and clinical protocol for every session. Therefore, the elements follow, one upon the other, without interpolated discussion. Each new element begins with the heading "Session:" followed by a title.

The "Rationale" section at the beginning of each skills training session after the first one (which is largely introductory) is designed for presentation to clients and discusses the benefits of the skills to be taught in that session—first in general terms, and then as specifically related to recovery from alcoholism and prevention of relapse. Sometimes questions are posed to solicit group members' experiences relevant to a topic, in order to further capture their interest in learning the new skill.

The "Rationale" section is followed by a "Skill Guidelines" section. It is important that the guidelines be presented as such and not as inflexible rules. The goal of the group is not only to teach specific coping strategies, but also, of equal importance, to encourage a flexible application of the strategies that is consistent with each individual's goals and with situational parameters.

Following the "Skill Guidelines" section in many sessions are sections titled "Modeling" and "Behavior Rehearsal Role Plays." Under "Modeling," we present standard vignettes that are used to demonstrate the skill guidelines. First a scene is described, along with the goals of the protagonist. Therapists usually enact each scene twice— once contrary to the skill guidelines and once consistent with them.

The "Behavior Rehearsal Role Plays" sections consist of individually tailored role plays that allow clients to practice the relevant skills. The rehearsals may be videotaped and played back for the entire group. At least two client dyads should engage in role plays each session. The other group members provide feedback and support. Such feedback and support should initially be modeled by the therapists.

At the end of the book, there is a section entitled "Reminder Sheets and Practice Exercises." This section includes the Reminder Sheets and Practice Exercises for each of the sessions in Chapters 2 and 3, which are intended to be distributed as handouts to clients. A few of the exercises describe hypothetical situations, which remove the demands of *in vivo* interaction and allow more time for appraisal of a situation and the formulation of responses. More complex exercises prompt clients to apply the skill guidelines in actual situations. Regardless of the type of exercise, clients are expected to bring written responses to the following session, where the practice exercise is reviewed. A review period at the start of each session provides clients with an opportunity to appraise their own behavior change efforts and to receive constructive feedback from the therapists and other clients.

Woven throughout the text of the handbook is additional material that we have found helpful, either in the conduct of our groups or in the training of our therapists and students. We have inserted this material where we feel it will be most helpful to practicing clinicians.

So as to keep this information distinct from the handbook per se, we have "boxed" these points throughout the text.

Before we begin with the actual program content, a word is necessary about the style in which these units are written. They are addressed to therapists who may be using this program, providing direct suggestions as to how to present the material to the clients. Thus, the pronoun "you," when used in the model presentations and instructions within the following clinical protocols, refers to the clients; "we" refers to both clients and therapists. Interrogatives are questions that the therapists may pose to the clients to stimulate group discussion. Finally, note that some of the text is worded in a "therapist's voice" as if a therapist is speaking with clients. This material is indented and usually occurs in the "Rationale" and "Skill Guidelines" sections.

## Session: Introduction, Group Building, Problem Assessment

In many ways, the first session will be one of the hardest sessions to lead. People coming to the group really don't know what to expect; they are waiting to be told what to do and aren't talking much as a result. The first session should therefore be largely dedicated to getting people comfortable with one another, responding to one another, and oriented to the general rationale, goals, and procedures of the group.

The session begins with an introduction of the therapists, and a statement that today's session will include an overview of what this skills group is about and what the group will be doing over the upcoming sessions. This is followed by a quick exercise for people to learn the names of at least a few people in the group. Some people already know one another, and this can go fairly quickly. The instructions are as follows:

> We're going to spend a few minutes learning each other's names. It will take too much time for us to learn everyone's name today—that will come with time—but we're going to have you learn the names of at least two other people. Here's how we'll do it. We're going to go around the room, and each person will say his/her name. The first person will give his/her name only. The second person will give his/her name and the name of the first person as well. The third person will give his/her name and the name of both the first and second person.

Starting with the fourth person, he/she will give his/her name and the names of the two people before him/her. This will continue until we return to the first person, who will then repeat his/her name and the names of the two people before him/her. The last person to do this will be the one who originally went second.

## Ground Rules

The following rules apply to both inpatient and outpatient groups unless otherwise specified. Review the following points briefly. For outpatient groups, hand out the "Group Member's Contract" (see "Outpatient Aftercare Considerations" section of Chapter 4).

### ATTENDANCE

Explain scheduled meeting place and time. Hand out calendars. Outpatient clients are asked to commit themselves to attend at least the first four sessions. If they wish to withdraw after that, they should discuss their reasons with the group before deciding. Attendance has been part of the "required treatment" for our inpatients (see "Inpatient Treatment Considerations" section of Chapter 4 for elaboration of this point).

### PROMPTNESS

Each client is asked to arrive promptly for each group session. If, for some urgent reason an outpatient must be late or absent, he/she should call in advance to notify the group leaders.

### ALCOHOL AND DRUG USE

Therapists can set forth the group policy on abstinence as follows:

This group is designed to help people who are working on being abstinent from alcohol and mood-altering drugs. You are not alone if you have some ambivalent feelings about accepting abstinence as a goal. However, for this group to function well, every member has to be willing to work on remaining abstinent, at least for the duration of the program.

For outpatient groups, the following points are made:

Any difficulties encountered in working toward an abstinence goal (in the form of fears about drinking/drug use, or actual drinking/drug use) should be discussed with the group. You may continue to attend the group even after an episode of alcohol or drug use, as long as you are willing to work toward renewed abstinence. However, we ask that you not come to a session if you are under the influence of alcohol or drugs. There are two reasons for this: (1) We cover a lot of new information here, and it's hard to concentrate, stay on topic, and remember what was done in group if you have been drinking or using drugs. (2) You may be disruptive to other group members who are actively participating in the session.

In order to avoid unnecessary accusations, guessing, or discussion about whether someone has had something to drink, group leaders may request a breath or urine test at any time. Anyone under the influence of alcohol or drugs will be asked to leave the session and arrange safe transportation home. It is important that clients not view this as a punishment, and anyone asked to leave will be encouraged to return to the next session and to continue in the group.

CONFIDENTIALITY

The therapists explain that confidentiality is essential for a successful group.

EATING AND SMOKING IN GROUP

Therapists should make their own rules regarding smoking, eating, and coffee drinking during the group.

## Cravings and Slips

Clients who have been out of treatment for some time may have experienced strong cravings, slips, or relapses. Encourage them to discuss these experiences, and reinforce clients for their self-disclosure of problems. Avoid "drunkalog" storytelling; get clients instead to focus on the preslip high-risk situation and on cognitive–affective reactions to the slip. Try to limit this to 15–20 minutes of group time.

## Group-Building Exercise

The purpose of this exercise is to help group members get to know one another and to get them to think about their motivation and commitment to sobriety. List the following on the board:

- Whom do you live with?
- Describe a typical day.
- Describe the benefits of sobriety.

Split those present into groups of three (you may need one or two groups of two). Try to form groups of people who don't already know one another. Each group should decide on someone to speak first. Each member should briefly (1) name the people he/she lives with, (2) describe a typical weekday, and (3) state what he/she expects will be some of the benefits of sobriety for him/her. Each speaker will have 5 minutes (a therapist acts as timekeeper).

While the triads are talking, drift around the room and listen to what is being said. After all have had their turn, highlight some of what you heard as you listened in on the groups:

Some live with spouse and children, with parents, alone.
Some are employed, looking for work, taking care of children, retired, and so forth.
Benefits of sobriety: better health, money saved, improved self-esteem, clearer thinking, better at work, more responsible, and so on.

(Feel free to add items for group members to think about, even though you did not actually hear them in the groups.)

## Goals of Group

Throughout the following discussion of the group's goals, encourage clients to ask any questions they may have and to share examples from their own lives that exemplify the points made in this section.

We *all* have some problems getting along with family, friends, and coworkers; meeting strangers; and handling our moods and feelings. Everyone has different strengths and weaknesses in coping skills.

Interpersonal difficulties and negative feelings are often associated with drinking and relapse. There is evidence that much problem drinking occurs in these "high-risk" situations. They include such things as feeling frustrated with someone, being offered a drink at a party, feeling depressed, angry, sad, lonely, and so on. What examples of high-risk situations can you think of from your own lives?

*An important goal of this group is to teach some skills you can use to cope with your high-risk situations.* We will focus on ways to handle difficult interpersonal situations more comfortably and honestly (e.g., giving and receiving criticism, expressing positive feelings, starting conversations, refusing a drink, etc.). In addition, we will teach ways to handle negative feelings.

## Introducing the Practice Exercise

The purpose of this exercise in problem identification is to motivate clients' involvement in treatment by helping them see it as something that will address their particular needs. When reviewing these problem lists in the next session, the therapists will mention those elements of the program that will address each of the problems.

The therapists should hand out the "Practice Exercise" sheet and initiate a discussion of potential problem situations in the list, and how they could lead to relapse. If clients do not give adequate descriptions of situations, the therapists should provide examples, such as the following:

*Close/intimate relationships:* e.g., lack of communication, or arguments, with spouse or close friend.

*Loneliness:* e.g., when you're not at work you stay home alone and watch T.V.

*Anger:* e.g., little things seem to "bug" you a lot, and you find yourself angry much of the time.

*Anxiety or tension:* e.g., you feel tense or anxious when you have to meet new people or go into strange situations.

*Pressure to drink:* e.g., a friend at work offers to buy you a drink.

---

A key point to communicate in this first session is that the content of the program will be tailored to the individual needs of each client. It is essential that clients leave this session believing that there is something in this group for them. The message should be "You will learn how to cope better with *your* problems." First impressions are important, and if clients leave the session believing that the group is merely going to be an academic exercise, it will be difficult to convince them otherwise.

Since the therapists do not know the clients very well at this session, it is especially important that they remain attentive to clients' reception of the message. The practice exercise is designed to tie the content of this program with the needs of individual clients. Before this session ends, it is especially important to check that clients understand this assignment.

---

Refer to the end of the book for the "Practice Exercise" for this session (p. 195).

**Session: Starting Conversations**

Rationale

1. Conversation is an important first step in establishing both casual and more intimate relationships with people. It is a basic communication skill.
2. This is a difficult skill for some people, and easier for others (though there is always room for improvement).
3. What are some of the reactions you have had when a conversation with someone has gone poorly, been avoided altogether, or when it has gone well? Examples of reactions that might come up here include negative feelings of low self-esteem, frustration, anxiety, boredom, or feeling left out; or positive feelings after an enjoyable exchange, when another person is responsive and seems interested in you, when you find it interesting to hear what someone else has to say, or when you feel good about sharing some time with someone else.
4. There is a relationship between one's ability and comfort in making conversation and problem drinking:
   a. Some people drink because they feel it helps them to talk to people at parties, gatherings, and the like. They may feel uncomfortable meeting new people or socializing without having a drink first. Thus, it is important to become skillful at conversing without first having a drink.
   b. Some people avoid socializing or meeting people because of difficulty making conversations. This avoidance is likely to lead to loneliness, boredom, and feeling isolated, which are common drinking triggers (i.e., high-risk situations).
   c. Often, people who drink heavily have friends who drink heavily too. People who decide to quit drinking may feel lonely at first and may miss socializing with drinking buddies. It is especially important to begin to meet new people and to build new friendships, in order to reduce the temptation to return to the bar, club, or other drinking setting to socialize. The ability to engage comfortably in conversations is necessary for this purpose.

Skill Guidelines

1. Consider places where you could meet people. As a group, you may want to think of a number of such places and list them on the blackboard as a brainstorm exercise. Each of you can then select a situation from the list in which to try to meet people.

2. Some people have misperceptions that can be obstacles to starting conversation. Here are three common misunderstandings:
   a. That you should only talk about important and weighty mat-
      ters. Actually, it is not necessary to start a conversation by
      talking about world famine or national politics. In fact, such
      topics may make conversation more difficult. You don't have
      to solve the problems of the world in the first conversation.
      Conversation should be fun, a way of sharing ideas with or
      getting to know others in a comfortable way. Therefore, *small
      talk is OK*. Start small by picking a topic that the other person
      is able to respond to easily. Sports, the weather, asking who
      the person knows at the party, asking someone you meet on a
      bus or train where he/she is going—all these are good, simple
      conversation openers.
   b. That you are totally responsible for keeping up the conversa-
      tion. Conversation is a two-way process, with each person
      contributing about equally, so you should start with some
      topic that gives the other person a chance to respond easily
      and comfortably.
   c. That you should never talk about yourself. Some of us are
      trained that talking about ourselves is not polite, and often
      feel uncomfortable talking about ourselves because of that
      training. However, social psychology research has shown that
      people like others who self-disclose, who like similar things,
      and who have similar attitudes. The only way to know
      whether we share ideas and likes with others is to tell them
      about our ideas, likes, and dislikes, and to ask about theirs.
      By telling others about yourself, you open the way for them to
      tell you about themselves. Start sharing your likes and dis-
      likes; set the example. *It's OK to talk about yourself.*
          You can start to be open and share things about yourself
      while talking about "simple" things. If you're talking about
      cars, you can perhaps tell why you like a particular model of
      car. The amount or level of self-disclosure that is appropriate
      varies from setting to setting (e.g., a person you're meeting for
      the first time vs. an acquaintance you've been seeing more
      often and with whom you are developing a closer friendship.)
3. Here are some specific suggestions that make starting a conversation easier:
   a. *Listen and observe.* People give many clues that can help you
      decide what may be good topics for discussion. You may pick
      up clues from their conversations with others, or from things
      they seem interested in. (How can you tell whether someone
      is interested in or bored by certain things?) Also, approach

someone to start a conversation when he/she is not deeply involved in some other activity, in a rush, or in the middle of an ongoing conversation. If he/she is in a group of people, wait until there is a lull in the conversation. Don't be hesitant and shy, but don't barge in.

b. *Speak up.* Let the other person know that you want to talk by making eye contact and saying something first, rather than just standing there and waiting for him/her to talk to you. Perhaps his/her coffee cup is empty at a party. Ask who he/she knows there, and suggest that you refill your cups together. Recall the value of small talk: Conversation need not be "heavy."

c. *Use open-ended questions to prompt a response.* This is a technique that is easy to use and is very effective in both starting and continuing a conversation. "Prompting a response" means giving the other person a natural opening in the conversation. An open-ended question encourages discussion, whereas a closed question can be answered by simply saying "yes" or "no" (e.g., "What did you think of the movie?" vs. "Did you like the movie?" or "How do you think the Sox will do this year?" vs. "Do you think the Sox will win this year?"). By asking open-ended questions, you signal the other person that you want to talk with him/her.

d. The preceding skills will help you to get a conversation started. Then, it is very important to *check the reception of your conversation.* How is the other person responding? Are his/her responses to your questions getting shorter? Or is he/she throwing questions and comments back your way? Is he/she shifting his/her weight, looking at his/her watch, or looking past you? Or is he/she maintaining eye contact and leaning forward? Does it look as if he/she would like to get back to a magazine? Or has he/she closed it? If it looks as if the other person has had enough of the conversation, end it. You don't have to say everything in the first conversation. Remember, conversation should be fun and easy. When it's not enjoyable to either party, end it gracefully. Conversations can be very brief or fairly long. It's up to both of you to keep tabs on how it's being received. Another point in checking your reception is to be careful not to overwhelm your listener. If you get the feeling that a particular topic isn't interesting or is uncomfortable for the other person, switch to another one. Don't overwhelm your listener with too much talk or with topics that are not interesting to him/her.

e. *End the conversation gracefully.* When your conversation is coming to an end, or one of you has to leave, you can end a conversation gracefully by saying something pleasant about how you enjoyed talking with (and/or meeting) the other person. You can mention that you have to leave now, or that you see he/she has to get going, and maybe you'll see the person later. Basically, what is appropriate here is that you *leave your listener with the feeling that you enjoyed sharing conversation with him/her, and that your feeling is sincere.* People usually enjoy the feeling of sharing that comes out of a pleasant conversation, and the assertive person can let the other person know that he/she feels that way. In fact, it increases the likelihood that the other person will want to talk with you again.

---

In our experience, many alcoholics feel that they are good conversationalists. However, in most instances alcohol, or expectancies about alcohol, play a subtle or more obvious role in alcoholics' confidence and perceptions of their skill (alcohol expectancy effects are more generally covered in Chapter 1). In the absence of alcohol, many of our clients have come to appreciate the relevance of the content of this session.

Another important point is that situational demands can influence one's ability to use conversational skills. Attempt to explore a variety of situations with especially confident clients.

---

## Modeling

Therapists role-play two strangers who are sharing a seat on the bus. These two people frequently ride the same bus in the morning on the way to work, but they have never talked together before. Within this scenario, therapists should demonstrate the skills described above, and show how use of them might lead to making a new acquaintance.

## Behavior Rehearsal Role Plays

The first role play could involve group members interacting using the following scenario: Two people have just been introduced to each other at a party given by a mutual friend.

For subsequent role plays in this session, clients should use personally relevant scenes. Dimensions along which scenes might vary are (1) setting and (2) degree of familiarity—is the other person a stranger, an acquaintance whom the client wishes to get to know better, or a family member whom the client lives with (and watches

TV with, etc.) but doesn't usually share much light conversation with (e.g. about casual events of the day)?

Introducing the Practice Exercise

Therapists hand out the "Practice Exercise" sheet and explain as follows:

> By practicing these points on how to start, continue, and end a conversation, you'll find that those initial fears you had about walking up to someone and starting a conversation will lessen. You'll also find that it's easier and probably more fun for you. The effects of this lesson won't be immediate, but we all know that practice helps.
>
> Between now and our next session, you must, at the very least, start one conversation and record it on the "Practice Exercise" sheet. You are encouraged, however, to practice more than just once, whenever you have an opportunity.

Refer to the end of the book for the "Reminder Sheet" and "Practice Exercise" for this session (p. 196).

## Session: Giving and Receiving Compliments

Rationale

1. The satisfaction we get from relationships with others depends partly on sharing *positive* things with them. Thus, it is important to be able to tell others positive things, and to respond appropriately when they make positive comments. This applies to the relationships we have with all of the different people in our lives—with our spouses, children, parents, friends, neighbors, colleagues, coworkers, employees, employers, and so on. The types of positive things we tell others are varied. We might tell others that we like the color they chose for their new car, the way their new haircut looks, the helping hand they willingly give when a task needs to get done, the way they lend an ear when we need someone to talk to, their enthusiasm whenever we take a Saturday afternoon off together to do something fun, and so forth.
2. Despite the importance of giving compliments to building and maintaining relationships, people often fail to do it. Perhaps they start to take others for granted, or they assume that the

other person already "knows" how they feel, or they are uncomfortable doing it.
3. Some people who are very good at giving compliments nevertheless have difficulty receiving them. Likewise, some people who are good at accepting compliments have difficulty giving them.
4. How might the ability to give and receive compliments be related to your efforts to stop drinking?
   a. Relationship problems frequently accompany problem drinking. As the problems increase, the positive aspects of a relationship start to get overlooked. Making an effort to share positive comments with each other is one way to begin to change things for the better.
   b. Different people may be supporting your efforts to remain abstinent (e.g., friends, employer, family, etc.). By letting them know that you appreciate their support, you share a good feeling with them, and thereby also increase the likelihood that they'll continue to do things that are of help to you.

Alcoholism and depressed mood are often linked. If clients are feeling badly about themselves because of past drinking, they may have an especially hard time receiving compliments. However, clients should be reminded that rejecting a sincere compliment can make the other person feel bad and may discourage him/her from saying positive things in the future. By learning to accept compliments, clients encourage others to point out good things about them.

## Skill Guidelines

1. *Whenever possible, state your compliments in terms of your own feelings, rather than in terms of absolutes or facts.* For example, saying "That's a nice shirt" sounds as if you're stating a fact about the shirt. In contrast, saying, "I really like that shirt; I think it looks nice on you," conveys to the other person your own feelings. Even though both statements are positive, the latter one will be more effective and more valuable to the person, since it is stated in terms of your feelings. Furthermore, a person's feelings aren't right or wrong, whereas a person *can* be incorrect about facts. This difference makes it easier to accept compliments that are stated as feelings than compliments that are stated as facts. For example, if the other person dislikes the shirt, he/she can deny or debate the "fact" that it's a nice shirt. But if the compliment is stated as a sincere feeling, the "facts" of

the matter become irrelevant; the recipient can appreciate and accept the expression of positive feelings as a valuable message, whether or not he/she feels similarly about the shirt. Of course, positive statements are valuable to others only if those statements reflect our *sincere* feelings.

2. *In giving compliments, try to pick out specific things that you like.* For example, if a coworker has been covering for you while you take a coffee break, it's more effective to say something like "You know I really appreciate it when you cover for me while I go on a break. You really are a nice person," than to just say, "You really are a nice person to work with." Although the latter statement is nice to hear, it's probably hard for your coworker to know exactly what aspects of working together you like. Although general compliments are pleasant to give and receive, they are more effective if you also tell the person the specific things that you find particularly enjoyable or helpful. Specificity indicates to people that you have taken time to notice what they have done. It also helps identify to them the things they do that you find desirable, and makes it more likely that they will do them again.

3. *Accept compliments that are given to you; don't negate them or turn them down.* For example, if someone compliments you on a photograph you took, and you say something like "Oh, this dull thing? I think it's terrible. I was just using up the end of the roll of film and wasn't paying much attention to what I was doing," how is the person who is giving the compliment going to feel? Essentially, you are insulting him/her by implying that he/she has bad taste. You are implying that his/her opinion doesn't count for much, and the person may feel rejected.

4. Even if you disagree with the person's opinion, respond to it graciously and *indicate that you appreciate the positive feedback.* Accepting a compliment in this way isn't dishonest, since it doesn't imply that you share the positive feeling. It simply lets the other person know that you appreciate the compliment (e.g., "Well, thank you; that's very nice of you to say").

## Modeling

Therapists use the following role-play scene to contrast an ineffective and an effective way of giving a compliment:

1. Guest *insincerely* compliments host(ess) on *entire* dinner that night. As a consequence, host(ess) enthusiastically offers to pre-

pare the same meal for the guest again soon (much to the first person's dismay!).

2. Guest *sincerely* compliments host(ess) on the *specific* parts of the dinner that he/she enjoyed (e.g., the homemade soup and the dessert). As a consequence, host(ess) enjoys the compliment and offers to make those things again.

Therapists should solicit brief group discussion about the two different communication strategies demonstrated above.

## Behavior Rehearsal Role Plays

Guide clients in generating and practicing personally relevant situations. Problem areas might include failing to give compliments, negating compliments, giving too many compliments at a time (thereby making others feel uncomfortable), and so on. Encourage group members to consider a variety of situations in which these new skills might be applicable to them (e.g., work, family, friends). The "confederates" (those on the receiving end) in these role plays should practice appropriate responses for *receiving* compliments.

## Introducing the Practice Exercise

Spend a few minutes helping group members to anticipate interpersonal situations they may be in between now and the next session that will provide opportunities in which to practice these skills (e.g., at social events, phone conversations with others, at work, etc.).

Refer to the end of the book for the "Reminder Sheet" and "Practice Exercise" for this session (p. 197).

## Session: Nonverbal Communication

### Rationale

1. Nonverbal communication, sometimes called "body language," plays a large part in the messages we relay to other people. In contrast to verbal communication, which consists of the actual *words* used in speaking with someone, nonverbal communication refers to the *way* in which those words are projected. For example, during a job interview, one person might look down at

the floor or off in the distance, whereas a different person might look directly at the person being spoken to. What very different messages might the nonverbal behavior of these two job applicants convey to the interviewer? Might the nonverbal behavior affect which applicant gets the job offer?

2. Nonverbal behaviors can help or hinder communication with other people. The same words will be interpreted very differently by another person, depending on how those words are delivered. For example, if you fidget, rock back and forth, and speak in a whisper when you ask someone to repay the money he/she owes you, how likely is it that your words will be taken very seriously? Sometimes people say one thing with their words and something very different with their actions; that is, their nonverbal behavior contradicts their words, and the overall message ends up being very ambiguous (this is sometimes referred to as giving "mixed messages"). For example, if you appear hostile while claiming that you are not angry, what effect will you have on your listener?

3. Developing effective nonverbal behavior can make a world of difference in your interactions with other people. It will increase the chances that others will respond positively to you, will increase the likelihood of more satisfying communication with them, and will also help you to feel better about yourself.

4. People are often unaware of the nonverbal messages they send; they may act in automatic or habitual ways and may not be aware of the impact they are having on the other person. In this session, we will discuss several different components of nonverbal behavior and help you pinpoint those that can help you become a more effective communicator.

## Skill Guidelines

1. *Posture.* Developing a relaxed posture is important. Relaxed posture looks natural to others and feels natural to you. You should refrain from either slouching or sitting too rigidly. Try to find a comfortable position in which your back is resting against the chair and your arms are either on the arm rests or folded across your body. Remember, don't strike a rigid pose like a statue, but think about being relaxed and how good your body feels when you are relaxed. Other people will also recognize when you are relaxed, and they will not feel that you are afraid to talk with them.

Many people have difficulty assuming a relaxed posture when standing. An easy idea to remember is to distribute your weight evenly. This will prevent you from doing such things as rocking back and forth or swaying, which can be very distracting to your listener and indicates how nervous you might feel.

Some other messages which you may communicate to your listener through your posture are shyness or insecurity. To avoid this, you should stand or sit directly facing the person(s) you are speaking with, or at no more than a slight angle. Having your back toward a person or being turned away from him/her sends the message that you don't want to talk or that you are uncomfortable doing so. Try to have your body facing those you are conversing with.

2. *Personal space.* When conversing with someone, it is also important to maintain a comfortable distance between you—not too far away and not too close. Each individual has a "personal space" of about 1 square foot encircling his/her body. (This may vary from culture to culture.) If this space becomes too small, the listener may begin to feel anxious. Rather than concentrating on the conversation, either you or your listener may be trying to increase the distance between you. To alleviate this problem, try to remember that a comfortable distance is at least 2 feet—your square foot and the square foot of the person you are interacting with.

3. *Eye contact.* It is important to initiate eye contact as well as to receive eye contact while talking with others. Eye contact involves looking directly at a person's face while trying to catch his/her eye and acknowledging a smile, gesture, or other facial expression. When people talk to each other, they hold each other's attention not only by what they are saying, but also by frequently looking into each other's eyes. Not looking at a person while he/she is talking makes him/her feel that you aren't listening or that you aren't interested in continuing the conversation. *Eye contact indicates to a person that you are following what is being said and that you are interested in conversing.* However, overusing eye contact can be as disruptive as underusing it. If the other person feels that you are staring, he/she will probably begin to feel uncomfortable. Try to strike a happy medium in making frequent eye contact during your conversation (a little more than half of the time).

4. *Head nods.* A head nod is a relatively easy and effective nonverbal behavior that lets your partner know that you are listening

and following the conversation. By nodding your head, you can indicate agreement or understanding in a conversation.

5. *Facial expression.*
   a. Just as with other aspects of body language, it is important that your facial expression agrees with what you are saying (e.g., affection, sadness, concern, disapproval, etc.). As mentioned earlier, nonverbal behavior that is inconsistent with your words can weaken or change the overall message.
   b. A pleasant expression on your face can help to loosen up the conversation. This expression lets the other person know that you are enjoying speaking with him/her. If you habitually scowl or frown, this may be misinterpreted by your listener as disapproval or irritation at what he/she is saying. What effect will this have on the conversation? Being able to smile and laugh appropriately during a conversation conveys the message that you are a pleasant person to be around and to talk to. Consequently, the interaction will probably be more enjoyable for both of you.

6. *Nervous movements and hand gestures.* Some of your nervous movements will begin to decrease as you practice the communications skills that are covered in this program. However, nervous or distracting gestures that have become long-standing habits should be recognized, so that efforts can be made to change them. Examples of some nervous movements are playing with objects, tapping your feet, shaking your knee, or swinging your leg while your legs are crossed. These movements indicate to those around you that you are distracted or uncomfortable. By becoming aware of these movements, you will be better able to stop doing them. For example, if you know that you have a habit of playing with your mustache or hair while you speak, focus on resting your hands on the arms of your chair instead.

   Hand gestures can serve a good purpose when used effectively to emphasize the point of a verbal statement. However, too many hand gestures can distract from a conversation if a listener gets caught up in the gestures rather than the topic of conversation. Think of hand gestures as aids to communication and not just as something to do with your hands.

7. *Tone of voice.* A weak, hesitant voice; a cold, superior, demanding voice; or a flippant, sarcastic style can all affect how our words are interpreted. Imagine a situation in which one person is asking his/her spouse to try to get up earlier in the morning to avoid having to rush to leave the house on time. By using a calm, caring tone of voice to say, "I know it's difficult to give up an

extra half hour of sleep," the speaker demonstrates respect and understanding for the spouse's point of view. Yet if those same words were delivered in a cold, sarcastic tone of voice, the message would be very different and would be more likely to result in an argument than in a solution to the morning rush problem. Your tone of voice aids communication when it is firm, warm, and relaxed, and when you speak clearly without mumbling, yelling, or whispering.

---

Timing is an important aspect of nonverbal behavior that cuts across many of the above-mentioned elements. For example, eye contact, gestures, and head nods must "fit together." If not, the communication may be disrupted. It is difficult to teach appropriate timing per se. However, therapists can help clients whose timing is off by focusing on a particularly noticeable aspect of their behavior. For example, if a client's hand gestures are not particularly inappropriate in and of themselves, but simply do not fit with other aspects of his/her communication style, the therapists might coach the client not to use his/her hands as much. The net result should be a better fit between the client's nonverbal and verbal behavior.

Most alcoholics readily relate to this otherwise difficult topic of timing when asked to imagine what they might look like after having too much to drink. Although this usually generates some laughter, the image often helps get the message across. That is, timing is an important aspect of social interaction.

---

## Modeling

To demonstrate the effect that nonverbal communication can have on the impact of a verbal message, therapists should role-play the following scene, using three different styles of nonverbal communication (and the *same* verbal content). The scenario is as follows:

It is 9 P.M., it's been a long week, and Terry wants to get to sleep early tonight because he/she works an early shift and has to wake up before 5 A.M. tomorrow. However, it's impossible to fall asleep because the neighbors in the apartment upstairs are playing the TV very loudly. Terry decides to ask the neighbors to turn down the TV. He/she goes upstairs, knocks on the door, and says to them: "You may not realize it, but I can hear your TV downstairs in my apartment and it's pretty loud. I need to get to sleep so I can get up early tomorrow, and I'd appreciate your turning the volume down."

Using the exact same words, the therapists should repeat this scene three times with three different communication styles:

1. Hesitant speech; fidgeting; poor eye contact; apologetic tone of voice; slouched posture; etc.
2. Loud, hostile, demanding tone of voice; scowling/glaring expression on face; hands on hips; etc.
3. Relaxed but firm tone of voice; good posture; direct eye contact; etc.

After each of the three scenes, the therapists should ask group members to discuss briefly how the nonverbal elements may influence the effectiveness of Terry's communication with the neighbors.

> Just as production of nonverbal behaviors is important, so is reception of another's nonverbal behavior. Nonverbal behavior can often be a sign of underlying emotions and feelings. Being in tune with these feelings is important in most social interactions. Like many individuals, some alcoholics may be hypersensitive to subtle, nonverbal cues, and this could inhibit their behavior. Other alcoholics may not attend to these cues at all, and may thereby miss opportunities to engage in social interactions. Individual differences in sensitivity must be considered when trying to assist clients in improving their nonverbal skills.

## Behavior Rehearsal Role Plays

Have group members generate personally relevant scenes in which they have had, or expect to have, difficulty communicating with someone. During today's session, practice and feedback will focus on the nonverbal aspects of the interaction rather than on the verbal content. Inform clients that in subsequent sessions, as they focus on new verbal skills (e.g., criticism, drink refusal, etc.), the nonverbal aspects of those skills will continue to be dealt with. Today's session formally introduces and initiates practice with elements of nonverbal communication that will be used in conjunction with most other communication skills.

Refer to the end of the book for the "Reminder Sheet" and "Practice Exercise" for this session (p. 198).

## Session: Feeling Talk and Listening Skills

### Rationale

1. Feelings are something that all people have in common. Everyone has experienced sadness, anger, happiness, joy, frustration,

relief, enthusiasm, or fear at one time or another. These feelings may be tied to different situations for different people, and some feelings may be more frequent than others, but overall everyone experiences a wide range of emotions. This session focuses on two related skills: sharing our feelings, opinions, and attitudes with other people; and listening to other people in a way that lets them know that we care about and understand the feelings they share with us.

2. Although many people have difficulty expressing their feelings and/or listening attentively to others' feelings, both of these are communication skills that can be improved with practice. Practice can produce positive results for you; after a while, you will be able to use the skills more naturally and comfortably in your day-to-day interactions.

3. There are several benefits to sharing feelings with other people:

   a. Shy people who don't express their feelings or opinions often get mislabeled as being "cold" or "aloof." This can lead to a negative cycle in which others avoid a person who seems aloof, and the shy person then has even less opportunity to initiate discussions about feelings.

   b. Sharing positive and negative feelings can enhance relationships with family members and acquaintances whom we wish to know better. Sharing can be a means of moving conversations from small talk into more serious topics.

   c. A major way to get to know someone better is to share feelings about something. For example, how did you feel about growing up in a small town? What did you think of the movie that was on TV last night? How did you feel about the trip to the beach that you took last weekend? How are you feeling about having to get your income taxes done within the next week? What are some of your long-term plans/interests (e.g., career development, learning to play the guitar)? Sharing your feelings with another person will help him/her feel closer to you and will let you discover things you have in common with each other. The more you know about each other, the more friendship and liking for each other can increase. This applies not only to new acquaintances, but also to family interactions. Even though people may see their families daily, many people report feeling "out of touch" with their spouses or children; conversation at home revolves around such topics as "What's for dinner?" As mutual sharing of feelings decreases, family members feel distant, as if they no longer know much about each other.

   d. Your own self-disclosure conveys the message that it's OK to talk about feelings. It lets others know that they can share something meaningful with you. This mutual trading of feelings and experiences is a major way in which trust and affection are built between people.

e. Often, other people are relieved to find out that they aren't alone in feeling something (e.g., sadness). Thus, sharing information about your feelings can be an important source of support for another person. This works both ways: If you share negative feelings with others, you may be surprised and relieved to find that they too have had similar feelings or experiences.

4. *Listening attentively* when another person shares feelings with us is important if we are to get to know and feel close to him/her. Use of this skill has several positive consequences: It lets the other person know that we are interested in, and want to understand, what he/she has to say; it encourages the other person to talk further about himself/herself; and it helps us to learn things about the other person that we would otherwise miss.

5. Relationship between these skills and problem drinking:

a. Many drinkers who have used alcohol to try to deaden unpleasant feelings find that sobriety initially comes with an increased awareness of negative feelings. By talking with friends or family about these feelings, you are likely to receive their support and feel closer to them as a result.

b. Some drinkers report that they use alcohol to help them express positive feelings (e.g., affection, caring, closeness). For these people, sharing positive feelings without drinking will be one step toward continued abstinence.

c. Being intoxicated makes it nearly impossible to be a good listener, since it interferes with your ability to concentrate on and remember what the other person is saying. Although you may have been a very good listener in the past, this skill may not return right away after a month or so of abstinence. You are no longer intoxicated, but your listening skills may have become rusty through disuse. Thus, practice is important, whether you are learning or relearning this skill.

d. Many drinkers report feelings of loneliness. At times, drinking is used to try to cope with the loneliness; at other times, the loneliness may result from the drinking itself, which has alienated the drinker from close friends and family. In either case, learning to cope with loneliness will help to prevent relapse. Feeling talk and listening skills are one way to decrease loneliness, since they help you to build friendships and to feel closer to your family.

Skill Guidelines

1. *Feeling talk.*
   a. *It's OK to talk about your feelings.* Feelings are something we all have in common. We have also all had experiences that were in some way notable: notably bad, wonderful, happy, and so on.
   b. *It is important to share both positive and negative feelings.* Some people are more comfortable sharing only positive feelings, and some only negative feelings. However, people will get to know you better if you share a range of your feelings rather than only one kind (e.g., always focusing on how angry you are at your neighbor, at your boss, or at your kids).
   c. The goal is not to share all of your innermost feelings with everybody. Rather, *appropriate self-disclosure* is the guide to follow. As you get to know and trust someone better, you will feel comfortable sharing more of your feelings with him/her. Others will probably feel uncomfortable hearing about very personal feelings if they only met you an hour ago. You will probably share more, or different, types of feelings with some people than with others. This is reasonable, since we have different relationships with the different people in our lives.
2. *Listening skills.* Listening is more than just sitting quietly or passively while someone else is speaking. It is an active skill because it involves trying to understand what the other person is communicating, rather than just waiting for your own turn to talk. The following suggestions can improve your active listening skills:
   a. *Nonverbal behavior.* Leaning slightly forward, maintaining eye contact, nodding your head, and sometimes giving a sympathetic touch or murmur all indicate to someone that you are interested and are hearing what he/she has to say. Looking at your watch, yawning, or watching others distracts the speaker and tells him/her that you're not very interested or tuned in to what he/she is saying. Nonverbal behavior is one of the first things that people notice when they monitor how they are being received.
   b. *Recognizing the nonverbal behaviors of the speaker* is another part of good listening. Good listeners "tune in to" the other person's feelings; they listen to the "message behind the words." The speaker's tone of voice or facial expression may provide a lot of extra information beyond what is being said in words. For example, if someone is talking about a wedding,

he/she will probably describe the bride's dress, the reception hall, the food, and the decorations. But what if the speaker looks sad or seems subdued when talking about the wedding? A good listener might ask how the person felt, whether he/she had a good time, whether it brought back memories of other weddings, or what the wedding meant to the person. The good listener may also ask specifically about the speaker's sad expression, thereby helping the other person to talk about what the experience meant to him/her.

c. Verbal ways of telling someone, "I hear you, I'm tuned in to what you're saying," are to *ask questions* about feelings, to *paraphrase* what was said, and to *add comments* (e.g., "Wow, that must have been exciting!"; "Yes, it can be pretty lonely when you're all alone in the house").

d. A good listener will *share similar experiences or feelings* with someone who is telling him/her about something. This is part of the pleasureable give-and-take of a conversation. However, it is best to wait for the other person to complete his/her train of thought before adding your own feelings or experiences. *Timing* is once again important. The person who interrupts what someone is saying isn't being an effective listener. You should listen for an appropriate time to talk so that your comments will be a way of telling the other person that you hear what he/she is saying.

## Modeling

The therapists role-play two friends who are conversing about the skiing trip one of them recently took. The speaker, the one who went skiing, is enthusiastic about the trip and is attempting to share positive feelings about it (e.g., the relaxation of a weekend away from town, the freedom and exhilaration one feels during a downhill run, the sense of accomplishment and pleasure after skiing down a difficult trail, etc.). However, the "listener" displays poor nonverbal skills, asks many annoying questions about the price of the lift tickets and lodging, forgets the name of the ski resort and has to ask again, complains about how it's always cold when one goes skiing, and starts talking about his/her own Florida vacation plans. In short, the listener fails to attend to the feelings expressed by the speaker, resulting in the speaker's waning enthusiasm and ultimate termination of the conversation.

The therapists ask group members to briefly discuss "what went wrong" in this scene and to suggest what could have been done better. The therapists then repeat the scene, this time incorporating group members' suggestions and modeling more effective listening skills.

### Behavior Rehearsal Role Plays

Group members should select personally relevant situations in which they have had or anticipate having difficulty expressing their feelings. Each role play serves a dual purpose: One person practices talking about feelings, and the other person practices attentive listening. Make sure that the person practicing "feeling talk" is talking about his/her own feelings and not relating a story about someone else's feelings. In some of these role plays, the listener can play himself/herself rather than portraying someone in the speaker's life. Since clients may find it difficult to do this in front of the whole group, have the group members pair up and do this role playing concurrently in separate parts of the room. Halfway through the exercise, ask the clients to switch roles. Circulate around the room to monitor performances.

---

Many of our clients have brought up feelings related to the loss of trust they experienced with significant others over the course of their drinking years. Those who have tried the techniques outlined in this session prior to this group sometimes complain that the techniques simply do not work for them. We have found that a discussion regarding the building or rebuilding of relationships is helpful. Emphasize the point that it takes time and effort to communicate feelings effectively, especially when there is a history of manipulation and broken promises. No single encounter should be expected to change things dramatically. Clients may be initially disappointed at their lack of progress because of the skepticism of others. They should be encouraged not to give up or become bitter, but to persist until, little by little, trust is rebuilt.

Although such discussions about feelings have proven very helpful, it is equally important to emphasize the skill components of this session. Since many clients prefer to talk about feelings rather than practice skill components, therapists should ensure that adequate role playing occurs in this session.

---

Refer to the end of the book for the "Reminder Sheet" and "Practice Exercise" for this session (pp. 199–200).

## Session: Introduction to Assertiveness[1]

> Since the concept of "assertiveness" has been popularized over the past several years, some clients believe they "know it all" going into this session. Furthermore, novice therapists may be surprised over the misconceptions that many of these clients have about assertiveness.
>
> One technique we have found helpful in introducing clients to this session is to begin by soliciting clients' definitions of the word "assertiveness." Writing these definitions on a blackboard will help make the point that there are some differences of opinion. After discussing the various responses, therapists can begin to shape a definition that is consistent with the one advocated in this session. Furthermore, some clients may be able to articulate an appropriate definition, but upon direct observation during role plays, it becomes apparent that their behavior is not consistent with their definition.

Rationale

1. "Assertiveness" means recognizing your right to decide what you will do in a situation, rather than acceding to what someone else expects or demands. It also means recognizing the rights of the people you deal with, which must be respected.
2. "Rights" refer to the following:
   a. You have the right to inform others of your opinions.
   b. You have the right to inform others of your feelings, as long as it is done in a way that is not hurtful to them.
   c. You have the right to request others to change behavior of theirs that affects you.
   d. You have the right either to accept or to reject anything that others say to you, or request from you.
3. There are a number of different interpersonal styles: passive, aggressive, passive–aggressive, and assertive.
   a. *Passive* people tend to give up their rights if it appears there might be a conflict between what they want and what someone else wants. They also usually fail to let others know what they are thinking or feeling. They habitually bottle up their feelings, even when the situation doesn't require it, and consequently are often left feeling anxious or angry. Sometimes they feel depressed by their ineffectiveness, or hurt because they wish others had drawn them out or figured out what

[1]This session has been adapted from the *Problem Drinkers Project Manual* by L. Dean, E. Dubreuil, B. S. McCrady, C. P. Paul, and S. Swanson, 1983, unpublished manuscript, Providence, RI: Butler Hospital. Used by permission of the authors.

they wanted. People have no way of knowing what the passive persons wants, and so they do whatever they wish, and the passive person seldom gets his/her needs met. In addition, others may come to resent the passive person for not communicating.

b. *Aggressive* people act to protect their own rights, but in doing so they run over others' rights. Although they may satisfy their short-term needs, the long-term effects of aggressiveness are often negative. Because they disregard others while they achieve their goals, they earn the ill will of other people, who may seek to "get even" at some later time.

c. *Passive–aggressive* people are indirect. They may hint at what they want, make sarcastic comments, or mumble something, without ever directly stating what is on their minds. Or they may act out what they want to say, such as by slamming doors, giving someone the "silent treatment," being late, or doing a sloppy job. Sometimes they may get what they want without having to deal directly with others. However, as often as not, people around them do not get the message and become confused or angry, so the passive–aggressive person ends up feeling frustrated or victimized.

d. The *assertive* person decides what he/she wants, plans an appropriate way to involve other people, and then acts on this plan. Usually, the most effective plan is to clearly state one's feelings or opinions, and directly request the changes that one would like from others, while avoiding threats, demands, or negative statements directed at others. However, a usually assertive person may decide in certain circumstances that a more passive response is the only safe one (e.g., with a totally insensitive boss), or that an aggressive response is necessary (e.g., in confronting a "pusher" who won't back off after several polite requests). However, what is unique about assertive people is that they adapt behavior so that it *best fits the situation;* they do not always react in the same habitual manner to all situations. Assertive people generally feel satisfied with their actions, and are generally well regarded by others.

Assertiveness is the most effective way you have to let others know what is going on with you, or what effect their behavior has on you. By expressing yourself, you can resolve uncomfortable feelings that otherwise might remain and build up. Since being assertive often results in correcting a problem that is a source of stress and tension, being assertive can lead to your feeling more in control of your life. The

assertive person usually does not feel like a victim of circumstances. However, remember that your goals can't be met
in *all* situations; it isn't possible to control how the other
person will respond. Nevertheless, dealing assertively has
two benefits: It increases the chances that your goals will be
met; and you feel better about your own role in the situation
than you would if you had behaved in an aggressive, passive,
or passive–aggressive manner.

## Skill Guidelines

1. *Take a moment* to think before you speak. Decide what you are
   reacting to. What did the other person do? Try not to make
   assumptions about the other person's intentions. Don't assume
   that he/she must know what is on your mind.
2. Plan the most effective way to make your statement. *Be specific
   and direct* in what you say. Address the problem at hand without
   bringing in extraneous issues. Be positive without making excuses or apologies. Don't put the other person down; blaming
   others only causes them to feel defensive, and they will be less
   likely to hear your message.
3. Pay attention to your use of *body language,* including eye contact, posture, gestures, facial expression, and tone of voice. Make
   sure that your words and your expression communicate the
   same message. In order to get your point across, speak firmly
   and be aware of your appearance, your voice, your expression,
   and so on.
4. Be willing to *compromise.* Others will hear you if you let them
   know that you are willing to work things out. No one has to
   leave the situation feeling as if he/she has lost everything. Try to
   find a way for both of you to "win." Give others your full attention when they reply to you; try to understand their point of
   view; and seek clarification when necessary. If you disagree with
   something, discuss it with the other person. Don't dominate
   others or submit to them. Strive for a sense of equality in your
   relationship.
5. If you feel that you're not being heard, you may need to *restate*
   your assertion. In some instances, persistence and consistency
   are necessary parts of assertiveness.
6. Changing a habitual way of responding requires conscious
   efforts and a willingness to endure the unnatural, awkward
   process of learning to respond in a new way. Someone who is
   habitually nonassertive will have to initially force himself/
   herself to act more assertively. Otherwise, a nonassertive re-

sponse will occur almost automatically. The first step in becoming assertive is to become aware of your habitual response and make a conscious effort to change.

## Modeling

Group leaders demonstrate passive, passive–aggressive, aggressive, and assertive responses to the following situation: A person has borrowed a good friend's car for the day and has returned it without refilling the gas tank. The borrower returns the car keys, thanks the lender for the car, and enthusiastically starts telling the lender about his/her day. (A good way to start off the assertive response is for the therapist playing the lender to show sincere interest in how the borrower's day went and then to say something like "I'd like to talk with you about something; do you have a few minutes?") After each of the modeling scenes, ask the group what type of behavior was demonstrated and whether the "lender's" goals were met: first, to get the tank refilled; and second, to keep the friendship.

## Behavior Rehearsal Role Play

Group members should generate practice scenes from among situations they have personally found difficult (e.g., refusing a request, expressing discomfort, asking a favor, etc.) (Note: Problems with criticism and anger are taken up in other sessions.) Although the therapists have modeled several inappropriate responses to provide examples of them, clients should practice only assertive responses, to strengthen that behavior.

Refer to the end of the book for the "Reminder Sheet" and "Practice Exercise" (p. 201).

## Session: Giving Criticism

Several sessions in this program focus on problems due to differences or conflict with other people, and the angry feelings that may accompany them. Two sessions in this chapter provide an opportunity to practice skills for giving and receiving criticism, and in Chapter 3 two sessions address coping with anger in ourselves and anger from others.

Since criticism is often viewed as a wholly negative or unpleasant event, an important goal of this session is to present criticism as a potentially *constructive* communication skill that can produce *positive* results for both parties involved.

Rationale

1. At times we all come into contact with things people do that we find disagreeable or objectionable. It is important to be able to tell other people these negative things, and to request changes, without hurting their feelings unduly and without producing needless fights and arguments.
2. Yet to tell people negative things is often very difficult for many people. Some people fail to give criticism because they feel that to do so is "not nice," and they wish to avoid hurting the other person's feelings. Some fail to give criticism because they feel that it's better to live with the objectionable behavior than to risk losing their tempers and starting a fight when confronting the other person. This reluctance to give criticism is usually the result of years of experience with *destructive* criticism. The skills to be practiced in this session are intended to help you give constructive criticism—to seek changes in others' objectionable behavior without unnecessarily hurting their feelings or starting an argument.
3. There are several reasons for learning to give constructive criticism:
   a. Sometimes people do things that irritate others around them, and they don't even know it. This can limit their ability to interact successfully with people, and therefore can be a serious personal drawback. By telling the people about their disagreeable behavior (e.g., interrupting, being chronically late, not returning borrowed items, etc.), you may very well be doing them a favor by pointing out something they were previously unaware of.
   b. By repeatedly not giving someone constructive criticism when it is called for, you are likely to end up feeling very stressed and uncomfortable about your relationship with the other person. After a while you may feel angry, frustrated, or resentful, and these feelings will probably be reflected in your day-to-day behavior toward the person.
   c. Being able to give constructive criticism may not only result in positive changes in the annoying behavior, but may also help you and the other person feel good about your ability to discuss potentially difficult topics with each other.
4. Relationship between this skill and problem drinking:
   a. Many problem drinkers report that they drink when they feel frustrated with or angry at other people. They feel that they cannot speak up and deliver criticism without having some-

thing to drink first. Practicing giving constructive criticism while sober will reduce the likelihood that you will feel the need to drink when you wish to comment on someone's disturbing behavior.

b. Other heavy drinkers report that they usually refrain from giving criticism altogether, and instead attempt to block out the other persons' objectionable behavior, or retaliate by becoming intoxicated. Anger, frustration, and resentment, resulting from failure to give constructive criticism when it is called for, are common high-risk situations. Thus, practice at giving constructive criticism will reduce the likelihood of drinking in response to others' objectionable behavior.

c. Many individuals report feeling "hot-tempered" when they have been drinking heavily. Thus, sobriety will make it easier to give criticism in a constructive rather than a destructive way, if the skill has been practiced sufficiently.

## Skill Guidelines

1. *Calm down first.* If you are feeling very angry or feel as if you are on a short fuse, take a minute to slow down and calm down before speaking.

2. *State the criticism in terms of your own feelings, not in terms of facts or absolutes.* Consider the following example: You have gone to a party with your spouse or a friend. However, when you arrive at the party, your partner leaves you alone; he/she seems to be entirely absorbed in what is going on at the party and is not paying any attention to you. If you say to him/her, "How can you just ignore me like that? That's the rudest thing anyone could ever do!", then you are stating the criticism in terms of facts or absolutes. In contrast, saying something like "When you ignore me, it makes me feel as though you don't want to be here with me," is a way of stating the criticism in terms of your own feelings. It's less likely to make the other person feel defensive and less likely to start a fight. A good way to remember how to state the criticism in terms of your own feelings is to use the following type of phrase: "When you do X, I feel Y." Notice how this is different from saying, "X is a bad thing to do."

3. *Give the criticism in a clear and firm, but not angry, tone of voice.* If criticism is seen in the context of an emotional outburst, it is much less likely to be listened to and is less likely to be effective. Sarcasm or anger may be effective in punishing the other person, but that is not the goal of constructive criticism.

4. *Direct your criticism at the person's behavior, not at the entire person.* We can all accept that we may do various things that might be annoying to other people. However, it is more difficult to take the criticism, and we are much more likely to get defensive and argumentative, if someone criticizes us personally and calls us names. Engaging in an objectionable behavior does not make someone a bad person; thus the criticism should not be a global attack implying that everything about him/her is bad. For example, imagine that you have come home from work and have found that your spouse has left dirty dishes all over the kitchen. There is a family rule that dishes will be rinsed off and left in the sink after they have been used. You go over to your spouse and say, "You big slob. What kind of a lazy oaf are you? I think you must have been raised in a barn." What effect is this likely to have on the listener and on the relationship. Because this criticism is directed at the spouse himself/herself, it is likely to cause needless bad feelings and fights, and the spouse is very unlikely to change his/her behavior. An alternative way of giving criticism focuses on the behavior and not on the person: "I don't like to come home from work and find dirty dishes all over the kitchen. We have made an agreement that dirty dishes will be rinsed off and put in the sink. I'd appreciate it if you'd remember to rinse them off and put them in the sink when you're done with them."

5. *Request a specific behavior change.* Sometimes we assume that other people know what they should do in order to please us. However, sometimes they don't know. What may seem completely obvious to us may not be at all obvious to others, and what seems to be stubbornness to us may simply be other persons' lack of knowledge about what we prefer that they do. So, besides stating your feelings about a particular behavior, you also need to tell the person specifically what you would like to have happen. For example, saying, "I'd like you to ask me my opinion more often," is much more informative and specific than simply saying, "I feel badly that you show no respect for my point of view."

6. *Be willing to work out a compromise with the person.* The goal isn't to "win" a battle, but to reach a mutually satisfying resolution. For example, you may be annoyed at your sister because she frequently asks you to babysit for her and then returns home many hours after she said she would. Instead of insisting that she *always* limit her outings to short periods of time, or *never* ask you to babysit at all, you might work out a compromise wherein

you agree to babysit for longer intervals on a once-a-month basis, at a time convenient to you and with plenty of advance notice.

7. *Start and finish the conversation on a positive note.* People are more willing to accept negative feedback and do something about it if they first have some positive interaction with the persons giving the feedback. For example, a supervisor criticizing an employee might phrase it as follows: "You know you've been doing really excellent work lately, so I was surprised when you turned in that job yesterday with several mistakes in it. It's going to have to be redone, but I'm sure a good worker like yourself will be able to make the necessary corrections on it." Similarly, finishing the conversation with a positive comment makes it a more pleasant interaction for both parties and conveys the message that the disturbing behavior hasn't adversely affected the entire relationship. For example, one friend says to another, "Thanks for agreeing to share the driving sometimes. I'm glad we could talk together about this. One thing I like about our friendship is that we can talk about things that bother us."

## Modeling

Therapists role-play people who live together and who both get ready at the same time in the morning to go to work. One of them often has to rush and is late to work because the other one uses the bathroom first and spends a long time in the shower, shaving, and so on. The one who is always rushed is annoyed at the other's behavior and decides to say something about it.

*Scene 1:* Demonstration of *destructive/aggressive* criticism: banging on bathroom door, yelling through door, name calling, and the like.

After Scene 1, the therapists ask group members to describe what went wrong, to imagine the likely consequences of such an interaction, and to suggest specific constructive alternative behaviors. The therapists then implement these suggestions in Scene 2 to contrast constructive criticism with the prior destructive criticism.

*Scene 2:* Demonstration of *constructive/assertive* criticism: better timing of the request (not during the morning rush), beginning and ending on a positive note, requesting specific behavior change, criticizing the behavior and not the person, and so forth.

Behavior Rehearsal Role Plays

Since receiving criticism is not covered until the next session, some group members may feel uncomfortable role-playing the recipient of the criticism in the present session. This may be handled as follows:

1. Therapists should acknowledge that this discomfort may arise, and stress that the recipient is not expected to demonstrate a skilled response yet. Besides, this may depict a more typical example of what group members will encounter in the "real world," since most of their acquaintances will not have had similar communication skills training. In addition, any discomfort the role-play recipient experiences can be shared with the group and the protagonist, as valuable post-role-play feedback.
2. Therapists may play the recipients of the criticism in these role plays if there is difficulty in having other group members play recipients.

Group members should be encouraged to generate a variety of types of scenes that are relevant to them (e.g., family, coworkers, friends, waiter, car mechanic, etc.) in which they have wished to give negative feedback.

> Some alcoholics respond to problems with others with either passivity or aggressiveness. This may be due to their lability during drinking and/or the "black-or-white" nature of their behavior when sober (e.g., passive) versus when drunk (e.g., "blowing up," aggressive). Because of these past extremes of behavior, we have noticed a tendency among some alcoholics to overcompensate to the other extreme when practicing these exercises, especially in the natural environment. They may be so eager to try out their newfound skills in assertiveness that they become aggressive as an overreaction to passivity or vice versa. Therapists should gently help such clients find the middle path, without becoming too critical and thereby dampening the clients' willingness to keep trying out the skills.

Introducing the Practice Exercise

Point out that the situation chosen should be of moderate difficulty. Instruct group members to identify whom they will criticize, to set specific goals for the criticism, and to think about how they will deliver the criticism *before* they approach the person.

Refer to the end of the book for the "Reminder Sheet" and "Practice Exercise" for this session (p. 202).

## Session: Receiving Criticism

Rationale

1. Critical statements are often encountered in everyday life; one of the most difficult things to do in our interactions with people is to receive criticism gracefully.
2. Criticism, if given and received appropriately, provides us with a valuable chance to learn things about ourselves and about how we affect other people. We all have room for improvement, and constructive feedback from others helps us to make positive changes in ourselves.
3. Another reason to practice receiving criticism gracefully is that doing so helps us to avoid unnecessary arguments and lets other people know that we are receptive to hearing their point of view. In contrast, the person who responds angrily to criticism will discourage others from speaking up again, which may lead to more damaging consequences in the future (e.g., an employee who cannot accept appropriate criticism may jeopardize his/her job and hinder his/her own professional growth; a spouse who cannot accept appropriate criticism jeopardizes the mutual understanding and give-and-take that contribute to a satisfying relationship).
4. There are two basic types of criticism that we may be exposed to, and neither one warrants an emotional or hostile reaction from us.
   a. *Constructive* (or assertive) criticism is the type that was described in the session on giving criticism. It is directed at behavior and not at the person. In this case, the other person describes his/her feelings with regard to something you are doing and asks you to change in some way.
   b. *Destructive* (or aggressive) criticism occurs when someone criticizes you as a person, rather than criticizing your behavior. This criticism is often related to the other person's emotional state or is a provocation to fight, rather than an appropriate reaction to your behavior.
   Whether the criticism is constructive or destructive, it is nothing to get emotional about, and it is particularly not worth fighting about.
5. Relationship between these skills and problem drinking:
   a. Interpersonal conflicts, and the resulting anger or other negative feelings, are high-risk situations for relapse to drinking. Failure to respond effectively to criticism can lead to serious

interpersonal conflicts, whereas having available an effective response can reduce conflicts and the probability of drinking.

b. Problem drinking has probably disrupted your functioning in multiple ways (e.g., as a parent, spouse, worker, etc.), and thus has made you susceptible to a variety of criticisms about your behavior. This increased likelihood of receiving critical feedback makes it especially important for you to be able to respond to it in a productive way. (Note: Receiving criticism about drinking per se will be practiced in another session. Since it can be especially difficult, we will focus on it only after first practicing how to receive criticism on other topics.)

## Skill Guidelines

The main goal in receiving destructive or constructive criticism is to prevent escalation into a fight. When possible, a second goal should be to try to change the nature of the criticism and to help the other person to communicate more productively with you. Even some destructive criticism, albeit presented in an ineffective and potentially hurtful way, may contain useful information that we can learn from.

1. *Don't get defensive, don't get into a debate, and don't counterattack with criticism of your own.* Doing so will only escalate the argument and decrease the chance of effective communication between the two of you. Consider the following situation: Someone heading out on a fishing trip is being criticized by his/her spouse for going fishing. The spouse replies, "Who are you to say whether fishing is good or bad? You know nothing about it." This kind of statement is quite offensive and directs attention away from the feelings between the husband and wife that are leading to the argument.

2. *Sincerely question the other person in order to clarify and refine the criticism so that you're more clear about its content and purpose.* By asking for more information about critical statements, you encourage straightforward criticism given in ways that are likely to improve the communication between yourself and people that you care about. To continue with the example of the fishing trip, a nondefensive reply, and one that would help to clarify the criticism, would be something like this: "I don't understand what it is about my going fishing that makes you unhappy. Could you tell me what it is?"

3. *Find something in the criticism that you can agree with and restate the criticism in a more direct fashion.* This is particularly impor-

tant when the criticism is 100% correct. Instead of responding to this with guilt or hostility, assertively accept and admit those things that are negative. To continue with the fishing example, the spouse going fishing might say, "You're right, I have been leaving you alone often on weekends." This approach takes away much of the negative impact of the criticism and allows the other spouse to be more objective in responding to negative feedback.

4. *Propose a workable compromise.* This consists of proposing some behavioral change to meet the criticism. Consider the "fishing trip" interaction: A workable compromise might be proposed in which the spouse would go fishing this week and go out with the other spouse to the movies next week.

5. *Reject unwarranted criticism.* There are some times when criticism is unjustified. In these situations, it is important to reject the criticism politely but firmly, in a way that is not demeaning to the other person. For example, a husband arriving home from work might say angrily to his wife, "This house looks like a cyclone hit it, and the kids have not eaten yet. I sometimes think that all you do is sit around at home while I am at work." An appropriate response for the wife might be to say, firmly but not angrily, "I realize that the house is a mess and I am behind schedule in feeding the children, but I have been sick all day and do not appreciate your criticism."

## Modeling

Therapists demonstrate effective responses to criticism: A store manager provides destructive criticism to a store clerk about the inadequate job the latter has been doing during the last few days (e.g., slow service, reading on the job, etc.). The clerk accepts responsibility for some elements in the harangue, asks for clarification of other points, and proposes a reasonable solution. A brief group discussion should be conducted after the demonstration.

## Behavior Rehearsal Role Plays

Give group members an opportunity to practice responding to both constructive and destructive criticism. Scenes should involve topics that the "receiver" has been criticized on in the recent past, or anticipates being criticized on in the near future. Protagonists should provide the role-play partner with sufficient description of the "criticism" being portrayed and its delivery, so that the scene approximates the real-life situation encountered by the protagonist.

Although the primary focus of this session is on receiving criticism, the "constructive" scenes also give the role-play partners additional practice in giving criticism.

Refer to the end of the book for the "Reminder Sheet" and "Practice Exercise" for this session (p. 203).

## Session: Receiving Criticism about Drinking

### Rationale

1. Since this session is an extension of the earlier session on receiving criticism, several of the general points remain applicable, particularly the notion that failure to respond assertively to criticism can result in needless emotional upset and arguments. These negative consequences, in turn, further increase the probability of drinking.
2. Sometimes criticism about drinking will take the form of accusations or inquiries (e.g., "You're home late. I know you've been drinking again"). Even when you have made a sincere decision to stop drinking and are fully engaged in treatment, it may take time for others in your life to increase trust and to reduce their own excessive vigilance about recurrence of drinking episodes. Sometimes this vigilance will result in unfounded criticism, but occasionally the criticism may be accurate. In either case, it is important to be able to respond to the criticism in a way that facilitates productive communication and does not start a fight. Similarly, even if the criticism is delivered in a destructive way, you need to be able to respond assertively and effectively.
3. Sometimes the criticism about drinking will focus on historical events or on the negative consequences of past drinking. It may be either destructive or constructive (e.g., "You were a horrible person during all those years you were drinking. You wrecked our home and family," or "I'm happy about all the good changes you're making now, but sometimes I still feel sad and frustrated about all that we suffered in the past when you were drinking. If you would start to eat dinner with us again and listen to the children talk about their day at school, I think that would help me feel more hopeful and positive about us"). However the criticism is phrased, it is important to be able to respond to it effectively and to focus on here-and-now solutions without getting sidetracked into a nonproductive rehashing of past conflicts.
4. During the initial period of sobriety, criticism about drinking

may be occasioned by some other behavior besides drinking that is disturbing the other person. For example, your spouse may be upset about your isolating yourself in the den after work or about your quick temper. However, instead of directly criticizing those behaviors that are disturbing, he/she may not mention them at all and instead may focus on past drinking or on present risk of drinking as the issue. This misdirected criticism may occur because drinking has been associated with those other behaviors in the past, or perhaps because it is easier and more automatic to criticize drinking than to focus on the other problems. Regardless of why the criticism was misdirected, the correct topic will not get raised unless you can respond appropriately to the initial criticism and not get sidetracked into a discussion about alcohol when it is not relevant. By refraining from getting defensive and by asking questions for clarification about what specific behaviors are upsetting your spouse, you have a better chance of accurately refocusing his/her criticism.

## Skill Guidelines

The general guidelines for receiving constructive and destructive criticism are applicable here (see "Rationale" and "Skill Guidelines" for that session). Some specific examples follow:

1. *Finding something to agree with.* If you have not been drinking but your spouse says to you, "You're home late. I know you've been out drinking again," you might respond by saying, "You're right, I am home later than usual today. I can see why you're worried, since when I used to drink I'd often get home late."

2. *Propose a workable compromise.* If your spouse angrily accuses you of drinking because he/she is worried about relapse and can't tell whether you've been drinking or not, a compromise such as the following might prove mutually satisfying: "If you're worried that I've been drinking, I'd appreciate it if you'd tell me that you're worried and just ask me in a calm, concerned way, rather than jumping to conclusions and angrily accusing me. I know you are concerned about me, but it sometimes doesn't come across that way. For my part, I'll speak up sooner and tell you why I'm feeling depressed, or call when I'm going to be home late. That way you won't have to wonder what's going on. Also, if I ever do have a slip, I'll talk about it with you right away and won't try to hide it from you like I used to. I'm pretty optimistic that if we both make these changes, the accusations and suspicion will lessen and we'll both feel better. How do these suggestions sound to you?"

## Modeling

The therapists role-play a situation involving an employee who is being criticized by his/her supervisor. The supervisor knows of the employee's drinking history and treatment involvement. The employee has maintained sobriety for several weeks, but has had a difficult afternoon at work today and has made some errors. He/she has had nothing to drink today. The supervisor points out the errors and expresses constructive concern that perhaps the employee drank during lunch and that the errors are due to the alcohol use. The therapists demonstrate an effective response to this criticism.

## Behavior Rehearsal Role Plays

In generating role plays, prompt group members to consider various types of drinking-related criticism that they have received or can anticipate receiving. Some dimensions along which the criticism might vary include:

- Person delivering it (e.g., employer, coworker, spouse, parent, child, sibling, or friend).
- Constructive versus destructive (see session on receiving criticism for distinction between these).
- Accurate versus unfounded.
- Focused on inquiries about possible recent drinking versus focused on past drinking episodes and their consequences.

---

Since many clients have received criticism about their drinking, the content of this session is usually quite familiar to most people in the group. Sometimes clients will have received the criticism while intoxicated, but at other times they will not have been drinking. Since there is likely to be some emotional response to the content of this session, it is important for the therapists to be aware that some clients may be so angered by memories of inappropriate criticism that they may not hear the message of the session.

Clients' anger can be used as an opportunity for therapists to empathize with them about being falsely accused. At the same time, therapists can ask clients to discuss the reasons why others might be suspicious. This may help clients understand that the suspiciousness might have a history rooted in the clients' own past behavior. Therapists can go on to gently confront clients about the fact that their erratic behavior was likely to have resulted in distrust on the part of others.

Once again, this illustrates the need for consistency in behavior over time, as well as the necessity for clients to be prepared to make repeated efforts to earn back the trust of others, even if some of the accusations against them were false.

---

Refer to the end of the book for the "Reminder Sheet" and "Practice Exercise for this session (p. 204).

## Session: Drink Refusal Skills

### Rationale

1. Being offered a drink or being pressured to drink by others is a very common high-risk situation for alcoholics who have decided to stop drinking. Have you received such offers or pressure? In what situations?
2. Being able to turn down a drink requires more than a sincere decision to stop drinking. It requires the specific assertiveness skills to act on that decision.
3. The social use of alcohol is very common in our culture, and it is encountered in a wide variety of situations and settings. Thus, even the person who totally avoids bars and old drinking buddies will still find himself/herself in situations where others are drinking or are making plans to go drinking. For example, family gatherings, office parties, restaurants, and dinner at a friend's home are only a few of the settings in which alcohol may be encountered. A variety of different people could offer you a drink, such as relatives, new acquaintances, dates, carpool partners, and waiters and waitresses. The person may or may not know of your drinking history. An offer to drink may take the form of a single casual offer of a drink, or may involve repetitious urgings and harassment. Different situations will be more difficult for different individuals.
4. Practice in refusing drinks will help you to respond more quickly and more effectively when real situations arise.

### Skill Guidelines

The precise nature of an assertive response to an invitation to drink will vary, depending on who is offering the drink and how the offer is made. Sometimes a simple "No, thank you" will be sufficient, At other times, additional strategies will be necessary. In some cases, telling the other person about your prior drinking problem will be useful in eliciting helpful support; at other times, it will be unnecessary to share that information.

*Nonverbal behaviors:*

1. Speak in a *clear, firm,* and *unhesitating voice.* Otherwise, you invite questioning about whether you mean what you say.

2. Similarly, making *direct eye contact* with the other person increases the effectiveness of your message.
3. *Don't feel guilty.* You won't hurt anyone by not drinking, so don't feel guilty. In many social situations, people will not even know whether you are drinking or not. You have a right not to drink. Stand up for your rights!

*Verbal behaviors:*

1. "No" should be the first word out of your mouth. It cuts the pusher off early. When you hesitate to say "no," people wonder whether you really mean it.
2. Besides saying "no," *suggest an alternative:*
    a. Suggest something else to do (e.g., go for a walk or a drive if you want to get together to talk, instead of going out for a drink to talk; go out to the movies instead of going drinking on a Saturday night).
    b. Suggest something else to drink or eat (e.g., ginger ale, coffee, orange juice, dessert, a sandwich, etc.).
3. *Request a behavior change.* If the person is repeatedly pressuring you, ask him/her not to offer you a drink any more. For example, if the person is saying to you, "Oh, come on, just have one drink for friendship," an effective response might be, "If you want to be my friend, then don't offer me a drink."
4. After saying "no," *change the subject* to something else to avoid getting drawn into a long discussion or debate about drinking. For example, you could say, "No, thanks, I don't drink. You know, I'm glad I came to this party. I haven't seen a lot of these people in quite a while, including yourself. In fact, I've been wondering what you've been up to lately."
5. *Avoid the use of excuses* (e.g., "I'm on medication for a cold right now"), *and avoid vague answers* (e.g., "Not tonight"). Both of these imply that at some later date you will accept an offer to drink. Although it is preferable to avoid excuses, their use may be defensible under certain circumstances.

## Modeling

Therapists role-play a situation in which the protagonist is offered a drink at a brother's birthday party. Someone hands him/her a drink and says, "Here, help us celebrate," and then ignores the protagonist's first refusal by saying, "Oh, come on, one drink won't hurt you." The therapists demonstrate an effective and assertive way to handle the situation.

### Behavior Rehearsal Role Plays

Group members are generally quite good at generating appropriate scenes to practice in this session. Occasionally, someone may state that he/she hasn't encountered any difficult situation yet and so has nothing to suggest for a role play. Encourage him/her to think ahead and to anticipate potential difficulties that could arise. Alternatively, have him/her role-play a typically difficult situation and demonstrate an effective response to it. Some role-play scenes will require using more than one role-play partner—for example, a group of people sitting around the table at a restaurant offering multiple prompts to drink.

In some of the later scenes, role-play partners may be very insistent, but most of the role plays should be of only moderate difficulty. Be sure to include a variety of scenes, involving coworkers, parties, restaurants, old friends, and new acquaintances.

---

In drink refusal role plays, the client asked to play the role of the drink pusher often becomes overly enthusiastic in attempting to outsmart the client playing the role of the refuser. Although this may prove to be fun, and therapists should tolerate some bantering, it is important to ensure that more subtle, realistic, and challenging situations are also presented.

---

Refer to the end of the book for the "Remainder Sheet" and "Practice Exercise" for this session (p. 205).

## Session: Refusing Requests

This session is based on the work of H. Fensterheim and J. Baer (1975).

---

Although this session does not teach anything dramatically new, in our experience it addresses a problem encountered by many alcoholic clients. Their feelings of guilt about the past, and their lack of confidence in applying newly acquired skills, leave them reluctant to disagree with others or deny their requests. However, failure to do so can leave clients feeling imposed upon, critical of themselves, or angry. Therefore, this concrete example of the application of assertiveness skills is provided, in order to help clients develop their abilities and confidence to cope with potentially awkward or difficult interpersonal situations.

---

Rationale

1. When people make requests or place demands on you, you will have to decide whether or not you want to go along with them. One consideration should be whether honoring a request will conflict with other activities that you give high priority. For example, you may have decided, as part of your program of recovery, that you will spend more time with your spouse/ children/family, that you will allocate an hour each day to try new leisure activities, and/or that you will develop new friendships with sober people. You may feel that fulfilling the request that has been made of you will conflict with one or more of these priorities. There also may be other reasons why you do not want to fulfill the request: You may feel that this person has imposed upon you too much lately; you may dislike doing that kind of activity; or you may not feel comfortable lending out what has been requested. You should evaluate every request made of you before giving an answer. Remember, you have the right to decide your priorities.

2. You also have the right to refuse requests made by others, without feeling selfish or guilty. If you decide that you want to refuse a request, you must be able to stand up for yourself by saying "no." If you can't state this simple word when you want to say it, you begin to lose control of your life. The inability to say "no" has several consequences:
   a. It distracts you from your more important priorities. Doing things you don't want to do may rob time and energy from the things that you really want to accomplish.
   b. Resentments build up. If you allow others to exploit you, you may eventually overreact when someone makes a small request.
   c. It leads to poor communication between you and others. It is dishonest and causes misunderstandings.
   d. You lose self-respect. You hate yourself for your weakness.

3. People often feel considerable discomfort when refusing requests. Even with practice, you may find that you still feel uncomfortable in this kind of situation. This is natural; many of us never feel entirely comfortable refusing someone else's request. However, it is important that you do it anyway, despite the discomfort that it may cause you. In the long run, the consequences of not refusing when you want to are worse than the short-term discomfort of saying "no."

4. People passively accede to requests for many reasons. They may

fear social rejection; they may feel that being a good wife/ husband means doing whatever their spouse wants; or they may find themselves unable to refuse, or even question, an assignment given by their boss. People may believe that they have no alternative but to say "yes" in such situations. In reality, however, they usually have more options than they realize. These options can be discovered through discussion and negotiation with the other person.

5. There is a big difference between agreeing to a request out of choice and agreeing out of coercion. If doing a favor may inconvenience you, there is still nothing wrong with saying "yes" if you believe that the friendship or the activity is important enough to you to accept some discomfort. Saying "yes" becomes a problem when it is in your best interest to say "no," but instead you end up agreeing to do what was asked.

6. There is often a direct connection between the inability to say "no" and drinking. The feelings of resentment, loss of self-respect, or distance from others that build up when you are not assertive are the kinds of negative emotions that often set the stage for a relapse. Developing effective, assertive ways to handle requests that are made of you can be an important element in preventing a relapse.

## Skill Guidelines

1. There are various reasons why you may refuse a request made of you:

   a. The request conflicts with other priorities. You need to have some idea about your time priorities: How much time do you want to devote to what? If you agree to the request, will it hinder your efforts to meet a goal of yours? Establishing your priorities will make it easier to determine whether you have the time to take on any new commitments.

   b. Perhaps the person making the request has a bad "track record" with you—perhaps he/she has made too many requests of you, failed to pay you back on time, or the like.

   c. Perhaps you are just not in the mood at the present time to fulfill the request. It is OK to state this, and inform the other person that you may be willing to do it at some other time.

2. Your refusal will be more acceptable, and will be less likely to cause problems with the other person, if you acknowledge his/ her feelings or position. By paraphrasing what he/she has said in making the request, you give the message that you have

been attentive and that you understand the need, but that nevertheless you are not going to honor the request. People can accept a rejection with less resentment if they feel that they have been heard and taken seriously.

3. Be firm in your refusal. Say "no" clearly and get right to the point, without long explanations.

4. Although it is not necessary to do so, you may decide to give your reason for refusing. If you do, state it in terms of your own priorities, needs, or feelings, and be brief. (An exception to this would be if you were refusing a request made by your boss. Your boss is human and will probably accept a reasonable refusal, but you may have to provide a bit more explanation than to other people. "I'm not in the mood right now" just won't do.)

5. Sometimes you may want to negotiate a compromise. Although you may not want to spend as much time or do everything that has been asked of you, you may be willing to go part of the way. Since you also have the right to make requests of others, you may be willing to do what has been asked of you in exchange for some favor from the other person. Compromising should be done if you really want to help the other person out, but not to the entire extent requested or in exchange for something else. However, be careful that you not use this as a "copout" when you really want to say "no."

6. Pay attention to your use of body language. Your tone of voice, posture, eye contact, gestures, and so on can help you to make your point. Or your body language may encourage the other person to continue to pester you, if it is not consistent with what you are saying.

7. If someone does persist, and continues to plead with you or even escalates his/her requests, calmly repeat your refusal. Do not escalate in terms of increased voice volume, threatening gestures, etc. Continue to repeat your response in the same calm manner until the other person backs off.

## Behavior Rehearsal Role Plays

Ask group members to generate scenes from their own experience. They may use situations in which they have had difficulty refusing requests in the past, or in which they anticipate having a problem. The situations may involve family members, neighbors, friends, or coworkers, who may be asking for help, requesting a loan, trying to sell something (e.g. a raffle ticket), and so on.

Note that this exercise requires one of the players to make a request. Although this skill is not explicitly covered in this program, the therapists should attend to the use of assertiveness skills when the request is made, and, if necessary, comment on the choice of words, use of body language, and so forth.

## Introducing the Practice Exercise

Have group members brainstorm their priority lists and begin to record them during the session. Some suggested items that might be included are attendance at Alcoholics Anonymous (AA) and aftercare group meetings, spending more time with family, allowing some leisure time each day, and so on. They should complete the lists outside the group, as well as work out their refusal to a hypothetical request.

Refer to the end of the book for the "Reminder Sheet" and "Practice Exercise" for this session (p. 206).

## Session: Close and Intimate Relationships

This session builds on the skills taught in a number of prior sessions, and therefore in some ways constitutes a review of them. Included in this category are assertiveness skills, giving and receiving criticism, giving compliments, and active listening skills. An attempt is made to coordinate the application of these skills in response to problems that often arise within the context of close and intimate relationships.

## Rationale

1. Thus far, we have outlined a number of different communication skills and discussed their application to a variety of situations. We have talked about how improved communication can enhance interactions with strangers, new acquaintances, family, spouses, coworkers, friends, and neighbors. Sometimes it is more difficult to handle problems that come up in close relationships than it is to handle problems that come up with strangers or acquaintances. Since close and intimate relationships can be areas of particular difficulty for people, this session provides further practice in using effective communication in these areas of your life. The strategies discussed in previous sessions will be reviewed, and we will focus on applying them within a marital or romantic/committed relationship.
2. There are any number of possible barriers to intimacy in rela-

tionships. Can you generate some examples as a group? (These might include distrust, anger, poor self-esteem, fear of failure, withdrawal/isolation, sex-role typing, etc.)

3. Effective communication within close/intimate relationships is important for several reasons. Among them are the following:

   a. It helps you and your partner to feel closer to each other.

   b. It promotes better understanding of each other's point of view and increases your ability to solve difficulties and conflicts.

   c. It decreases the likelihood that resentment and bad feelings over something will build up and affect other areas of your life as well (e.g., daily bickering over finances or the in-laws may lead to more pervasive negative feelings and subsequent avoidance of sex and affection).

   d. Drinking and relapse are less likely to occur when you have an effective alternative way to respond to difficulties in a relationship.

---

A discussion of communication in intimate relationships should address sexual issues as well as other aspects of the relationship. However, people can be uncomfortable discussing sexual issues, especially in a mixed-gender group setting. Behavior rehearsal role plays on this topic may also be difficult, so it is important that therapists present some hypothetical examples and didactic material on communication about sexual topics. The purpose of this is twofold: to sensitize group members to the critical role of communication within the sexual relationship, and to begin to desensitize them to talking about this topic by addressing it in a comfortable and direct way.

---

## Skill Guidelines

1. *Don't expect your partner to read your mind.* That is, don't expect him/her to know what you think, want, or feel without your telling him/her. Mind reading is especially likely to be expected with sexual topics, where partners are often reluctant to talk about things because they have learned to view sex as a taboo subject or they feel they "should not have to ask" for what they like. However, failure to communicate directly about sex with your partner can limit the pleasure you both receive from your sexual relationship and can lead to unnecessary problems and anxieties. Sexual performance varies between individuals, and also from day to day, week to week, or mood to mood for the

same individual (e.g., satisfaction can depend on position, amount and type of sensual touching in addition to intercourse, type of atmosphere, etc.).

Since no one can read someone else's mind, clear communication about likes and dislikes is important. For example, you are in bed with your partner and you are both interested in making love. However, after a while you become reluctant about making love because you wish that your partner would engage in more sensual caressing prior to intercourse. You don't point this out because of embarrassment, or because you feel that he/she "should know what I want." Lovemaking proceeds as usual, and eventually you are dissatisfied and irritable because it wasn't as pleasureable as you had hoped it would be. Such failure to communicate may result not only in dissatisfaction with your sexual relationship, but also possibly in eventual sexual dysfunction. By becoming preoccupied with worries about what is or isn't happening during your sexual encounters, you become less able to focus on feelings of arousal, thus making erectile failure or lack of orgasm fairly likely. Lack of erection or orgasm does not mean that a particular sexual encounter cannot be enjoyable; the occasional absence of one or the other is *not* to be viewed as a problem. However, a *pattern* of noncommunication and preoccupation with thoughts that distract from focus on one's arousal can contribute to dysfunction in the form of *chronic* erectile failure or lack of orgasm.

2. *Don't let things build up.* Frequent contact with a person increases the chance that some of his/her behaviors may bother you. Since the cumulative negative impact of saying nothing about a repeated annoyance can be great, it is important to *give constructive criticism at an early point.* (You might think back at this point over the skill guidelines for giving criticism.) Consider the following example of letting things build up. Suppose that for a long time your partner has not been doing what you think he/she should do to be helpful around the house. He/she comes home from work, usually says hello, and sits down to watch the news on TV. He/she expects dinner to be ready just as the news on TV is over, and also expects that the house will be in reasonably good order by then. In the meantime, you have worked hard all day too. You have had no time for relaxation. You have never complained about all the work you have had to do or about your partner's expecting everything to go his/her way. On occasion you have felt some resentment, but you have tried to overlook it because you didn't want to start an argument. You

have rationalized that it was "such a little thing, anyway." However, on one occasion, quite suddenly, you are feeling so tense and annoyed that you have a blowup over something very small. Your partner forgot to pick up the milk at the grocery store on the way home as he/she had agreed to do, and you yell and say, "You never do anything around here; you're lazy." What are the possible consequences of such a blowup? How might speaking up earlier have prevented this?

3. *Use your skills in receiving criticism* to minimize unnecessary fights, to reach mutually acceptable solutions to problems, and to make self-improvements based on feedback that you receive. (Therapists at this point should briefly review the skill guidelines for receiving criticism.)

4. *Express your positive feelings.* (Briefly review skill guidelines for giving compliments.) Many couples have difficulty expressing positive feelings within their relationship, particularly if the level of criticism has been increasing. When criticism occurs in the absence of any expression of positive affect, good feelings get overlooked, and negative feelings become more salient. One reason why people become reluctant to express positive feelings is that they feel that to do so would contradict the criticisms they have made. For example, a partner may refrain from saying that a dinner is good if he/she has criticized his/her partner for serving it an hour later than expected.

An important point that we sometimes forget when dealing with people who are very close to us is that we can each have, at different times, different reactions to a loved one's behavior. Sometimes we may have a positive reaction and sometimes a negative reaction. However, it is not inconsistent to verbalize both of these aspects of our reactions to another person's behavior. A problem arises when we assume that positive verbalizations aren't important, because "he/she knows how I feel even if I don't say it." For example, suppose that after a hard day at work you feel tense, and you angrily criticize your spouse in a destructive way about his/her habit of smelling your breath for alcohol when you arrive home. Later in the evening, you realize that you have been upset and that you didn't deliver the criticism in a constructive way. However, you do not apologize and you fail to say, "I was upset, but I love you and didn't mean to hurt your feelings by being so quick-tempered before," because it would make you feel as if your comments about his/her smelling your breath were unfounded. This failure to express your new feelings will make it even more difficult for the two of you to begin productive communication about your respective concerns (i.e., your own work, your tensions, and your mutual problem of how to handle questions about alcohol use).

A couple's sexual relationship is another important area where failure to express genuine positive feelings can lead to needless upset. A common experience is the situation where one partner is feeling very tired or upset about the day and is not in the mood to respond to the sexual advances made by the other partner. If the nonresponsive partner only states his/her negative feelings and turns away, the other partner may end up feeling hurt and unwanted, and wondering whether something else is wrong. A more accurate and more mutually satisfying way of responding to the situation would be for the distressed partner to share his/her positive feelings as well: "I really enjoy our touching and lovemaking, but right now I'm feeling pretty upset about some problems I had during the day and don't feel very sexy. I'd feel better if we could sit and relax together a while. That often helps me to unwind."

5. *Be an active listener.* (Briefly review skill guidelines for listening skills.) This helps build the closeness, affection, support, and understanding that make your relationship with your partner more satisfying to both of you. Active listening is important, whether your partner is discussing his/her feelings about everyday issues (e.g., a movie, a newspaper article, etc.) or about more major topics (e.g., career goals and satisfaction, quality/quantity of leisure time, pleasures and responsibilities of parenthood, etc.).

---

Although the intent of this session is not to focus exclusively on sexual behavior, the topic of sexual dysfunction may be elaborated on. Indeed, survey research suggests that from 15% to 30% of problem drinkers have secondary orgasmic dysfunction or impotence. This may be related to episodes of sexual activity while severely intoxicated and/or to anxiety following several dysfunctional episodes when intoxicated. As is typical in problems of sexual dysfunction, the anxiety can perpetuate the problem independently of the original events. Therapists may wish to schedule an individual evaluation session with clients who appear to need more intensive work in this area. We recommend that if problems require treatment, referral be made to a qualified professional.

If sexual problems go undetected or untreated, the associated anxiety and poor self-esteem can be a precipitant of further alcohol abuse.

Behavior Rehearsal Role Plays

All role plays should deal with salient topics within group members' close relationships. A fair amount of time may be spent on scenes involving giving and receiving criticism, since group members often identify this as an important area. Therapists should also prompt clients to generate scenes involving compliments, talking about feelings, and active listening, since deficits in these areas may otherwise be overlooked or neglected. One strategy for generating role plays is to ask group members to think of interpersonal situations in which use of a particular skill (e.g., receiving criticism) would be beneficial to them. A second strategy that also works well involves asking group members to recall any times in the recent past when they felt angry, anxious, or sad within a close relationship. This focus on feelings will help clients in recalling relevant situations and aid in suggesting particular communication skills that the individual could practice, to cope with such feelings.

Therapists should remember to evaluate the nonverbal as well as verbal aspects of each role play.

Introducing the Practice Exercise

If time permits, have clients discuss the first three items in the "Practice Exercise" assignment.

Refer to the end of the book for the "Reminder Sheet" and "Practice Exercise" for this session (pp. 207–208).

## Session: Enhancing Social Support Networks

This session is adapted from J. Depue (1982).

Rationale

1. Before the conclusion of this group experience, it will be helpful to think about how you can replace some of the support you have received here. Over the long run, it is possible to develop and maintain a network of people in your daily lives who can provide this much-needed support. Those who have a network of supportive people usually feel more confident about their ability to manage their lives and cope with problems.

2. Your social support network consists of those people in your life—family, friends, and acquaintances—who help you to cope with problems. Usually such helping relationships are two-way streets, in that others also gain support from you.

3. Although we all strive to achieve some degree of independence and self-sufficiency, it is also important to be able to offer support to and accept support from one another. Support makes a big difference in one's ability to cope. Research has shown that people facing a personal crisis (e.g., major surgery, chronic illness, job loss, death of a loved one, etc.) do much better if they have support from the people around them.

4. There are many stresses associated with problem drinking: emotional, interpersonal, financial, medical, and so on. Your chances of coping effectively with these are better if you have a good social support network. Staying sober, dealing with the problems that prior drinking has created, and managing the troublesome situations that used to trigger drinking are far more difficult in the absence of support from others.

5. For a variety of reasons, people often feel that they do not have the support they would like. Some don't know how to seek it out or have been reluctant to do so because of society's emphasis on self-reliance. (This is particularly true for many men, who find that asking for help is inconsistent with the "macho" image they have learned to maintain throughout their lives.) Many problem drinkers have found that their social support networks have deteriorated over the years because of social withdrawal, isolation, or interpersonal conflicts resulting from their alcohol use.

6. The communication strategies we have practiced so far in this group will help you build and maintain supportive relationships with others. In this session, we will identify specific ways in which interactions with people can be a source of support.

## Skill Guidelines

After you have decided on a problem that you would like some help with, there are three basic steps to take.

1. Consider *who* might be helpful to you. This list may include the following:
   a. People who are already important in your life and are usually supportive.
   b. People who presently are neutral (they do not hinder or help), but who could potentially have a more supportive role (e.g.,

an acquaintance you haven't yet approached for help; an AA member whom you might ask to be your sponsor; a relative who knows very little about your predicament).
c. People who are presently hindering your efforts to resolve problems but who could also become supporters, with some effort on your part (e.g., a spouse who tells you that you're hopeless and you'll never change; a friend who laughs off your problems).

2. Consider *what* type(s) of support you would like. This list may include the following:
   a. *Help with problem solving.* This could come from someone who can expand your thinking about options and help weigh the choices, or someone who has coped with a similar problem.
   b. *Moral support.* This includes recognition and positive feedback for what you do, as well as messages of understanding, encouragement, or hope, (e.g., a neighbor who is in "the same boat" and will help you feel less alone).
   c. *Helping with tasks or sharing the load as needed* (e.g., family cooperation with household chores, help from a coworker in getting a job done before a deadline, etc.).
   d. *Information or resources* (e.g., about local clubs and community activities, apartments for rent, jobs available, etc.).
   e. *Emergency help* (e.g., small loans, shelter, needed items, transportation, etc.).

3. Consider *how* you can get the help you need. Although dependable relationships take time and effort to develop, the following factors help to build a social support network:
   a. *Ask for what you need.* Let the other person know how he/she can help you. Whether you're asking for help with a task, for advice, or for moral support, the more specific and direct your request, the more likely it can be filled as you wish.
   b. *Add new supporters.* For one reason or another, you may find that your current group of helpers does not provide the kind of help you need for the problem at hand. You may need certain information about a new career field, or may be the first in your group going through a major transition, such as retirement. You'll need people who can give you an accurate picture of what to expect. You may simply wish for a new source of moral support who will understand your situation. People usually enjoy sharing their experiences, and your first request may open the door for a new friendship. For example,

"Hi, we've got a mutual friend. Joe Baker tells me you're working in real estate. I've been thinking about going for a license. You could probably answer some of my questions to help me decide. Could we get together?"

c. *Lend your support to others.* Reliable support requires a two-way street. A mutually supportive relationship is more reliable and satisfying than is a situation where one person always gives and the other always receives. Helping someone else out will not only benefit the recipient, but will also strengthen your own coping skills.

d. *Be an active listener.* This communication skill is one that we have discussed in earlier sessions. Whether you're giving support to someone else or receiving a friend's advice on your own problems, it's important to pay attention and make sure you hear accurately. Active listening includes attentive nonverbal behavior, not interrupting, asking questions for clarification, paraphrasing what you heard to make sure you understood, and responding to the speaker's nonverbal message as well as to his/her words.

e. *Give feedback.* Your friends and family won't always give you the most constructive or satisfying help the first time you ask, even though they're trying. They need your guidance about what was or was not useful. Also, by thanking them for their support, you're more likely to get their help again. For example, you might say this: "I really appreciate your helping me think through my choices objectively, even though you have strong ideas about what I should do." Or "I know you're trying to make me feel better when you say 'It'll all work out,' but you would be more helpful if you'd help me come up with some ideas for what to do."

## Modeling

Therapists demonstrate ineffective and effective ways of asking someone to share the load:

Indirect request—"This clutter is driving me berserk."

Nonspecific request—"I could use your help more around the house."

Direct and specific request—"I'd feel much less pressured if we could work together to straighten out the house. Would you please sort through these papers while I do the laundry?"

Behavior Rehearsal Role Plays

Role plays may be done in the context of the "Practice Exercise" assignment.

> For people who do not have good supports, it is not easy to build them. A single session devoted to this topic only begins to set the stage for a process that may take months or years to complete. It may be necessary to set the goal of building new networks as part of a more comprehensive community outreach program. Therapists should be aware of existing community resources such as self-help groups and voluntary organizations. A comprehensive treatment program that addresses these issues, conducted by Azrin and colleagues, is described in the final chapter of this book.

## Introducing the Practice Exercise

Leave plenty of time to work on this exercise during the group session. Ask clients to discuss and answer the first four questions in Exercise 1, identifying a problem, potential supporters, and ways to get support. Also discuss the first two questions in Exercise 2, identifying someone who needs support and what help you could give. If time permits, have clients role-play ways to ask for and give support.

Refer to the end of the book for the "Remainder Sheet" and "Practice Exercise" for this session (pp. 209–210).

# 3

Coping Skills Training:
Part II. Intrapersonal Skills

## General Introduction

The coping skills strategies covered in this chapter can be divided into three general categories: skills for coping with specific intrapersonal problem situations, general lifestyle modification strategies, and relaxation training. Skills for coping with specific problem situations include managing thoughts about alcohol, awareness of and management of anger and other negative mood states, cognitive restructuring exercises, planning for emergency situations, and coping with persistent problems. Lifestyle modification strategies include skills for identifying and coping with problems through systematic problem solving, avoiding high-risk situations through more intelligent decision making, and improving the balance of enjoyable versus obligatory activities in one's daily schedule. Finally, relaxation training provides a means for coping with tension, anxiety, and cravings to drink, and can also be used to help clients to "cool down" as part of anger management.

The program elements covered in this chapter have more of a cognitive focus than those in the preceding chapter, which have both cognitive and behavioral aspects. Some of the material in this chapter is complex and may pose difficulty for clients who suffer from cognitive and memory deficits in the first weeks and even months following detoxification. However, we feel that the skills contained in this chapter are essential to a comprehensive rehabilitation program. Our clinical experience has borne out the feasibility of including these materials, especially when the more complex cognitive restructuring skills are presented in the later phases of a treatment program. Repeated practice of specific techniques, and use of examples from clients' personal material or concerns, help with retention of skills. Frequent review of cognitive material over several sessions enhances understanding further and reduces the likelihood of forgetting due to neuropsychological impairment.

Although there could be an advantage to delaying some of this material as long as possible to allow for clients' neuropsychological recovery, a good case can also be made for presenting some selected skills early in the training sequence. For example, in an outpatient setting, staying sober is necessary for clients' very participation in this program, so the unit on managing thoughts about alcohol should come very early in the program (see Chapter 4 for discussion of sequencing). Problem solving is another unit that can advantageously be presented early, although it is one of the more abstract concepts in this handbook. It can help clients to cope with a variety of problems that occur in their daily lives, and also provides a framework for the therapists to structure group discussion of problems that clients bring into sessions. Thus, once introduced, it can be used in subsequent sessions to structure discussion of whatever topic or case example arises. This kind of repetition over time, using a variety of problem situations, ensures that the more abstract problem-solving skills are eventually incorporated into the clients' repertoire. Toward the end of the treatment program, therapists should "fade out" giving direct advice, and instead help clients to become their own problem solvers.

The order of topics in this chapter generally proceeds from the simpler to the more complex. However, problem solving is introduced early because it will be useful in subsequent sessions. Furthermore, the session on managing thoughts about drinking provides material that all alcoholics can readily use, and it is considered a good way to introduce the concepts of cognitive restructuring and self-control. Relaxation training is a simple, concrete skill that can be mastered easily and used for coping with a variety of high-risk situations. Although we have begun to move away from spending several lengthy sessions on full-blown formal relaxation training (e.g., 30 minutes of deep muscle relaxation), using briefer relaxation techniques allows more flexibility for incorporating relaxation into other cognitive coping strategies (e.g., to help clients calm down when angry). It is also recommended that clinicians consult the program sequences for inpatient and outpatient programs that are discussed in Chapter 4, prior to deciding on the exact sequence of sessions they wish to use in their clinical work.

## Session: Managing Thoughts about Alcohol[1]

### Rationale

1. Thoughts about drinking are normal; almost anyone who stops drinking will occasionally think about starting up again. There is no problem with thinking about drinking, as long as you don't *act* on those thoughts. You may feel guilty about the thoughts (even though you have not acted on them), and you may try to get them out of your mind. The purpose of this session is to identify those thoughts or feelings that can lead you to drinking, and then to learn some new ways to catch yourself before you actually slip. Sometimes the thoughts are obvious, but sometimes they can creep up on you almost without being noticed.

2. The following are some common situations in which ex-drinkers may have thoughts about resuming drinking. (You can probably provide examples of your own as well.)

   a. *Nostalgia.* Some recovering alcoholics think about drinking as if it were some long-lost friend. For example, "I remember the good old days when I'd take a few six-packs down to the lake and go fishing." "What's New Year's Eve without a drink?"

   b. *Testing control.* Sometimes, after a period of successful sobriety, ex-drinkers become overconfident. For example, "I bet I can drink with the guys tonight and go back on the wagon tomorrow morning." Curiosity can also be problematic. For

[1]This session has been adapted from *Relapse Prevention: A Non-Smoking Maintenance Program*, by R. Brown and E. Lichtenstein, 1979, unpublished treatment manual, Eugene, OR: University of Oregon. Used by permission of the authors.

example, "I wonder what it would be like to have just one drink," or "Let's see if I can leave a six-pack in the refrigerator, just for guests."

c. *Crisis.* During stress or crisis, an ex-drinker may say, "I *need* a drink," or "I can only handle this with a few drinks in me," or "I went through so much upset, I deserve a drink," or "When this is all over, I'll be able to stop drinking again."

d. *Feeling uncomfortable when sober.* Some people find that new problems arise after they become sober, and they think it would help to resume drinking in order to end those new problems. For example: "I'm being very short-tempered and irritable around my family—maybe it's more important for me to be a good-natured parent and spouse than it is for me to stop drinking right now," or "I'm no fun to be around when I'm not drinking. I don't think I should stop drinking, because if I do, people won't enjoy or like me as much."

e. *Self-doubts.* You may doubt your ability to succeed at things. For example, "I just have no willpower," or "I tried to quit many times before and none of those efforts worked out; why should I expect this one to last?"

---

It is often difficult for clients to grasp the material on analyzing and changing thoughts. Introducing the concept of cognitive analysis and restructuring can be particularly difficult for alcoholics in treatment. If the concept is not understood from the outset, then many of the benefits of cognitive coping skills can be lost.

Clients may initially be unaware of the thoughts and feelings that precede the decision to have a drink. They may simply state that they are not aware of any thought/feeling triggers, and that they "just start drinking and that's all." They may admit that logically, *something* must have caused them to drink, but it seems to be some powerful, usually external force that occurs "in a flash" so that they do not know or remember what comes over them. Such statements may help clients protect themselves by denying personal responsibility for their actions and attributing their behavior to forces "beyond their control." This lack of awareness makes it difficult for clients to identify the actual antecedent events and to initiate the use of appropriate coping skills.

In order to help clients begin to grasp cognitive concepts, the idea of "slowing down the action" (as in an instant replay on TV or a slow-motion film sequence) is useful. Once clients feel comfortable examining the chain of thoughts that might have led to a previous relapse, the notions of self-monitoring (or self-awareness) and of modifying one's thoughts (cognitive restructuring) can then be more readily introduced. The primary goal is to gradually make clients more aware of their thought processes and of their ability to control or stop thoughts that may set the stage for drinking, and to replace these with more adaptive coping thoughts that enhance abstinence.

3. Try to identify your own specific resumption thoughts and rationalizations for drinking. What thoughts about alcohol preceded your last drinking episode after a period of sobriety? For each of you, which thoughts about alcohol seem to be the most frequent or the strongest? Under what circumstances do these resumption thoughts tend to occur? As a group, list these resumption thoughts on the board.

## Skill Guidelines

All recovering people have thoughts about drinking at one time or another. Here are some ways to manage thoughts about drinking.

1. *Challenge them.* Use other thoughts to challenge the resumption thoughts. For example, "I cannot have just one drink without increasing my risk of more drinking," or "I don't have to drink to unwind after work; I can use relaxation exercises instead," or "I can still go fishing and have other good times without drinking—it may feel a little strange at first, but in time I will feel more comfortable."

2. *List and recall benefits of not drinking.* Thoughts about the personal benefits of sobriety can help to weaken your excuses for drinking. Benefits to think about include better physical health, improved family life, greater job stability, more money available for recreation and paying bills, increased self-esteem, sense of self-control, and so on. It is important to pay attention to these positive aspects of sobriety and to the progress you are making, rather than focusing on what you seem to be giving up. Add more items of your own to the list of benefits. You might also carry a card listing the benefits of sobriety, to be reviewed whenever you catch yourself being persuaded to drink.

3. *List and recall unpleasant drinking experiences.* Try to recall the pain, fear, embarrassment, and other negative feelings associated with drinking. Make a list of unpleasant experiences associated with drinking, such as blackouts, hangovers, fistfights, arrests, withdrawal, liver problems, and so forth. Try to conjure up an *image* of a specific unpleasant experience. Make a list of the negative effects of drinking on the reverse side of the card listing the benefits of sobriety. At moments of temptation, take out the card and read it over slowly three or four times. One needs to counteract the "pros" of drinking with the "cons" of drinking and the "pros" of sobriety.

4. *Distractions.* Think about something unrelated to drinking, to stop thoughts about drinking. For example, think about

pleasant, enjoyable topics (holiday plans, vacation spots, loved ones, relaxation, enjoyable hobbies, etc.). Focusing on a task you want to get done is another constructive distraction. Add more items of your own to the list of possible distracting thoughts.

5. *Self-reinforcement.* Remind yourself of your success so far—for example, 2 weeks of abstinence, becoming actively involved in treatment, staying in the treatment program. Again, add more items of your own to this list.

6. *Decision delay technique.* Put off the decision to drink for 15 minutes. Most urges to drink are like waves: They build to a peak and then decline. If you wait a while, the wave will pass. Try imagining that you are a surfer riding the "wave" of craving until it subsides, or use another image that is effective for you.

---

Some clients and clinicians find imagery exercises to be a potent force in controlling thoughts and urges to drink. A client who feels that he/she is about to be overwhelmed or engulfed by urges to drink can be helped by imagining scenes that portray urges to drink as storms that will end with calmness, mountains that can be climbed, or waves that can be ridden. Every client can find a personal image to help him/her maintain control until the urge peaks and then dissipates. Other useful images include being a warrior or explorer who can "slice through" urges (e.g., the enemy, the thick tropical underbrush) and carve out a path to safety. Images can be made more vivid by using relaxation techniques and by referring to all the senses (e.g., seeing the thick green jungle, hearing the sword swishing through the leaves, smelling the tropical plants, etc.). Photographs or images of loved ones (e.g., children) can also be used to distract the alcoholic who is craving a drink. Interested clinicians may want to make use of imagery enhancement exercises or other handbooks on imagery training (e.g., Lazarus, 1977).

---

7. *Leave the situation or change the situation* in which you started having thoughts about drinking. Try a different activity, such as a hobby or physical exercise.

8. *Call someone* who in the past has been helpful talking you through a situation. It is important that the person can really be helpful. Consider individuals such as your AA sponsor or a friend.

## Exercise in Group

Use the coping techniques listed under "Skill Guidelines" to help the group members develop individualized strategies they can employ to combat craving (refer to material generated earlier by the group during discussion of point 3 of the "Rationale"). Although this session does not include any explicit modeling or role playing, clients can be asked to imagine a difficult high-risk situation as vividly as possible, and then to practice coping with the thoughts and the craving for alcohol.

## Introducing the Practice Exercise

Ask clients to write out lists of (1) personal benefits of not drinking, and (2) the unpleasant effects of drinking. Distribute 3 × 5 cards and instruct the group members to transfer their completed lists onto them, in accordance with the suggestion in points 2 and 3 of the "Skill Guidelines."

Refer to the end of the book for the "Reminder Sheet" and "Practice Exercise" for this session (p. 211).

## Session: Problem Solving

### Rationale

1. People often find themselves confronted by difficult situations. A situation becomes a problem if the person has no effective coping response immediately available to handle it.
2. Problems are part of everyday life. They arise in dealings with other people (e.g., handling social situations, feelings about others, etc.), and out of one's own thoughts and emotions (e.g., the way one looks at a situation, self-critical thoughts, desires for the future, etc.). Think of examples from among the problems you have described in previous sessions.
3. Effective problem solving requires recognizing that you face a problem situation, and resisting the temptations either to respond on your first impulse or to "do nothing." Coming up with an effective solution requires that you pause to assess the situation, so that you can decide which actions will be in your own best interest.
4. Sometimes the problem situation may involve wanting to drink such as at a party. At other times, the problem itself may not involve drinking, but your tendency may be to act impulsively to find a quick and easy solution. If you don't find a good solution, then the problem can build up over time, and the pressure may eventually get to you and trigger drinking. Drink-

ing may appear to be an easy way out. Effective problem-solving strategies must therefore be a part of everyone's program for sobriety, since the occurrence of problems can easily set the stage for a relapse.

## Skill Guidelines

The overall problem-solving approach is adapted from T. J. D'Zurilla and M. R. Goldfried (1971).

1. *Problem recognition.* (This element was adapted from Intagliata, 1979.) "Is there a problem?" The first task is to recognize that a problem exists. What are some of the clues that indicate that there is a problem?
   a. Clues you get from your bodies (e.g., indigestion, craving).
   b. Clues you get from your thoughts and feelings (e.g., feelings of anxiety, depression, loneliness, fear, etc.).
   c. Clues you get from your behavior (have you been meeting your own standards for performance at work, in your family, with friends?).
   d. Clues you get from noticing the way you react to other people (e.g., anger, lack of interest, withdrawal, etc.).
   e. Clues others give you (e.g., they appear to avoid you, to criticize you).

---

Problem solving is a skill that can be used to develop a flexible coping repertoire in situations that have not been previously encountered. Problem recognition is crucial, especially when the impulse is to minimize or deny problems. The very act of sitting down, formally analyzing a problem situation, and coming up with a range of possible solutions can also be a direct form of coping. It can be used as an alternative to drinking when one is faced with a difficult situation. Situations requiring solutions can be alcohol-specific (e.g., at a party where drinks are available), general (e.g., family illness, conflict at work), intrapersonal (e.g., feeling confused, lonely, depressed, tense), or interpersonal (e.g., family argument).

The idea of formal training in problem solving is used to accelerate the process of developing higher-order coping strategies that go beyond situation-specific skills. This enhances generalization of coping skills beyond the treatment situation and, in effect, encourages clients to "become their own therapists" when they are on their own.

---

2. *Identify the problem.* "What is the problem?" Having recognized that something is wrong, try to identify the problem as precisely as possible. Gather as much information and as many facts as

you can to help clarify the problem. Be concrete, and define the problem in terms of behavior whenever possible. Try to break it down into specific parts—you may find it easier to manage several parts than to have to confront the entire problem all at once.

3. *Consider various approaches.* (This element is adapted from Bedell, Archer, & Marlowe, 1980.) "What can I do?" It is important to develop a number of solutions to a given problem, because the first one that comes to mind may not be the best. The following methods will help you to identify several approaches that could be useful in solving a problem, so that you will be more likely to settle on a good solution and implement it effectively.

   a. *Brainstorming.* Generate solutions without stopping to evaluate how good or bad the ideas are. It is more helpful to write them down, so that they can be reviewed when deciding which one to try. Write down all the ideas you get; do not stop to evaluate whether they are good or bad. More is better. This helps you get all your ideas out into the open so you can decide how well they solve your problem without rejecting any of them too hastily.

   b. *Change your point of view or frame of reference.* It helps to step back and get a little distance from the situation. Imagine that you are advising a friend about what to do. A different perspective may help you generate more alternative solutions, or may help change your attitude toward the problem.

   c. *Adapt a solution that has worked before.* Perhaps you can think of a solution that worked well for you in a similar situation, or ask someone else about solutions that have worked for them in the past. An old solution will probably have to be modified to fit your present needs, but it can give you a good starting point.

4. *Select the most promising approach.* Think ahead. "What will happen if . . . ?" Identify the most probable outcomes for each possible approach; be sure to include both positive and negative outcomes, both long- and short-term consequences. Consider what factors in your life may be used as resources to help you implement each approach, and what factors may interfere with each approach. Arrange all the potential solutions according to their consequences and their desirability. The solution that maximizes positive consequences and minimizes negative ones is the one to implement first.

5. *Assess the effectiveness of the selected approach.* Implement your decision. "How did it work?" Remember that the solution may not be immediate—you may have to keep working at it. Evaluate the strengths and weaknesses of your plan as you proceed by asking yourself: "What difficulties am I encountering? Am I getting the results I expected? Can I do something to make this approach more effective?" If, after you give the plan a fair chance, it doesn't seem to be resolving the problem, move on to the second-choice solution and follow the same procedure.

## Behavior Rehearsal Role Plays

Clients should work through the problem recognition stage, to identify problems that they would like to work on. Select one at a time, have the client describe it as accurately as possible, and have the whole group brainstorm solutions, which should be listed on the blackboard. Then have the group reason through the process of weighing the alternatives to select the most promising one. Have them articulate both advantages and disadvantages for every alternative, as a means of combating black-and-white thinking. Prioritize the alternatives. If it seems appropriate, role-play and evaluate the effectiveness of the most promising one(s).

If the group has difficulty coming up with appropriate problems to work on, present the following hypothetical problem to the group:

Your landlord is always crabby when he comes to collect the rent. One of the windows in your bedroom was cracked when you moved in; during a cold night, it cracked all the way, and a section is now out. When he comes to collect the rent, you mention it to him. He screams at you and accuses you of breaking the window, saying it was never cracked. Whenever he was crabby before, you simply let it go, but this time he says you must pay to have the window replaced.

Present various definitions of the problem and have clients select the best one:

The problem is that your landlord is a real grouch.
The problem is that his screaming has made you feel real down and hurt.
The problem is that you don't have enough money to pay for a new window.
The problem is that your window is cracked and should be repaired by the landlord. (Correct)

Consider various approaches to solving the problem and have clients select the most promising one. Demonstrate the brainstorming process and the factors that go into selecting the apparent best solution.

Refer to the end of the book for the "Reminder Sheet" and "Practice Exercise" for this session (p. 212).

### Session: Increasing Pleasant Activities[2]

Rationale

1. This session focuses on the role of pleasant activities in coping with lifestyle problems. "Lifestyle" is a word to describe the usual pattern of one's day-to-day activities.
2. Many alcoholics feel a void in their lives after they stop drinking. If you had a life composed of eating, sleeping, working, and drinking, and then you stopped drinking, you're left with just eating, sleeping, and working. The absence of pleasant leisure activities can be a major problem.
3. Research has shown that the number of pleasant activities a person engages in is directly related to the occurrence of positive feelings. Likewise, the fewer pleasant activities a person engages in, the more likely it is that negative feelings such as boredom, loneliness, and depression will occur. This suggests that pleasant leisure-time activities may be a powerful tool for controlling these negative feelings.
4. Many people spend most of their time meeting obligations that are not necessarily pleasant but that must be performed (e.g., a job, housework, yardwork, errands)—things they "should" do, rather than things they "want to" do. If your lifestyle is full of "shoulds" and totally lacking in "want tos," you may start to believe that you "owe" yourself a drink or drug as a reward for working so hard. It is best to achieve some balance between activities you should do and those you want to do (Marlatt & Gordon, 1985).

Skill Guidelines

1. *Develop a menu of pleasant activities.* The first step in changing your lifestyle is to target some pleasant activities that you want

[2]In order to conduct this session, therapists will need copies of the Pleasant Events Schedule. These can be obtained by contacting Dr. Peter M. Lewinsohn, Oregon Research Institute, 1899 Willamette, Suite 2, Eugene, OR 97407.

to initiate or increase in frequency. One way to do that is to brainstorm a list of activities and pick out some that are pleasant for you. People are very different with respect to the specific kinds of activities they experience as pleasant. We will now pass out copies of the Pleasant Events Schedule; read it through and check off items that you personally find pleasant.[3] The checked items can form a "menu" of pleasant activities. Some of the pleasant activities may be things you used to enjoy, but haven't done in a long time. Other items on your menu may be things you have wanted to try but never got around to.

2. Some pleasant activities can become "positive addictions" (Glasser, 1976). If a negative addiction (e.g., alcohol) can be described as an activity that feels good at first but results in feeling bad later on and causes harm in the long run, a positive addiction (e.g., jogging) is an activity that may not feel so good at first, but becomes more desirable as time goes on and is very beneficial in the long run. A positive addiction is an activity that meets the following criteria: (a) It is noncompetitive; (b) it does not depend on others; (c) it has some value for you (physical, mental, or spiritual); (d) you can improve with practice (but you are the only one who is aware of your progress); and (e) you accept your level of performance without criticizing yourself. Examples include relaxation, meditation, exercise (jogging, swimming, skiing, cycling, etc.), hobbies, reading, cultural activities, and creative skills (music, art, writing, etc.).

3. The next step after completing your menu is to *develop a pleasant-activities plan.* Try scheduling a small block of time each day (30–60 minutes) for pleasant activities. Begin this "personal time" by sitting quietly and mentally reviewing your menu of pleasant activities. You probably will not want to do the same thing every day. One day you may feel the need for relaxation, another day for exercise, and a third day for gardening or music. Schedule some time each day, but do not schedule the activity, so that what you do in your personal time does not become another obligation.

4. As a group, let's discuss the following strategies for, and obstacles to, increasing one's rate of pleasant activities (adapted from Lewinsohn, Antonuccio, Steinmetz, & Teri, 1984):

    a. *Commitment.* Putting a pleasant-activities plan into action requires a strong commitment. You must be willing to es-

---

[3]The original Lewinsohn scale (MacPhillarny & Lewinsohn, 1971) contains some pleasant events that are not appropriate for alcoholics. These should be deleted from the list prior to using it.

tablish priorities and perhaps also rearrange other activities in your life.

b. *Balance.* The goal is to achieve an adequate balance between the activities you "should" do and the activities you "want to" do. Note that balance is not the same as equality: There will likely be more "shoulds" than "want tos." "Balance" refers to each individual's degree of satisfaction with his/her daily life.

c. *Planning.* What problems or circumstances could interfere with completing your plan? How will you take care of competing demands on your time?

d. *Pleasantness.* Be sure to choose activities that you find highly enjoyable.

e. *Anxiety.* Anxiety can interfere with your engaging in or enjoying pleasant activities. This may dissipate with time, or you may need to choose other activities.

f. *Control.* If you stick to your plan, you will achieve a measure of control over your daily schedule. You will also add some activities that you find enjoyable and rewarding.

### Introducing the Practice Exercise

This assignment asks group members to write out a list of pleasant activities based on the Pleasant Events Schedule items. They should also make appointments with themselves for "personal time." *After* their personal time, they should record their activities.

Refer to the end of the book for the "Reminder Sheet" and "Practice Exercise" for this session (p. 213).

## Session: Relaxation Training: I. Deep Muscle and Imagery Techniques

> Relaxation training sessions can also be used, in part, to review previous materials, since it is not necessary to take up the entire session with relaxation skills training.

### Rationale

1. Today's session focuses on the use of relaxation techniques in coping with stress, tension, and anxiety.

2. Chronic difficulties in coping with stress or tension can result in a variety of negative consequences. Examples of such consequences include insomnia, irritability, difficulty concentrating, cardiac problems, headache, overeating, smoking, getting into arguments, and being impulsive.

3. Alcohol abuse is another possible negative consequence of chronic difficulties in coping with stress. Stress and anxiety are high-risk situations for many problem drinkers. That is, stress and anxiety frequently precipitate drinking bouts and relapses. An important step in staying abstinent is learning to use stress as a signal to cope in some other way, rather than as a signal to drink. It is important to recognize your stress signals or triggers as early as possible, before they build up to the point where you become desperate to do anything—including drinking—to get rid of the discomfort. When you recognize these signals, you can use other ways of coping to reduce your tension. Relaxation is one coping skill that can be very useful during times of stress. What thoughts, feelings, or physical signs are your tension signals? (Examples include "I am going nuts over this work assignment—it's really getting to me," or getting a tense feeling in the neck and shoulders.)

4. There are several ways in which relaxation can be used to cope with stress:
   a. To decrease tension in *specific* stressful situations (e.g., nervous about upcoming job interview, angry at the children, etc.).
   b. To decrease one's *general* level of daily tension.
   c. To decrease tension prior to going to sleep.
   d. To decrease the urge to drink.
   e. To increase one's ability to think clearly and rationally in a problem situation (e.g., when very angry or when surprised by some unexpected event). It is easier to think positively if you are relaxed first.

5. The relaxation skills that we will learn here use three basic techniques: reducing muscle tension, breathing exercises, and pleasant images (i.e., creating a relaxing scene in your mind).

6. Several sessions will be devoted to learning and practicing relaxation skills. During the early stages, the procedures will take up to 25 minutes to practice. After that, we will work on gradually fading out some of the steps, so that eventually you will be able to relax much more quickly and in a variety of situations. At first you should not attempt to use relaxation to actually cope with stressful situations; simply focus on *practic-

*ing* the skills and exercises. Like any other skill, such as riding a bicycle, it becomes more useful and automatic only after a period of practice. After several sessions, you will be ready to begin using your relaxation skills in many everyday situations.

7. Relaxation skills can be taught in three steps. First, you will learn to become more aware of tension and relaxation by tensing and relaxing eight specific muscle groups. This step is taught today. In future sessions, you will learn to "let go," or relax the eight muscle groups without tensing first. In the third step, through individualized planning, you will choose the relaxation techniques that work best for you. By that time you should be able to use briefer techniques, such as a calming word or image, and should be able to relax a selected muscle group (e.g., jaw, neck) rather than your whole body.

Therapists may want to omit some of the more formal relaxation exercises and use only the abbreviated techniques. The skills can also be interspersed with other sessions throughout the program, rather than given in a series of consecutive sessions in isolation. There are numerous handbooks of relaxation techniques, as well as audiotapes, available. Therapists may want to use some of these support materials, since the relaxation instructions that follow are an abbreviated summary of the most common, basic techniques. The tapes can be useful to therapists who wish to hear the tone of voice and pace of experienced relaxation therapists, but they should not be used in sessions as a substitute for the personal touch of the therapist. Tapes can also be made during a session, duplicated, and given to clients to use at home.

## Preparations for Relaxation Induction

1. Today we will guide you through a tension–relaxation exercise so that you can get a good idea of what it involves, and can begin to practice it on your own. The exercise is often called "progressive relaxation" or "deep muscle relaxation."
2. Progressive relaxation involves alternately tensing and relaxing various muscle groups in order to identify sensations of tension and substitute the sensations of relaxation.
3. As stated earlier, this is a skill that is learned gradually and with practice. We will not be doing anything to you; you will be in control and learning how to relax yourself. It is important that you not expect too much too soon. It is quite possible that you will feel little effect the first few times, although some people do feel deeply relaxed the first time.

4. We will now demonstrate the method of tensing each muscle group, with you imitating our behavior. Before beginning, we should point out the following:
   a. During the tension phase, the idea is to produce a *moderate* amount of tension, not to strain the muscles by tensing as hard as possible.
   b. Release the tension immediately on cue (i.e., as soon as [leader's name] says "Now").
   c. The pace of the demonstration will proceed more rapidly than will the actual relaxation induction.
5. We will now hand out a subjective rating scale to each of you. Estimate and record your *present* degree of tension–relaxation, using the 0–100 scale. This is done privately and should take only a minute. We will discuss the self-ratings after the exercise.
6. It is best to lie on the floor on mats or blankets for this practice. We will turn off some of the room lights.

Rating Scale

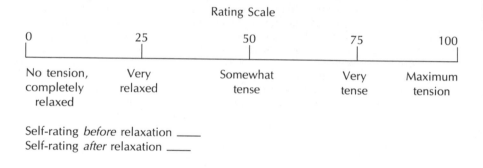

| 0 | 25 | 50 | 75 | 100 |
|---|---|---|---|---|
| No tension, completely relaxed | Very relaxed | Somewhat tense | Very tense | Maximum tension |

Self-rating *before* relaxation ____
Self-rating *after* relaxation ____

NOTES TO THERAPISTS ON RELAXATION INDUCTION

1. Conduct two tension–relaxation cycles for each muscle group before proceeding on to the next muscle group. Allow 5 seconds of tension and 15–20 seconds of relaxation for each cycle.

2. In relaxation training, how the therapist says things is as important as what is actually said. It is not necessary to talk continuously during the full 5 seconds of the tension phase or the full 15–20 seconds of the relaxation phase. The therapist should begin the session in a conversational tone and become a bit louder and more intense during the 5-second tension instructions. Over the course of the rest of the session, the therapist's voice should show a progressive reduction in volume and speed, becoming calm, soft, and rhythmic.

3. The therapist who is guiding the relaxation induction should

tense somewhat and relax a lot in synchrony with the group members. This will automatically improve voice tone. (If there is a cotherapist who is not guiding the induction, he/she should join the group members in doing the relaxation induction.)

4. Notice that each tension–relaxation cycle consists of the following:

- Brief instructions on how to tense the muscles.
- Instructions to tense up, hold the tension, and study it (5 seconds).
- "And now relax, feel the tension flowing out of your body."
- Relaxation patter (i.e., instructions to tune in to the feelings of relaxation, to notice the difference between the tension and relaxation, and to enjoy the contrast) (15–20 seconds).

Follow the directions for "Timing and Patter" and "Muscle Groups" (see below) as you guide the relaxation induction. During the relaxation patter, use a variety of the statements provided, but don't try to use all the statements in each phase. The statements can flow together in nearly any combination, as long as the patter remains rhythmic and does not become overly routine and predictable.

5. After the tension–relaxation cycles are completed, continue the induction with the directions on "Imagery" and on "Breathing."

TIMING AND PATTER

*Tension: 5 seconds*

Study *(feel, note)* the tension. That's right, hold it, study it, tight, hard, feel the tension in your _____. Concentrate on the tension, how it feels, where it's located.

*Relaxation: 15–20 seconds*

And relax: Just let go, further and further, get rid of all the tension, tune into the feelings of relaxation, deeper and deeper. Just enjoy the feelings in the muscles as they loosen up, smooth out, unwind, and relax, thinking about nothing but the very pleasant feelings of relaxation flowing into your _____. See if you can let go a little bit more. Even though it seems as if you've let go as much as you possibly can, there always seems to be that extra bit of relaxation, letting all the tension go. Notice what it's like as the muscles become more and more deeply relaxed, calm, peaceful, and relaxed. There's nothing for you to do but to focus your attention on

the very pleasant feelings of relaxation flowing into your _____.
Focus on (concentrate on, notice) the difference between the tension and the relaxation. Enjoy the contrast.

## MUSCLE GROUPS

We will proceed through eight groups of muscles, first tensing each
for 5 seconds and then relaxing each for 15–20 seconds.

Settle back as comfortably as you can, take a deep breath, and
exhale very slowly. You may feel most comfortable if you allow
your eyes to close. Notice the sensations in your body; you will soon
be able to control those sensations. First, focus your attention on
your hands and forearms. . . .

- Squeeze both hands into fists, with arms straight.
- Flex both arms at the elbows; push upper arms into the floor.
- Shrug shoulders toward head. Tilt chin toward chest.
- Clench jaw, gritting your teeth together.
- Close your eyes tightly.
- Wrinkle up your forehead and brow.
- Harden your stomach muscles, as if expecting someone to
  punch you there (continue to breathe slowly as you tense your
  stomach).
- Stretch out both legs, point your toes toward your head, and
  press your legs together.

## IMAGERY

Now, as you continue to sit quietly, breathing slowly and steadily,
I'd like you to imagine the following scene: You are walking
through the woods on a very pleasant, sunny day. You're all alone,
feeling relaxed, calm, and totally peaceful. Look all around you.
Look up at the tree above you. Notice how full and green the
branches are. Stop for a moment to take a deep breath and smell
the fresh country air. . . . As you walk farther on, you notice, over to
the right, a narrow babbling brook running through the woods. It's
a small, shallow stream, and you can hear the water over the stony
bottom. The sound of the brook has a relaxing effect on you, and
you feel very calm. Let yourself relax and enjoy the surround-
ings. . . . Notice the fallen leaves on the ground. Pick up one of the
leaves, one of the larger ones, and hold it in your hand. Rub it
between your thumb and finger. Feel the texture. Look at the leaf

closely. Notice the colors. Bring it up to your nose and smell it. Take a deep breath. Now let the leaf drop from your hand. Continue walking slowly along. Feel the relaxation in your body—the heavy, warm feelings in your muscles. . . .

Just in front of you, the woods come to an end. You see a clearing ahead. As you get closer to it, you notice that you're standing at the edge of a huge meadow. The meadow has green grassy hills as far as the eye can see. Throughout the meadow are beautiful wild flowers of every color and description. As you walk into the meadow, you notice the bright blue sky, and you can feel the warmth of the sun on your skin. You feel a slight warm breeze on your cheek. It's very gentle, very relaxing. . . . You walk slowly toward a huge oak tree in the middle of the meadow. When you get there, you lie down under the tree. As you lie down, you're amazed to find that the ground is very, very soft. As you look up through the branches of the tree, you notice again how blue the sky is. There are just a few white fluffy clouds drifting by. You get the feeling that you're floating right along with those clouds. As you lie there looking at the sky, you feel more relaxed than you've ever felt before. Your muscles are warm and relaxed. You feel calm and peaceful, without a care in the world.

## BREATHING

Take a deep breath and exhale very slowly. For the next few minutes, continue to breathe slowly and steadily, keeping your body completely relaxed, limp, and heavy. Each time you exhale, slowly and softly say the word "Relax" to yourself. Imagine the word "Relax" each time you exhale. Do nothing more than that for the next 2 minutes.

## END OF INDUCTION

Now I'd like you to think of that 0–100 scale where 0 is complete relaxation and 100 is maximum tension. Consider approximately where you would place yourself on that scale, and remember it so you can jot it down after you've opened your eyes.

Now I'm going to count backward from 5 to 1, and with each number you are to become more and more fully awake. When I say "1" you'll be wide awake, still feeling very comfortable and relaxed but fully awake and alert: 5 . . . 4 . . . 3 . . . 2 . . . 1. Eyes open wide and awake.

Postrelaxation Comments

- Have group members record postrelaxation scores on their rating sheets.
- Provide the group with positive feedback for doing well on the exercise (regardless of whether or not subjective ratings of tension decreased from before to after the exercise).
- Respond to any questions or comments by group members about the relaxation induction.

Introducing the Practice Exercise

1. Clients should practice progressive relaxation exercise (all eight muscle groups, two times each muscle group) for 20–30 minutes two or three times before the next meeting. To do this, clients will need to arrange to have about 30 minutes of quiet time in a room where they will be uninterrupted. They should identify days, times, and location for relaxation practice prior to leaving this group session and should record these relaxation appointments on the "Practice Exercise" sheet. If feasible, it is suggested that clients be given a cassette tape with the induction, for practice between sessions.

2. Instruct clients to conclude each relaxation practice by spending a few minutes imagining a pleasant, relaxing scene:

> The scene used today is but one example of how to gain a calm sense of relaxation by simply closing your eyes and picturing yourself in pleasant, peaceful surroundings. Different people may find other scenes even more relaxing. For example, some people enjoy imagining themselves at the beach, a park, a lake, the mountains, or the like. It can be a place you've been to before and always liked—for example, lounging in a canoe that's tied to a shade tree on the riverbank, listening to the ripple of the water and waiting patiently for the fish to bite. Or the scene can be a place that you've never been before—an imaginary place that you create. The more detail you use, the better you will be able to really get into the scene when you use it later to relax.

See Lazarus (1977) for details on use of imagery techniques in therapy. The only requirements for the scene are that (a) it is relaxing, peaceful, and serene; and (b) the client is alone in the scene.

3. In addition to or as an alternative to imagery, therapists may ask clients to pick a calming word or phrase that they can focus on or repeat to themselves while enjoying the concluding part of relaxation training. This word or phrase can then be used in everyday situations

to help them calm down during periods when daily hassles or negative thoughts are causing problems.

Refer to the end of the book for the "Practice Exercise" for this session (p. 214).

## Session: Relaxation Training: II. Letting Go

Rationale

1. The ultimate goal of progressive relaxation training is to learn the skill of controlling excess tension as it occurs in "real life." Obviously, you will not be able to stop and run through a complete tension–relaxation procedure every time tension occurs. Today we will practice "letting go" of tension in your muscles without tensing them first. After practicing in a reclining position, we will use the "letting go" technique while sitting, standing, and during activities.

2. Relaxation in a nonreclining position involves relaxing those muscles that are not necessary for ongoing activities. For example, while sitting at the table and eating dinner, you can relax your forehead, shoulder, chest, and leg muscles. While standing and talking with someone, you can relax facial, shoulder, arm, and hand muscles. The result of using this technique is that you will be able to perform most daily activities with a minimum of tension and a maximum of relaxed comfort.

3. To achieve this goal, it is necessary to abbreviate the relaxation procedure so that it can conveniently be used in a variety of situations. Two procedures for relaxing in stressful situations are (1) letting go of muscle tension, focusing on "trouble spots"; and (2) steady breathing and reciting "Relax" or some other word that you have associated with relaxation. Initially, you should practice both procedures, but you may come to prefer one or the other.

---

Therapists are encouraged to read and use the ideas presented in *The Relaxation Response* by Benson (1975). The relaxation response is a popular technique for achieving relaxation without much elaborate practice and in a brief period of time. It can be easily incorporated into everyday situations and can be used multiple times per day.

## Group Exercise

Relaxation through "letting go" employs the same eight muscle groups that we used in the previous procedure. First, focus your attention on any tension you can detect in those muscle groups. Then you should recall the feelings that were associated with release of that tension during the tense-and-release procedure. Then relax your muscles as completely as possible, releasing as much of their tension as you can.

We will take about 10 minutes to practice letting go of tension in a reclining position, and then we will ask you to apply this skill while sitting, standing, and performing other activities.

### "LETTING GO" INDUCTION

You are resting comfortably with your eyes closed, all parts of your body supported so that there is no need to tense any muscles. Just let go as best you can. [Pause]

Concentrate on the feelings in your hands and forearms and let go of any tension that is there . . . letting the muscles relax and unwind. . . . Relax the muscles in your hands and forearms further and further . . . letting them become more and more deeply relaxed.

Focus now on the muscles in your upper arms and biceps. . . . Allow them to smooth out, unwind, and relax . . . allowing any tension there to melt away, and just noticing what it's like as the muscles become more and more deeply and comfortably relaxed.

Now relax the muscles of your shoulders and neck, feeling the warm, pleasant feelings of relaxation flowing into those muscles . . . feeling the soft heaviness, the calm relaxation as you let go further and further . . . more and more relaxed. . . . Tune in to the feelings of relaxation . . . letting all the tension go.

Now pay attention to the muscles in your face, beginning with your forehead and brow. Let your forehead loosen up, smooth out, and become peacefully relaxed . . . enjoying the very pleasant feelings of relaxation. . . . Let your eyes be light and comfortably closed . . . letting any tension or stress simply drift away. . . . Your jaws and cheeks relaxed, teeth separated. . . . Notice the warm, comfortable feelings of relaxation spread throughout your face. . . .

Allow the relaxation to spread to the muscles in your stomach as you let go of any tension that is there. . . . See if you can keep letting go a little bit more. Even though it seems as if you've let go as much as you possibly can, there always seems to be that extra bit of relaxation. . . .

Notice the muscles throughout your legs . . . in your thighs, calves, and shins. . . . Let go of any tension or tightness that you find there, letting the tension melt away . . . and enjoy the calm, peaceful feelings of relaxation flowing into your legs and down to your feet.

As you continue to rest quietly, breathing slowly and steadily, think about your own safe, peaceful scene. It may be in the mountains, at the ocean, a lake, a grassy meadow, a garden, or anywhere else that is pleasant and relaxing to think about. . . . Place yourself in that imaginary scene and enjoy it fully. . . . Look around you, noticing the pretty sights and colors. . . . What peaceful, pleasant sounds can you hear? . . . Breathe deeply as you take in any lovely scents, aromas, or fragrances drifting by. . . . I will remain quiet for the next few minutes as you continue to relax, unwind, and enjoy your own peaceful scene. . . .[Two minutes of silence.]

Take a deep breath and exhale very slowly. For the next few minutes, continue to breathe slowly and steadily, keeping your body completely relaxed, limp, and heavy. Each time you exhale, slowly and softly say the word "Relax" to yourself, or some other word that you have associated with relaxation. Imagine the word each time you exhale. Do nothing more than that for the next few minutes. [One minute of silence.]

## Introducing the Practice Exercise

Begin to apply your new skill in daily living. Start relaxing during relatively slow, nonstressful activities. Try relaxing, for example, while reading. Allow all muscles to relax except for the ones that you absolutely have to use for the activity. Is it possible for you to be very relaxed while you are:

- Watching TV, a movie, or a play?
- Playing cards, chess, checkers, or other table games?
- Sitting and talking with others?
- Waiting in line?
- Riding a bus?
- Driving? (many people tense up unnecessarily when driving)

Once you can relax during these slower activities, begin relaxing during some more demanding ones:

- Shopping
- Doing housework

- Fixing the car
- Having a conversation while standing
- Playing ping-pong or pool

Eventually, you may use your relaxation skills during the fastest, most demanding activities you can think of:

- Jogging (Yes, you can relax while you run—athletes do!)
- Running to catch a bus (you don't need tension in your face)
- Standing in a crowded place
- Rushing to finish a project or assignment
- Playing tennis, football, or some other sport
- Talking to a very angry person
- Taking care of an emergency

It *is* possible to relax and move rapidly. Athletes and dancers are trained to remain loose as they perform. If some of your muscles are tight and tense, they will keep your other muscles from doing their jobs smoothly. In addition, you lose a lot of energy for nothing.

For the time being, try using relaxation skills only while engaged in slow, nonstressful activities. Pay special attention to your "trouble spots." These are muscles that tend to get particularly tense (e.g., jaw, neck, hands, etc.).

Refer to the end of the book for the "Practice Exercise" for this session (p. 215).

## Session: Relaxation Training: III. Relaxing in Stressful Situations

Rationale

1. Today we will focus on learning ways to apply your relaxation skills to real-life stressful situations. We began learning relaxation skills by tensing and releasing muscle groups to enhance awareness of tension and to achieve a deep level of relaxation. We also paired a word, such as "Relax," with the slow breathing associated with this state of deep relaxation. Next, we practiced "letting go" of tension without first tightening muscles, so our relaxation technique would be brief and convenient to use in a variety of situations. Then we practiced "letting go" of tension

while sitting, standing, and performing nonstressful activities. Today we will begin to practice using our relaxation skills to cope with stressful situations and negative moods.

2. Relaxation skills can be useful for coping with a number of negative moods, such as anger, stress, tension, fear, and anxiety. Brief relaxation techniques can be used *during* stressful encounters, and can also be useful just *before* and *after* confronting stressful situations.

3. Relaxation skills can help you stay sober because they provide an alternative to drinking as a means for coping with stress, or with the craving to drink that could follow a stressful situation.

4. Recall the three techniques: letting go of muscle tension; steady breathing; and relaxing imagery or a favorite relaxing word or phrase. Which of these techniques or combination of techniques is personally most effective for you? You may have noticed that relaxing imagery is not appropriate for situations requiring vigilance (e.g., when driving, operating machinery, talking to others, etc.). However, the imagery technique may be appropriate for situations involving boredom, rote tasks, or feelings of helplessness (e.g., sitting in a dentist's chair). Letting go, steady breathing, and the relaxing word are useful in a wider variety of situations.

## Group Exercise

One effective way to practice relaxation as a coping skill is to use imagery to generate a negative mood, and then apply relaxation skills to control it. This type of practice allows you to see for yourself how relaxation skills can reduce negative moods.

### MOOD SCENE DEVELOPMENT

Think of an activity, event, or situation that occurs reasonably often and that you're familiar with—a real situation that puts you in a negative mood. If you have difficulty identifying a specific mood-arousing event, just remember the last time you were in a negative mood, how it felt, and what was happening.

The following are characteristics of good mood scenes:

1. *Scene-setting details.* These should replicate a precise event; they include descriptions of the location, participants, time of day, and so on.

2. *Time limitation.* Scenes should be limited to an event of a few moments rather than a lengthy time sequence.
3. *Mood-arousing details.* These details add the cues that arouse a negative mood state (anger, anxiety, etc.). The details associated with the mood state can include thoughts, feelings, and physiological signs (e.g., dry mouth, butterflies in the stomach, or a pounding heart).
4. *No descriptions of avoidance, escape, or defensive behaviors.* You should try to avoid the tendency to minimize, deny, or rationalize the mood or situation.

An example of a good, detailed mood scene is as follows: "I'm listening to my spouse, who is angrily blaming me for being late for dinner. I'm at the front door, am being confronted and I'm thinking . . . 'I'm really in for it this time, I should have left earlier' . . . and I'm also feeling anxiety inside me, my stomach is knotting up and I want to hide away. The argument is mainly one-sided, and the words thrown at me are . . ." (quoted from Suinn, 1977, p. 3). On the other hand, a poor example of a mood scene is this: "I become anxious when people are angry with me." This scene lacks the details that define a precise event.

## IMAGINAL ANXIETY MANAGEMENT

After each client has decided upon a mood scene, the therapist conducts a differential relaxation induction with clients seated, including steady breathing and a peaceful imagery scene. The mood scene is then called for by the therapist:

> In a moment, I'm going to have you switch on the negative mood scene that you identified for yourself. All right, switch on that scene right now. Really be there . . . let the scene develop as realistically as possible. Allow yourself to experience the negative mood again; just let it build. Hold the scene for about 10–15 seconds. . . . Now, while you're still in the mood scene, reinitiate relaxation by letting go of muscle tension, or steady breathing and reciting the word "Relax." That's fine, now continue that relaxation. . . .

On the first presentation, the therapist should hold the mood scene only briefly to avoid too much anxiety arousal (about 10–15 seconds). The mood scene is repeated several times (as time permits), with a slightly longer exposure (20–30 seconds) followed by relaxation.

Postrelaxation Interview

Determine whether negative mood arousal was achieved, as well as whether relaxation was eventually re-established. Ask clients what anxiety management techniques were most effective (letting go, or steady breathing while reciting a word such as "Relax").

Introducing the Practice Exercise

To begin with, clients should be told to use the abbreviated relaxation procedures (letting go, steady breathing, reciting a relaxing word) to help cope with *moderately* stressful situations. Caution clients not to attempt to use relaxation in highly stressful situations until the skill has been well practiced. It is important that they experience some success with the technique at this stage.

Refer to the end of the book for the "Practice Exercise" for this session (p. 216).

## Session: Awareness of Anger

Rationale

1. This session deals with anger. What is anger? Anger is a normal human emotion. However, there is a distinction between anger as a *feeling* and some of the behavioral *consequences* of anger, such as aggression, impulsive actions, passivity, and passive–aggression.

   The following is a cognitive–behavioral model of anger:

   Trigger $\rightarrow$ Angry thoughts and $\rightarrow$ Behavior
   event feelings

2. There are both constructive and destructive effects of anger. Anger itself is neither good nor bad. It can be an intense feeling, and the reaction to that feeling can be constructive or destructive.

   *Destructive effects:*

   a. Anger causes mental confusion. It leads to impulsive actions and poor decision making.
   b. Aggressive reactions to anger inhibit communication, mask

other feelings, create emotional distance, and trigger hostility in others. Can you think of some examples in your life of how aggressive behavior has backfired?

c. Passive reactions to anger leave you feeling helpless or depressed, reduce self-esteem, mask real feelings with an appearance of indifference, are a barrier to communication, and build resentments that may spill out at the slightest provocation in a furious tantrum or drinking.

*Constructive effects:*

a. Feelings of anger signal problematic situations and energize you to resolve them.

b. An assertive response to anger increases your personal power over distasteful situations, helps you communicate your negative feelings and their intensity, can be used to change destructive aspects of a relationship, helps avoid future misunderstandings, and may strengthen a relationship. An assertive response helps you to increase the constructive effects and decrease the destructive effects of angry feelings.

3. Relationship between anger and problem drinking: Many problem drinkers report that they drink when they feel angry or upset at another person. Studies of people who relapsed after alcoholism treatment have revealed that many took their first drink when they were angry.

## Skill Guidelines

The first step to managing your anger is to become more aware of the feeling. Increased awareness can help you to identify angry feelings early, before they grow and get out of hand.

1. Become more aware of situations that trigger anger.

a. *Direct triggers:* a direct attack on you, whether verbal or nonverbal (e.g., being told what to do, physical attack, obscene gesture, unfair treatment), or frustration resulting from inability to reach a goal.

b. *Indirect triggers:* observing an attack on someone else, or your appraisal of a situation (e.g., feeling that you are being blamed, thinking that someone is disapproving of you, or feeling that too many demands are being made of you).

2. Become more aware of internal reactions that signal anger.

a. *Feelings:* Do you feel frustrated, irritated, annoyed, insulted, treated unfairly, agitated, "on edge," "wound up"? These less intense feelings often precede anger, and therefore should be attended to before they build and become more difficult to control.

b. *Physical reactions:* muscle tension in the jaw, neck, arms, hands; headache; pounding heart; sweating; rapid breathing.

c. *Difficulty falling asleep:* This may be due to angry thoughts and feelings stored up during the day.

d. *Feeling tired, helpless, or depressed:* This can also can be a sign of anger. It may be that past attempts to express anger have not been effective. You may then have given up trying and become depressed.

## Exercise in Group

Each group member should list personal anger triggers and internal reactions to them. Pull for a variety of situations (e.g., at home, at work, shopping, recreation, driving) and for a variety of other persons involved (e.g., family, friends, coworkers, strangers). In addition, pull for a variety of internal reactions that signal anger (as in point 2 of the *"Skill Guidelines"*).

> It is well known that many alcoholics have difficulty managing and expressing anger. They may be particularly uncomfortable with anger expression because of previous drinking situations where extreme expression of anger has occurred. They may have overreacted themselves or managed to get others very angry at them. In other cases, a family history of alcoholism, violence, or child abuse may be relevant. Alcoholics can be exquisitely sensitive to the topic of anger expression and management. Some may become very quiet or depressed about memories of angry or violent episodes. Clinicians may have to draw out the quieter members of the group to help them feel comfortable discussing the topic. Some clients may need more individual attention or specialized counseling to help them work through difficult memories.

## Introducing the Practice Exercise

The goal of this week's exercise is to increase clients' awareness of anger by paying attention to anger trigger events and internal reactions that signal anger.

Refer to the end of the book for the "Reminder Sheet" and "Practice Exercise" for this session (pp. 217–218).

### Session: Anger Management

Rationale

1. The preceding session was devoted to awareness of anger and of the events that trigger anger. (You may wish to review the "Reminder Sheet" from the preceding session.) Today's focus will be on techniques that can be used to control anger.
2. Anger is not caused by trigger events alone, but by our thoughts or beliefs about those events.

No: Events → Anger

Yes: Events → Thoughts → Anger

3. Example:

| Event | | Thoughts |
|-------|---|----------|
| Your spouse is acting quiet and withdrawn when you arrive home. | → | I must have done something wrong. She's mad at me again, and we're in for a fight. |

    What feelings and behaviors might follow from these thoughts? What are examples of positive or constructive thoughts that would probably lead to quite different feelings and behaviors?
4. Review last week's "Practice Exercise" and select examples that identify triggers, thoughts, and behavior. Which reactions were inappropriate or destructive reactions? Which were examples of constructive self-control? Do you begin to see the role of thoughts in determining reactions to triggers?

Skill Guidelines

1. Here are some suggested ways to think about anger triggers, so you can increase your ability to control your behavior. The first thing to do is *calm down*. As long as you keep cool, *you* will be in control of the situation. Here are some phrases to help you cool off in a crisis:

| | |
|-------|----------|
| Slow down. | Chill out. |
| Take it easy. | Deep-freeze. |
| Take a deep breath. | Relax. |
| Cool it. | Count to 10. |
| Easy does it. | |

Decide on one or two of these, or something similar, that you can say to yourself to help you cool your anger in a crisis.

2. After you've slowed yourself down, think about the situation:

What's getting me angry?

Is this really a personal attack or insult?

Am I angry because I'm expecting too much of myself or someone else?

Is someone trying to get me angry?

What are the positives in this situation?

Review the situation point by point.

3. After assessing what's making you angry, think about your options:

What is in my best interests here?

My anger should be a signal that it's time to do some problem solving.

What can I do?

Which option seems best? (Relaxation, communications skills, or other coping skills might be used in this situation.)

4. After trying to resolve the problem:

a. You may find that you cannot resolve the conflict, and you still feel angry. Remember that you can't fix everything. Thinking about it over and over again only makes you more upset. Try to shake it off—it may not be so serious. Don't let it interfere with your life. Use relaxation exercises to reduce your tension and anger.

b. If you succeed in resolving the problem, congratulate yourself: "I handled that one pretty well. I could have gotten more upset than it was worth, but I actually got through that without blowing my cool. I'm doing better at this all the time."

## Modeling

The therapists present the clients with the following scenario:

Your spouse (or friend, or teenage child) is helping you to wash and wax your car. In the middle of the job, he/she suddenly walks away, goes inside, and turns on the TV. You find yourself increasingly angry as you look at the work that remains and the mess that has to be cleaned up. You decide to confront your work partner.

The therapists should demonstrate an appropriate response to this situation, articulating their self-statements for anger management aloud:

Cool-down phrases
Thoughts about the situation ("What's getting me angry? Is this a
personal attack? Am I expecting too much?")
Thoughts about options ("What is in my best interest here? What
can I do?")

## Behavior Rehearsal Role Plays

Guide the group in generating positive-thinking alternatives to the
situations they wrote up for the preceding session's "Practice Exercise." Where appropriate, role-play the situation and have clients
"think out loud," using the calming reminder phrases and positive
thinking.

## Introducing the Practice Exercise

This exercise involves examining and recording one's reactions after
an anger situation.

Refer to the end of the book for the "Reminder Sheet" and "Practice
Exercise" for this session (pp. 219–220).

## Session: Awareness of Negative Thinking

## Rationale

1. The way we think influences how we feel and behave. Many
   times we assume a negative thinking style about events that
   could just as easily be interpreted as neutral or even positive.
2. Thinking negatively can lead to all sorts of negative emotions
   and tension that can then lead to drinking as an escape. For
   example: "My boss must really hate me for being unreliable, so
   there is no chance he will ever promote me. I may as well stop
   trying to do such a good job, or perhaps I should just quit work."
3. Negative thinking can become a self-fulfilling prophecy, leading
   to chronic low self-respect, anger, depression, fatigue, stress,
   anxiety, or boredom. For example, if you think about giving up
   or quitting work, you may start slacking off and eventually get a
   warning or be fired. You must therefore learn to recognize your
   negative thoughts and moods as signals to stop and to change
   the negative thinking, rather than as signals to give up on yourself and drink. Your thoughts are sometimes called "self-

statements" or "self-talk." Negative thoughts are sometimes referred to in AA jargon as "stinking thinking."

4. Usually, changing your thinking doesn't make you feel better
   instantly. It takes time and practice before you learn to catch
   yourself thinking negatively, and develop positive thinking to
   change your moods and feelings of self-worth. Just because you
   don't notice feeling much better the instant you change your
   thinking doesn't mean it's not working.

5. The following is called the "ABC" model of thinking and feeling
   (Ellis, 1975):

| A | → | B | → | C |
|---|---|---|---|---|
| Events | | Thoughts | | Feelings/behavior |

Can you think of examples from your own life that illustrate this
model?

Often people feel helpless and unable to change the way they feel.
They say, "I can't do anything about it. I just feel depressed and tired
all the time—leave me alone!" They seem to be saying:

| A | → | C |
|---|---|---|
| Events | | Feelings |

This A-C model is not the whole story. You *can* learn to recognize and then control or change your feelings by changing your
thoughts. The thoughts that lead to negative moods/feelings are
called either negative thoughts or negative self-talk.

## Skill Guidelines

1. The main steps to changing your negative thinking are these:
   a. *Catch yourself thinking negatively.* You must learn what kinds
      of negative thinking habits you have learned over the years
      and have come to use automatically. You must be able to
      recognize them when they occur. Your moods might be a
      signal. For example, if you are feeling depressed, you prob-
      ably were thinking negatively just before that and didn't even
      know it.
   b. *Stop the negative thinking pattern* and substitute a more posi-
      tive or reasonable set of thoughts. That is, challenge or re-
      place negative thoughts with positive or neutral thoughts
      (this will be covered in more detail in the next session).

2. Can you think of negative thoughts that might be behind some negative mood states or other common events? Here are some easy examples to start with:

| A Events | → | B Thoughts | → | C Feelings |
|---|---|---|---|---|
| Your kid broke a glass during breakfast. | → | _____ _____ _____ | → | Angry, upset |
| Your boss wasn't very friendly today and seemed not to notice that you were even there. | → | _____ _____ _____ | → | Tense, worried, depressed, upset |

Another way to get a list of intervening thoughts is to recall previous events that led to strong emotions or drinking. Examples of such thoughts are these: "I am a stupid idiot, I can't do anything right"; "He must hate me"; "Everything I do is wrong"; "If I blow this, I am a total failure"; "I should never do that"; "People are always out to get me"; "I am always letting people down"; "I must do everything perfectly and never make mistakes"; "Everyone should love me all the time."

3. It may be helpful to categorize the list of thoughts you have generated as a group. One system uses the guidelines provided by Ellis (1975) and includes these categories:

   a. *Unrealistic goals* (perfectionism): "I must, should, have to do everything right"; or "Other people should always be reliable, trustworthy, friendly, on time."

   b. *Catastrophizing:* "If things don't work out exactly the way I expect, then it's useless, awful, terrible, the end of the world."

   c. *Overgeneralization:* "I can never be on time"; "I am always and forever going to be depressed."

   d. *Expecting the worst:* "I will never get my act together"; "This marriage is doomed to fail"; "I know nobody really likes me"; "Even strangers won't ever like me if they get to know me."

   e. *Self-putdowns:* "I don't deserve better"; "I am stupid, unreliable, weak"; "My dad always said I was no good."

   f. *"Black-and-white" thinking:* Goes with perfectionism and catastrophizing. "If I am ever late for work at all, then I will

get fired and never ever get another job for as long as I live";
"If people don't totally love me, then they must hate me";
"Either I am all good or I am all bad."

## Behavior Rehearsal Role Plays

Clients may become more proficient and more comfortable analyzing
cognitive sequences by talking them out aloud. Have each of them
practice with personal examples.

## Introducing the Practice Exercise

Have each group member identify his/her negative thinking patterns
for at least one event that has led to strong emotional feelings or
urges to drink in the past. Recognizing these thoughts will help to
develop awareness of negative thinking, and then to teach cognitive
restructuring in the next session. Go over the "Practice Exercise"
sheet with the group and answer questions about it. Have the group
write down one or two examples of events that led to negative thinking, and their negative thoughts.

Refer to the end of the book for the "Remainder Sheet" and "Practice
Exercise" for this session (p. 221).

## Session: Managing Negative Thinking

### Rationale

1. In the sessions on awareness of negative thinking, anger, and
   anger management, you have become more aware of how
   thoughts can influence your feelings. Review the ABC model of
   thoughts and feelings:

   | A | B | C |
   |---|---|---|
   | Events | Thoughts | Feelings/ |
   | | | behavior |

   Review your "Practice Exercise" from the session on awareness
   of negative thinking and list the negative thoughts that you
   came up with.
2. Now we are going to learn ways to stop negative thinking and
   replace it with more healthy positive thinking. You may not

notice it at first, but with repetition and practice, this will gradually help you to begin to feel less moody, depressed, frustrated, angry, tense, or upset, and to feel better about yourself.

3. People or events cannot get at your thoughts or change your mind unless *you let them* or want them to. You have total control of what you think or say to yourself. People don't upset you; you allow them to upset you. For example, if someone says you are a no-good jerk, you can let that upset you (in effect, you are saying, "I agree, I am no good"), or you can challenge, defend, or protect yourself ("I may act like a jerk sometimes, but I am really a good person who is trying very hard to be better," or "When I do one dumb thing, it doesn't mean that I am a total jerk forever").

## Skill Guidelines

1. Use the example below to begin skills training, or develop your own group's examples, using the "Practice Exercises" that were completed after the session on awareness of negative thoughts. List *some* of the positive alternative thoughts and have the group generate more.

EVENT (A):

It's your first week on a new job. You miss the morning bus that you take to work because you misread the bus schedule. You will be late to work today.

NEGATIVE THOUGHTS (B):

"I can't do anything right."

"I must be really stupid if I made a mistake with a simple bus schedule."

"Now my boss will think I'm an irresponsible person."

"I wanted to be really good (perfect) on the job and now this ruins it all."

"I'll probably get fired for being late. How will I ever pay the bills now? It'll take me another 6 months to (or, I will never) find a new job."

"The boss knows I'm a recovering alcoholic, and he'll think I've been drinking again."

"Life isn't fair. Just when things start going good for me, something always happens to mess it all up."

NEGATIVE FEELINGS (C):

Scared, depressed, angry, anxious, worried, tense.
Will arrive at work feeling defensive, incompetent, and unable to focus on what to do.
Strong desire or urge to drink.

POSITIVE ALTERNATIVE THOUGHTS (B):

"Darn, I missed the bus. Well, don't get all upset about it. That won't do any good and will just get me thinking about booze."
"Nobody's perfect. Anyone could misread a bus schedule once in a while."
"I'd rather not be late, but if I am, it's not the end of the world."
"When I start to feel upset like this, that's my signal to stop, take a deep breath, relax, and think positive. What can I do about the situation right now?"
"I can call the boss and let him know that I'm late and on my way in. He'll probably appreciate my letting him know and won't have to wonder where I am."
"Even if my boss is a little angry at me, I've got plenty more days to show him that I'm a good worker. He'll get over it as soon as he sees that I'm usually reliable."
"I'm proud of myself for not flying to pieces over this the way I would have in the past."

POSITIVE FEELINGS (C):

Calm, confident, optimistic, relaxed.
In control of thoughts.
Not setting up a vicious negative cycle.
No urge to drink.

After group discussion of the examples of how to change negative thinking into positive thinking, explain that this is really a simple, three-step process:

- Catch yourself thinking negatively as soon as possible, before you get too upset or want to drink.
- *Stop* yourself—interrupt or break the chain of negative thoughts.
- Challenge the negative thoughts and substitute positive, more reasonable thinking.

2. *Demonstrate thought stopping.* Have the group members close their eyes and take a few deep breaths to relax. Have each member then imagine an event that led to bad/upset feelings. Have them use the five senses to create vivid images while keeping their eyes closed. Now ask them to consider the negative thoughts that led to the bad feelings, and then have them repeat the negative thoughts quietly to themselves over and over again: "Keep on saying the negative thoughts slowly to yourself. Try to get yourself feeling as upset as you were when the event actually happened. . . . Keep going."

Now, pause for 10 seconds and suddenly make a loud clap (with a ruler or open hand on a table), and at the same time loudly shout "STOP!" This should totally surprise the group members, who have up until then been sitting with eyes closed, concentrating on their negative self-talk and the event that upset them. This vividly demonstrates how a chain of thoughts can be disrupted. Calm everyone down and point out, "Thought stopping really stopped you thinking those negative thoughts, didn't it? It totally distracted you." Have the group members discuss their reactions and point out that the clients can do the same thing themselves—not out loud, but they can shout "STOP!" quietly whenever they become aware of negative self-talk. Once the chain of events is disrupted, they can challenge the negative self-talk and substitute more positive self-talk.

Draw the sequence on the blackboard and discuss it:

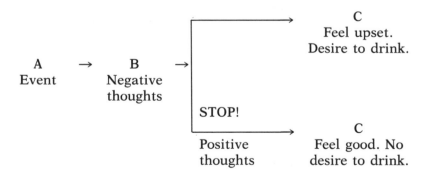

3. Discuss skills for substituting positive self-talk for negative. One helpful way to improve the ability to think positively and to come up with specific self-statements is to recognize that most of them fall into a few general categories. That is, there are a few basic types of positive self-statements, and if clients are aware of these basic types, they may be better able to come up with positive statements for any

given situation. (If you do not wish to cover all this in one session, just choose the most relevant categories for the group.)

a. *Recalling good things* about life and about yourself. For instance, what went well today, or what things do you usually do well? What's good about you as a person? What do you enjoy? What nice–thoughtful things has another person done for you?
b. *Challenging irrational beliefs and unrealistic expectations.* You can recognize these because they usually contain such extreme words as these:

   • Should, must, ought, have to
   • Awful, terrible, disastrous
   • Always, never, forever

   For example, compare "Others should always love and approve of what I do, and if they don't, then it is a terrible disaster" with "It's nice to have love and approval from others, but even without it I can still enjoy and accept myself."
c. *Decatastrophizing.* Often negative emotions are the result of predicting catastrophic consequences, or "projecting," in AA terms. These cognitions can be defused by examining the probability of the feared event; its degree of unpleasantness; your ability to prevent it from occurring; and your ability to accept and deal with the worst possible outcome.
d. *Relabeling the distress.* Tell yourself that the anxiety, frustration, or anger is a signal to use your coping skills, rather than a signal to get upset and drink. To use physical pain as an example, pain can be an important signal that there is a problem that needs treatment. A pain in the tooth signals you to seek treatment, thus preventing the infected tooth from getting worse. Although pain is uncomfortable, it is often an important signal that alerts us to take constructive action, so it should not be ignored. Similarly, feelings of emotional distress, though uncomfortable, are important signals that the situation and your thoughts or actions may need constructive change. In the past, you may have drunk or done other destructive things to avoid paying attention to your feelings, with the result that things got even worse. Thus, relabeling distress as a valuable signal telling you to cope (and no longer viewing distress as a signal to give up, or drink) is a very positive step.
e. *"Hopefulness" statements.* Often, pessimism or optimism become self-fulfilling prophecies. Making positive self-statements and

giving yourself encouragement may lead to positive outcomes. For example, "I can change how I'm responding"; "I can handle this"; "I can have an effect on the situation"; "It'll probably turn out well in the long run, even though it's difficult now."

f. *Blaming the event, not yourself.* Making one mistake does not make you a dumb *person.* Everyone is human and makes mistakes sometimes. Blame the *event* or *behavior* only—not yourself as a person, and not for all time, just for that once.

g. *Reminding yourself to stay "on task."* Focus on what needs to be done. For example, "Don't think about being upset; just relax and think about what you have to do."

h. *Self-reinforcement.* When you've handled a difficult situation well, tell yourself so—pat yourself on the back with your positive thoughts. For example: "I started off really upset about Jim being late for our appointment, but I did a pretty good job of calming myself down. I'm proud of myself for bringing my feelings back to a manageable level."

## Exercise in Group

Ask a group member to share a recent experience that he/she found upsetting or disturbing in some way (perhaps the one identified in the "Practice Exercise" from the session on awareness of negative thinking). After the client has described the situation, his/her reaction to it, and negative thinking about it, encourage the group to work with him/her to generate more positive self-statements with which to handle the situation.

Refer to the end of the book for the "Reminder Sheet" and "Practice Exercise" for this session (p. 222).

## Session: Seemingly Irrelevant Decisions

### Rationale[4]

1. Many of the ordinary, mundane choices that are made every day seem to have nothing at all to do with drinking. Although they

---

[4]This section is adapted from "Cognitive Assessment and Intervention Procedures for Relapse Prevention" by G. A. Marlatt, 1985a, in G. A. Marlatt and J. R. Gordon (Eds.), *Relapse Prevention: Maintenance Strategies in the Treatment of Addictive Behaviors* (pp. 201–279). New York: Guilford Press. Copyright 1985 by The Guilford Press. Used by permission.

may not involve making a direct choice of whether to drink, they may move you, one small step at a time, closer to being confronted with that choice. Through a series of minor decisions, you may gradually work your way closer to the point at which drinking becomes very likely. These seemingly unimportant decisions, that may in fact put you on the road to drinking, are called "seemingly irrelevant decisions" (SIDs).

2. People often think of themselves as victims: "Things just seemed to happen in such a way that I ended up in a high-risk situation and then had a drink—I couldn't help it." They don't recognize how perhaps dozens of their "little" decisions, over a period of time, gradually brought them closer and closer to their predicament. It's relatively easy to play "Monday morning quarterback" with these decisions and see how you set yourself up for relapse, but it's much harder to recognize when you are actually in the midst of the decision-making process. That is because so many choices don't actually seem to involve drinking at the time. Each choice you make may only take you just a little bit closer to having to make that big choice. But when alcohol isn't on your mind, it's hard to make the connection between drinking and a minor decision that seems very far removed from drinking.

3. The best solution is to think about every choice you have to make, no matter how seemingly irrelevant it is to drinking. By *thinking ahead* about each possible option you have and where each of them may lead, you can anticipate dangers that may lie along certain paths. It may feel awkward at first to have to consider everything so carefully, but after a while it becomes second nature and happens automatically, without much effort. It's well worth the initial effort you will have to make, in the increased control you will gain over your own sobriety.

4. When faced with a decision, you should generally choose a low-risk option, to avoid putting yourself in a risky situation. On the other hand, you may for some reason decide to select a high-risk option. If you make this choice, you must also plan how to protect yourself while in the high-risk situation.

5. To illustrate how some seemingly minor decisions can lead to a relapse, one client called "Sam" (not his real name) had been treated for compulsive gambling. His gambling had caused him numerous marital and financial problems. When asked to describe his most recent relapse, he said, "There's not much to tell. I quit gambling for 6 months, but then I was in Atlantic City and began gambling again." Obviously, Atlantic City is a high-risk

city for anyone trying to quit gambling. When asked to describe what led up to his arrival in Atlantic City, he told the following story:

He and his wife decided to take a car trip down the East Coast from Hartford, Connecticut, to Washington, D.C. On the return trip they were heading up I-95, and as they got close to the New Jersey line, Sam began to feel restless. He and his wife got into an argument about their travel route: He claimed it would be worth the added time if they made a slight detour and took the scenic Garden State Parkway instead of the New Jersey Turnpike. Since Sam was driving, he prevailed, and they turned off I-95 at the Atlantic City Expressway to get to the Garden State Parkway. As they approached the Garden State Parkway, Sam decided he was tired and persuaded his wife to continue past the parkway into Atlantic City, just to get a breath of ocean air, to see the boardwalk, and to stretch his legs on the beach.

When they arrived in town, Sam parked the car directly in front of one of the larger casinos. Needing money for the parking meter, he ventured into the casino—just to get some change for a quarter. Since he only needed a dime for the parking meter, he decided to try his luck by dropping the remaining change into a nearby slot machine. That was all it took to trigger an episode of heavy gambling; it took his wife almost 3 days before she could drag him out of town and back on the road home. By that time, however, he had wagered away all of their remaining vacation money, and they had to make it home on their gas credit card alone. His Atlantic City binge was the start of a prolonged period of gambling, which continued for some months until he sought professional assistance.

Did Sam plan his own relapse? He strongly denied any *conscious* plan to resume gambling. Yet he made a number of seemingly irrelevant decisions that led up to standing in front of a slot machine in Atlantic City with a handful of change—an extremely high-risk relapse situation. Can you identify some of these decisions? They did not appear to be gambling decisions. They were decisions to take a scenic route, to take a break and see the boardwalk, to get change for parking. Since they appeared to be irrelevant to gambling, we call these "seemingly irrelevant decisions" or SIDs. However, in each instance, one of the available choices brought Sam one step closer to a high-risk situation in which relapse was all but inevitable.

6. By becoming aware of SIDs, you may be better able to take corrective action to avoid high-risk situations. It is usually much easier to decide to *avoid* a high-risk situation before you get too close to it than it is to resist temptation once you are in the midst of the high-risk situation. For example, it would have been easier for Sam to decide not to take the Garden State Parkway than to decide not to gamble once he was in the casino.

## Group Discussion

Describe examples of your own seemingly irrelevant decisions and how they could eventually lead to a relapse. Here are some examples of SID situations that could set up a recovering alcoholic for a relapse:

Whether to keep liquor in the house for guests.
Whether to go to bars to see old drinking friends, watch a sporting event on TV, play darts, eat a meal, or the like.
Whether to go to a party where people are drinking.
Where to go to get a snack (i.e., in a package store or at a gas station).
What route to take when driving (i.e., to go past, or detour to avoid, a favorite bar, package store, etc.).
Making (or not making) plans for the weekend.
Whether to tell a friend that you have quit drinking or keep it a secret.
Planning how to spend free time after work.
Whether to start conversations with people at AA or Narcotics Anonymous (NA) meetings.
Whether to ask housemates not to bring alcohol into the house.
Whether to participate in physical exercise on a regular basis.

## Exercise in Group

Ask clients to think about their last slip or relapse after a period of abstinence, and to describe the situation and events that preceded the slip/relapse. What decisions led up to the relapse situation? List decisions on the blackboard. After a relapse, as noted earlier, it is easy to play "Monday morning quarterback." By becoming aware of SIDs, clients should be able to set themselves up for sobriety.

Introducing the Practice Exercise

Today's assignment asks clients to identify SIDs among recent and upcoming decisions. Make the point that one does not necessarily have to choose the "safe" alternative, but that clients should at least be *aware* that they are making a choice that allows them to enter a high-risk relapse situation, so that they may make preparations to cope with it effectively.

Refer to the end of the book for the "Reminder Sheet" and "Practice Exercise" for this session (p. 223).

## Session: Planning for Emergencies

Rationale

1. It is important to plan how to handle crisis situations on your own.
2. Major life events and life changes can be very disruptive, and can lead to a relapse to drinking. Some such life events might include the following:

   • Social separations (e.g., divorce, death, child leaving home, close friend moving away)
   • Health problems
   • New responsibilities
   • Adjustments to new situations
   • Work-related events
   • Financial changes

   Can you think of other major events to add to this list? (Recurrent and persistent life problems are dealt with in another session.)
3. Life events do not necessarily have to be negative to lead up to a relapse. Positive life changes can also pose a risk—for example, moving, promotion, graduation, or other events that may leave you feeling "on top of the world" and perhaps a little *too* confident.
4. Major events happening to those close to you can also affect you. Family members or close friends may become upset or preoccupied with their concerns, or may begin to act differently toward you.

5. Describe a life event or life change that you can anticipate. As a group, list these on the blackboard. Consider how your event will affect your behavior and interactions with others.

## Skill Guidelines

1. The major life events listed on the blackboard can be considered high-risk situations that may increase the likelihood of a relapse. What specific strategies can you use to cope with these situations? Draw on skills discussed in previous sessions: problem solving, decision making, managing thoughts about drinking, feeling talk, anger management, mood management of negative thinking and feelings, relaxation, and increasing pleasant events.
2. Begin to prepare a generic emergency plan for coping with any number of possible stressful situations that may arise unexpectedly. Include such strategies as problem-solving skills, calling people for support, increasing attendance at AA or NA meetings, and cognitive strategies. These are only a few examples, and you should provide as much specific detail as possible (e.g., names, phone numbers, locations of meetings, etc.).

## Introducing the Practice Exercise

Have clients write out an emergency plan. Encourage group members to be specific regarding whom they will call for support, what AA meetings they will attend, and so on. When reviewing the plans that the clients develop, play "devil's advocate" by challenging some of them, or suggesting that one of their options does not work out (e.g., "What if both of your support people are out of town?"). This provides an opportunity to test the range, depth, and flexibility of each client's current repertoire of coping skills. If necessary, some reminders of previous sessions' coping skills can be introduced.

Refer to the end of the book for the "Practice Exercise" for this session (p. 224).

## Session: Coping with Persistent Problems

### Rationale

1. It is important to consider how you have changed since the group began and what problems you continue to face. This can

help you to develop a strategy to maintain abstinence after this group has ended. In spite of the fact that you've completed this treatment program, you will find that you continue to face significant problems in life.

2. Here are some examples of life problems that can lead people back to alcohol and drug use:

*Lack of communication* in close/intimate relationships, or arguments with spouse or close friends.

*Boredom, loneliness, depression:* Too low a level of pleasant activities.

*Fatigue:* Lack of energy, no interest in going out to socialize or to support meetings.

*Anger:* Little things seem to bother you, unfair treatment from others.

*Anxiety or tension:* Discomfort in certain situations.

*Social pressure to drink:* Watching others drink or being offered a drink.

## Skill Guidelines

1. *Recounting of success experiences.* Ask group members to describe problems that they had at the beginning of the group, and the success they have experienced in resolving these problems over the course of these sessions. In addition, ask group members to describe the skills they have used in overcoming these problems. Press for specifics to enhance the opportunity for other members to learn from these experiences, particularly from the ways in which the various skills learned in the group have been brought to bear on specific personal problems.

2. *Review of remaining problems.* Now ask each group member to describe the most troubling or persistent problem that remains for him/her. Ask him/her to begin developing a strategy for resolving this problem, and call on all the group members to lend assistance by suggesting particular skills that might be appropriate. Draw on skills taught in previous sessions (have "Reminder Sheets" handy), such as giving and receiving criticism, feeling talk, compliments, problem solving, relaxation, and increasing pleasant activities. For example, a client may explain that although he has become increasingly assertive with his wife and is now able to express to her that he needs to have time to be alone, he and his wife are still having difficulty finding mutually enjoyable activities for their time together. Here,

the therapists may suggest that the client and his wife engage in the problem-solving process as follows: (1) Brainstorm a list of potential activities without censoring them; (2) rate each activity and rank them in order of mutual acceptability; (3) decide, on the basis of the rank ordering, which activities seem most promising to engage in; and (4) develop tactics to implement the chosen strategy.

## Behavior Rehearsal Role Plays

When appropriate, rehearse skills taught earlier in a role play.

## Developing a Practice Exercise

Work with each group member to generate his/her own individualized assignment. The goal should be to practice a skill that may help each of them to cope better with a persistent problem. No formal "Practice Exercise" is presented for this session.

## Final Session: Wrap-Up and Goodbyes

### Feedback

This session has been adapted from Sank and Shaffer (1984).

FEEDBACK TO GROUP MEMBERS

Therapists should model how to give positive feedback and suggestions for continued change. Their feedback to group members should be brief and nonjudgmental, and should project a positive view of the future. It may include reference to positive behavioral changes that have been made within the group or in daily living, progress toward stated goals, and contributions that group members have made to their peers or to the development of the group. The therapists may also use this as an opportunity to suggest future changes and areas for further development. Group members should be urged to build upon the growth they began during the group, and may wish to consider alternative means of support and development (AA, additional group therapy, individual therapy, marital therapy, etc.) that may be helpful now that this group is ending. This final contact with the group should be used to leave each member with an impression of what he/she has accomplished in the group and what further work lies ahead.

## FEEDBACK AMONG GROUP MEMBERS

By this time, the group members have shared many experiences together and discussed intimate aspects of one another's lives. They are therefore in a position to provide one another with valuable feedback regarding progress they have made and areas for additional growth, provided that this is done in a positive, supportive way. This structured opportunity for providing feedback is really no more than a continuation of what the group members have been doing in the preceding sessions as they collaborated to help each other. This final opportunity to collaborate provides an appropriate conclusion to the group's work, as well as an opportunity to take leave of one another. The conversation should be guided toward positive expressions of feelings, so that the group ends on an optimistic note. Exploration of issues that cannot be resolved in this session should be avoided.

## FEEDBACK TO THE THERAPISTS

Group members should be encouraged to provide comments, both positive and negative, regarding their reactions to the group experience as a whole and to the therapists in particular. This feedback should include recommendations to improve future groups, as well as comments on the therapists' style. Since this is a less accustomed role for them, group members may require some prompting to carry on this aspect of the discussion. Ask about group experiences that may have been especially helpful or meaningful, or particular sessions that stand out as valuable. What motivated group members to complete the "Practice Exercises" between sessions, and what factors stood in their way? Was too much time spent on certain skills, or were others that seemed to need more time given short shrift? Solicit suggestions for improving future offerings of this program. Regarding the therapists themselves, did they do anything that rubbed group members the wrong way, or were there ways they could have been more helpful? Were they open to comments and suggestions, and were they an effective team? Most clients will utilize this opportunity to provide appropriate, helpful feedback that will encourage the therapists; growth and/or refinements in the program. In rare instances, a client may abuse this opportunity, but prompt, assertive intervention can turn destructive criticism into an opportunity to model important skills to the group.

## Goodbyes

Allow plenty of time for group members to say goodbye in their own way. This process will undoubtedly have already begun during the feedback phases of this session.

# 4

_____

# Treatment Considerations for Inpatient and Outpatient Settings

## Introduction

The preceding two chapters have described, in detail, the basic elements of our coping skills training program. In an attempt to illustrate our approach, we have shared examples from our clinical experience and woven these into the descriptions. Yet there is obviously more to conducting coping skills training than we have presented thus far. A set of process/procedural issues has emerged from our clinical work that we feel are equally important to ensuring the effectiveness of the program.

In this chapter, we shall discuss treatment process issues as they pertain to conducting coping skills training groups with alcoholics. In addition, we shall consider several individual treatment considerations. Many of the issues to be discussed are not unique to our program with alcoholics (cf. Vannicelli, 1982). Indeed, we have discussed similar issues pertaining to treatment of other psychiatric populations (e.g., Monti et al., 1982; Monti & Kolko, 1985), as have other authors (e.g., Upper & Ross, 1985). Yet there are some key elements that are important in working with alcoholics, and these receive particular emphasis here.

In the context of behavioral skills training groups, "process" can have a somewhat different meaning than it does when it is used in more traditional group psychotherapy. Behavioral skills training groups are neither exclusively a didactic lecture series nor a client-centered process of exploration of whatever issues come up, but something in between. Since the goal of such a group is to educate clients rather than to explore feelings and underlying psychodynamic conflicts, many of the process comments in this chapter pertain to pragmatic issues of how to ensure the learning and practice of new behaviors. This requires more than the group's listening attentively to a didactic lecture. It is an engaging series of interactions between therapists and group members, and among group members themselves—one that is (we hope) relevant and even enjoyable.

A balance must be struck between allowing for group autonomy and ensuring that specific skills are taught and practiced. All group members must get a chance to build their actual skills during role plays and to receive constructive feedback, using relevant (client-centered) problems, rather than simply discussing or reflecting on material. As Bandura (1977) points out, active participation, modeling, and practice with positive, corrective feedback are the most effective ways to modify self-efficacy expectations and create long-lasting behavior change.

Despite this behavioral approach, many of the basic rules for conducting psychotherapy groups do apply. Therapists must use many traditional group therapy skills (e.g., establishing rapport, limit setting, empathy, etc.), while at the same time functioning as active teachers and role models for the group.

A number of unique problems are likely to arise in dealing with groups of alcoholic clients. An excellent review of these, and some suggested responses to them, are provided by Vannicelli (1982). It is based on a dynamic interactional model of group therapy with alcoholics (Yalom, 1974; Yalom, Block, Bond, Zimmerman, & Qualls, 1978), with descriptions of potential problems and suggested behavioral interventions that have proven to be helpful to our group leaders.

This chapter consists of four parts. First, we shall present general treatment process issues that apply to both inpatient and outpatient settings. These include topics such as therapist training; cotherapy teams; developing the rationale and techniques for role playing; between-session (homework) assignments; and incorporating significant others (e.g., family members) into the treatment groups. The next section deals with treatment process/procedural issues that are especially relevant to inpatient settings. These include topics such as integrating coping skills training with other inpatient treatment modalities, communication among staff members, neuropsychological factors that may be present after recent detoxification, and dealing with severe psychopathology. The following section presents considerations for conducting coping skills training as aftercare with outpatients. This section deals with issues such as the advantages of outpatient treatment, transition from inpatient to aftercare treatment, group ground rules, the order of topics, attrition, and termination. In a final section, we consider issues that are pertinent to conducting our program with individual clients in an one-on-one situation.

## General Considerations

### Responsibility for Change

Some have argued that if one accepts as fact that addictive behaviors are learned, it is equivalent to "blaming the victim" (Sontag, 1978). According to this line of reasoning, behavior theorists in effect hold addicted individuals personally responsible for having acquired and continued in their self-destructive behavior patterns. However, this perspective is based on the false assumption that individuals are somehow to be held responsible for their earlier learning experiences. Marlatt (1985c) counters this assumption:

> [B]ehavioral theorists define addiction as a powerful habit pattern, an acquired vicious cycle of self-destructive behavior that is locked in by the collective effects of classical conditioning (acquired tolerance mediated in part by classically conditioned compensatory responses to the deleterious effects of the addictive substance), and operant reinforcement (both the positive reinforcement of the high of the drug rush and the negative reinforcement associated with drug use as a means of escaping or avoiding dysphoric physical and/or mental states—including those associated with the negative aftereffects of prior drug use). In terms of conditioning factors alone, an individual who acquires an addictive habit is no more to be held "responsible" for this behavior than one of Pavlov's dogs would be held responsible for salivating at the sound of a ringing bell. In addition to classical and operant conditioning factors, human drug use is also determined to a large extent by acquired expectancies and beliefs about drugs as an antidote to stress and anxiety. Social learning and modeling factors (observational learning) also exert a strong influence (e.g., drug use in the family and peer environment, along with the pervasive portrayal of drug use in advertising and the media). Just because a behavioral problem can be described as a learned habit pattern does not imply that the person is to be held responsible for the acquisition of the habit, nor that the individual is capable of exercising voluntary control over the behavior. (p. 11)

Nevertheless, SLT-based *treatment* for alcohol abuse does require active participation by the individual client, as well as his/her assumption of responsibility for learning the necessary self-control skills to prevent future abuse. Through active participation in a training program in which new skills and cognitive strategies are acquired, an individual's maladaptive habits can be replaced with healthy behaviors regulated by cognitive processes involving awareness and responsible planning. Marlatt (1985c) states:

> As the individual undergoes a process of deconditioning, cognitive restructuring, and skills acquisition, he or she can begin to accept greater responsibility for changing the behavior. This is the essence of the self-control or self-management approach: one can learn how to escape from the clutches of a vicious cycle of addiction, regardless of how the habit pattern was originally acquired. (p. 12)

The interested reader is referred to Brickman et al. (1982) for an extensive discussion of the distinction between attribution of responsibility for the development of a problem and attribution of responsibility for a solution. Therapists should be prepared to discuss this distinction. They can empathize with the clients over their difficult history, and then instill hope for the future by suggesting that it is never too late to learn how to take care of oneself. This can be accomplished by learning self-management and coping skills that were lost or never learned adequately heretofore.

## Therapist Training

As is the case for all types of therapy, there is no substitute for a well-trained therapist. Since behavioral approaches to treatment are sometimes misunderstood to be applied in a "cookbook fashion"— without careful consideration of the training of the therapist and the unique needs of the individual receiving treatment—it is important to make clear from the outset that therapists must be experienced in psychotherapy skills as well as behavioral principles. In addition, they must have good interpersonal skills and be familiar with the materials, so as to impart skills successfully and serve as credible models. They must be willing to play a very active role in this type of *directive* group therapy.

We have delivered our treatment, for the most part, through cotherapist teams. A master's degree in a mental health discipline (e.g., psychiatric nursing, psychology), is generally considered as "entry level" for our therapists, although we occasionally employ bachelor's-level individuals as cotherapists. We also feel that some clinical experience in treating alcoholics is just as important as academic degree requirements. Usually 1 year of experience is the minimum that is acceptable for our therapist training program.

Therapist training consists of several stages. In the first stage, the individual usually observes every session of an ongoing group through a one-way-vision screen. A doctoral-level therapist supervisor will usually be present, along with the therapist trainee observing the group. This enables the supervisor to point out particular aspects of the group that he/she wants to emphasize. The trainee is encouraged to ask questions as they occur. Following each session, the trainee meets with the supervisor as well as the cotherapists to debrief for 10–15 minutes. In the second stage, after a therapist trainee has observed one full treatment cycle, he/she usually participates in a different group as a role-play partner or as a substitute therapist. Further feedback is provided after each session in this "hands-on" forum. In the third and last stage, the trainee is paired with an experienced therapist, and they form a cotherapy team of their own. In addition to the postsession debriefings, 1 hour of supervision per week is provided by the supervisor.

Since many of our treatment groups have been held in a group therapy room containing a one-way-vision screen through which trainees and supervisors can observe treatment, discussion of the "mirror" side of the screen has emerged as an issue we deal with during our first treatment session. The therapists explain who will be observing and why. To desensitize clients and to enhance trust and direct communication between therapists and clients, we encourage our therapists to invite the supervisor and trainee(s) into group for a moment to be introduced. Group members are then encouraged to ask questions. Our experience suggests that several minutes invested in this way during the first session usually satisfies any concerns that clients might have about being observed.

As part of our general training for therapists, we encourage them first to review the entire training program (Chapters 2 and 3 of this volume). In addition, we have assigned several key review papers as general background material. Chapter 1 provides an integrated overview of material we present to our trainees.

Prior to each treatment session, therapists are encouraged to reread relevant sections of the manual. To ensure that the main points of each session are covered, we recommend making an outline of them or highlighting them in the text. In presenting the didactic material, we suggest briefly paraphrasing the main points and listing them on a blackboard. To standardize the delivery of this material—

an important point in our treatment outcome studies (see Chapter 5)—we have developed large poster boards that summarize the "Skill Guidelines" section of each session. To save time and effort, we recommend that such poster boards be developed and used routinely. Indeed, we use ours on a regular basis, regardless of whether or not we are conducting a clinical trial. Even if poster boards are developed, we recommend that a blackboard be available as well.

Although standardization is essential when conducting a clinical trial, and covering all important points is desirable regardless of the intent of treatment (i.e., clinical trial or routine treatment), it is essential that the desire to comply with treatment format not lead to reading to clients from the text verbatim. As long as the major points are covered, a natural, free-flowing presentation style is preferred. It is crucial that clients not get the message that the therapists' agenda of adhering strictly to the manual is more important than the issues and concerns that constitute clients' personal agendas.

Indeed, if clients are not routinely involved and encouraged to provide their own material as examples, we have found that the groups become boring and the energy level for learning drops off dramatically. Therapists may experience burnout as a result. If a group is getting boring, it may be a sign of a burned-out therapist, since therapists must maintain a high level of energy and enthusiasm at all times. Effective reinforcement of clients for their active participation can help prevent burnout on the part of both clients and therapists.

The "Rationale" and "Skill Guidelines" sections of each session are intended to provide therapists with adequate background information to guide discussion of each topic. Although the topics covered usually generate group discussion that is meaningful, the discussion must be shaped by the therapists to prevent it from shifting focus onto other clinical issues (e.g., lengthy accounts of personal material). Since the treatment session can pass very quickly, it is important that the therapists keep the presentation of the "Rationale" and "Skill Guidelines" brief, to allow adequate time for the role plays, feedback, and group discussion.

As in other clinical work, use of appropriate self-disclosure and humor can be helpful clinical tools. As long as proper clinical judgment regarding timing and content is exercised, it can be helpful if therapists share with the group some of their own communication dilemmas and coping strategies. This demonstrates that group members are not alone in their efforts to achieve satisfying communication with others. It should be noted that "coping models" may have a greater impact on changing behavior than do "mastery models."

One self-disclosure issue likely to come up at the beginning of most group therapy programs for alcoholics is the question regarding the drinking practices of the therapists (Vannicelli, 1982). Therapists differ as to whether or not to answer this question directly; however, we agree with Vannicelli that the real concern that is usually being expressed is "Will you, therapist, be able to understand me, and can I get the kind of help here that I need?" (1982, p. 21). Thus, although we leave the specific answer to this question up to our therapists' judgment and individual therapeutic styles, we do encourage them to acknowledge to the client(s) asking the question that they hear the underlying message. How this question is handled has proven particularly important for our therapists, since many of our clients are only familiar with AA groups or other groups led by counselors who were themselves recovering alcoholics. Acknowledgment of the clients' underlying concern, coupled with an invitation to clients to judge the value of this program for themselves, usually is adequate.

A related concern involves alcoholics' expectations as to what the group is all about. Many alcoholics are familiar with AA groups, which are highly structured, or traditional psychotherapy groups, where an attempt is made to explore feelings and resolve conflicts. Although clients are informed that the exploration of feelings and resolution of conflicts can occur in this group, the emphasis should clearly be placed on skills training and behavioral rehearsal. Finally, we recommend that our therapists familiarize themselves with the similarities and differences between an AA approach and a behavioral approach to treatment (McCrady & Irvine, in press), so that they are prepared to clarify questions that clients might have. (See the "Outpatient Aftercare Considerations" section of this chapter for further information on how to prepare clients for coping skills treatment.)

## Cotherapist Teams

Our therapy program is led by cotherapist teams. We prefer that a male and a female team up together, regardless of the composition of the group, to ensure that models of both sexes are available. If there are no women in a particular group, as was often the case on our alcohol treatment wards at the Veterans Administration Medical Centers in Providence, Rhode Island, and Newington, Connecticut, then the presence of a female cotherapist is especially important to provide adequate modeling.

Therapists are encouraged to assume either a "content" or a "process" role for each session. The "content" therapist is responsible for ensuring that the necessary material for a particular session is adequately covered during the session. The "process" therapist is responsible for attending to and responding to process issues as they emerge during the session. For example, if one therapist is so involved in describing the skills for a particular session that he/she does not pick up on the fact that group members are bored and are not paying attention, then the process therapist may interrupt by suggesting a relevant example so as to stimulate more members to tune in. The therapists should shift process and content roles in alternate sessions to prevent boredom or role stereotyping. By dividing the work of the therapists according to process and content, we have found that most of the pertinent information gets presented in a way that is both effective and responsive to clients' concerns.

Good communication and cooperation between cotherapists are important; they not only affect the tone of the session, but also provide ongoing modeling for group members (e.g., how to disagree agreeably, how to listen, how to use nonverbal behaviors, etc.). Some cotherapists "click" at the outset and spontaneously work well together. Others need to work at working together. Elements to remain aware of in doing effective cotherapy include the following:

1. Knowing and accepting each other's role in a particular session (e.g., content or process).
2. Knowing each other's strengths and weaknesses with respect to role playing and communication skills.
3. Taking equal responsibility for various procedures across sessions, such as introducing new topics, providing feedback for role-play exercises, assigning practice exercises, being empathic and supportive, encouraging less verbal clients to become more actively involved in the group, and so on.
4. Communicating: Do the therapists track each other, look at each other, and ask each other for input at various points throughout the session? Do the cotherapists follow-up each other's comments and allow each other "room" to pursue a point?
5. Disagreeing amicably: How are disagreements handled? How do therapists articulate differences of opinion? How do they negotiate compromises?

## Guidelines for Behavior Rehearsal Role Plays

Behavior rehearsal plays a central part in the communication skills training program and is the main strategy by which group members acquire new skills. Each session provides a "safe haven" where members can practice and improve their communication skills prior to trying them out in the real world. Although some amount of group discussion during the introduction to each new skill is useful, therapists should discourage lengthy discussion about problem situations, and instead should focus on setting up and processing role plays.

It is normal for group members to feel a bit uncomfortable or embarrassed at first about role playing in front of the rest of the group. Therapists should acknowledge that this is a normal reaction and that behavior rehearsal becomes easier after a few experiences with it. After a while, participants are able to "get into" a scene more realistically and to focus on their role in it.

The group may try to resist the first attempt at role playing, but once the ice is broken, members usually become more comfortable. Resistance can take subtle forms, such as focusing on other issues or asking many questions. Therapists can acknowledge that they also feel uncomfortable role-playing in front of a group of strangers; they may have to take the lead and demonstrate the first role plays.

It may be very tempting to become sidetracked into exploring feelings or other group process issues by a resistant group or a few individuals in the group. Therapists should note which members seem most resistant, as these individuals may require additional work lest they sabotage each session.

Most role plays should be videotaped and then followed by constructive feedback. It is sometimes helpful to desensitize clients to the video camera by having them "play" with it at the beginning of the session when it is first introduced. This is particularly helpful with the more shy or suspicious clients. Our experience dealing with severe forms of psychopathology in skills training groups (e.g., Monti et al., 1982) suggests that even paranoid clients can learn that videotaping is harmless and helpful. If videotape feedback is to be maximally effective, it is important that the video equipment be in good repair and that the therapists be competent at operating it. If therapists are anxious about operating a videotape deck, this will create distraction and unnecessarily complicate the videotaping process. Therapists may erase the videotape at the end of each group session in front of the group to reassure members about confidentiality, especially if there are some suspicious members in the group.

Although video feedback is usually helpful, verbal feedback from therapists and group members is sufficient if video equipment is not available.

Therapists should encourage clients to generate and describe personally relevant scenes that are initially of only moderate difficulty. As clients demonstrate ability to handle these situations effectively, they should be encouraged to generate and practice more difficult ones. An adequate description of a scene will include specifying where it takes place, what the primary problems/goals are, whom the role-play partner should portray (boss, stranger, child, spouse, date, etc.), and relevant behaviors of the person portrayed so that the partner can act accordingly.

The following strategies are useful in helping group members to generate scenes:

1. The therapists can ask clients to recall a situation in the recent past where use of the new skill being taught would have been desirable (e.g., a client wanted to start a conversation but couldn't; another yelled at a neighbor about an unleashed dog tearing up the garden; another wanted to express positive feelings toward his/her spouse but couldn't without drinking first).

2. Therapists can ask clients to anticipate a difficult situation that may arise in the near future and that calls for use of the skill (e.g., a client's apartment has been cold this winter and he/she wants to ask the building owner to raise the setting on the thermostat; another client is going to a retirement party this weekend and will be offered alcoholic drinks).

3. The group leader can suggest an appropriate situation based on his/her knowledge of a group member's recent circumstances (e.g., "I know you've been wanting to get a sponsor at AA but have been shy about approaching someone about it. How about setting up a scene involving the end of an AA meeting at which the person you'd like as a sponsor is present. Where might he/she be standing? In a group of people? Alone at the coffee table?")

4. A group leader can use self-disclosure about a situation in which he/she has difficulty, in order to aid clients in thinking about situations from their own lives. For example, a therapist might say, "A person I live with always leaves the top off the toothpaste. It's certainly not a major problem, but it does bother me, and if I don't speak up about it I find that I start to get more irritated about it every day until I finally get real angry at him/her. Then we have an argument that could easily have been avoided if I'd just spoken up sooner and

said it differently. What kinds of 'little' things like this do you stew over until you get upset, rather than speaking up in the first place?"

5. The therapists can create a hypothetical situation for role playing. This approach should only be used as a backup in the rare instances when the other strategies are insufficient.

After a role play has been set up, it is essential that it be effectively processed. This task basically involves responding to each role play in a way that makes it a productive and encouraging learning experience for the participants. It is an opportunity for participants to receive social praise/recognition for practice and improvement, as well as constructive criticism about the less effective elements of their behavior. During this portion of the session, the therapists' primary goals are to identify specific problem areas and to shape and reinforce successive approximations to more effective communication skills.

Immediately after every role play, therapists should reinforce both role-play partners for participating. Then the following should be done:

1. The therapists should ask both of the partners to give their reactions to the performance (e.g., How does the protagonist feel about the way he/she handled the situation? What effect did the interaction have on the partner?)

2. The therapists should next ask other group members to offer comments, and should respond to those comments in a manner that encourages group members to focus on relevant issues in a constructive fashion (i.e., to remain task-oriented and not be destructive or threatening in their remarks). Initially, until therapists have modeled giving constructive criticism once or twice, they might solicit only positive feedback from group members (e.g., "What was *good* about the way John handled that situation?"). To the extent that group members offer supportive feedback and constructive criticism, they provide each other with a very valuable source of encouragement and ideas.

3. The therapists then offer their own comments about the role play. As already emphasized, these comments should be both supportive/reinforcing and constructively critical. If there are several deficiencies in a role-play performance, the therapists should choose only one or two to work on at a time. Both positive and negative feedback should focus on *specific* aspects of the person's behavior, since global evaluations do not pinpoint what was particularly effec-

tive or ineffective. Finally, the praise/reinforcement provided should always be sincere. Also, the therapists should refrain from being unnecessarily effusive, so that the value of the positive feedback is not undermined.

After initial reactions by role-play partners, group members, and therapists, additional feedback may be given by means of videotape playback of the role-play scene. Since immediate feedback is more effective than delayed feedback, it is a good idea to stop the tape to comment on appropriate or inappropriate behavior as it happens, rather than to reflect back on it after the tape is over.

Therapists may also have the role-play partners repeat a scene to give the protagonist an opportunity to try out the feedback he/she received the first time around. However, given the time limitations of the session, therapists will need to be attentive to striking a reasonable balance between doing repeat role plays, and moving on to a new scene to give other group members a chance to practice.

"Role reversal" is a role-play strategy in which the therapist (or a skillful group member) models use of the new skill, with the client playing the role of the target person (e.g., spouse, employer, neighbor, etc.). This strategy is particularly useful if a client is having difficulty using a skill or is pessimistic about the effectiveness of a suggested communication approach. By playing the "other," he/she has an opportunity to observe, and to experience firsthand the effects of the suggested skill.

## Homework

Homework is a powerful adjunct to treatment, because real-life situations can be utilized for out-of-group practice. This offers the distinct advantage of practice in actual problem situations, enhancing the likelihood that these behaviors will be repeated in similar situations (generalization). A preplanned homework exercise has been designed for every session of our program. Most require that the client try in a real-life situation what he/she has already role-played in the group session. The homework assignment also requires that the client record facts concerning the setting, his/her behavior, the response it evoked, and an evaluation of the adequacy of his/her performance. Homework exercises can be modified to fit the specific details of individual situations more closely, and extra homework assignments are sometimes given to help clients cope with problem situations they have encountered.

It should be pointed out that although the outpatient setting is perhaps more conducive to multiple opportunities for homework practice, the inpatient setting does provide some opportunities as well. Hospitalized clients should be encouraged to practice assignments with visitors and/or with other patients on their units. Passes provide further opportunities for completing homework. If no other individuals are available for practice, clients should be encouraged to approach members of the treatment staff as role-play partners.

Compliance with homework is often a problem in behavior therapy in general, and these groups are no exception. A number of steps are taken to foster compliance. The assignments are referred to as "Practice Exercises" to avoid the negative connotations often associated with the term "homework." When giving each assignment, the therapists provide a careful rationale and description of the assignment. They ask the group members what problems they can foresee in completing the assignment, and they discuss ways to overcome these obstacles. Clients are asked to identify a specific time that can be set aside to work on the homework assignment. Therapists review the preceding session's homework exercises at the beginning of each session, making an effort to praise all approximations to compliance with the assignment. Although problems that clients have with the exercises should certainly be discussed and understood, the main emphasis is on reinforcing the positive aspects of performance. For those who did not do an assignment, group suggestions are solicited as to what could be done to ensure compliance with the next assignment. No contingencies other than social praise or disapproval are imposed by the therapists to enhance compliance with homework assignments.

## Coping Skills Training with Significant Others

We have conducted many group sessions with clients' significant others or family members present in addition to the alcoholics themselves. Including significant others in skills treatment can greatly enhance maintenance and generalization of change (Monti & Kolko, 1985). There is also a growing literature on the role of family interaction and marital communication difficulties in the maintenance of alcohol abuse (Kaufman & Pattison, 1982; Paolino & McCrady, 1977). Maladaptive patterns of communication, lack of intimacy, and control struggles can be precipitants of drinking.

Several practical hurdles must be overcome in recruiting and retaining significant others in treatment. In one of our inpatient settings, a requirement for admission is to have at least one significant nonalcoholic member of a client's social network available to participate fully in treatment. The underlying philosophy of such a program is that involvement of social network members is an essential element of comprehensive treatment. Alcoholics are not accepted into treatment unless they meet this requirement. In practice, most alcoholics are able to come up with someone in order to satisfy this admission criterion. If a program is not willing or able to set such a stringent contingency on treatment, then it may be difficult to encourage some clients to identify such persons and place pressure on them to participate fully.

Another common problem is scheduling. Ideally, having family groups two or three times per week is desirable, but most significant others cannot make such a large time commitment. We found that an extended (3-hour) group session held once per week for several weeks is an acceptable compromise. This requires three sessions' worth of material to be provided at each extended session. Practice exercises corresponding to these sessions are discussed and distributed at the end of the evening. A short break of 10–15 minutes midway through the session helps to keep up concentration and break up the material.

The emphasis in these family sessions should obviously be placed on interpersonal skills training topics (i.e., the material presented in Chapter 2). The more individually focused cognitive and intrapersonal (e.g., relaxation) exercises can be provided to the alcoholics in separate sessions. Group size should be limited to 6 clients or 8 at most (i.e., 12–16 group members total).

A group coping skills training program can be beneficial to both clients and significant others for reducing dysfunctional interactions, but it does not necessarily result in all the changes in systems functioning that would be the goal of a family systems treatment (Steinglass, 1979). Nevertheless, there is often such a degree of mistrust and miscommunication between alcoholics and their significant others that the basic set of communication skills described in this book, directed at individual client and spouse behaviors, can be useful for changing interactions that could otherwise lead to relapse.

As an illustration, a spouse may challenge/criticize an alcoholic in a suspicious manner that, while intended to prevent drinking, may actually exacerbate the likelihood of drinking. The client and spouse can be taught directly, in role plays with each other, how to give and receive criticism in a more adaptive fashion. If the role play and feedback reduce misunderstanding and improve communication in each partner, then maintenance of sobriety is more likely.

Occasionally the relationship between a significant other and the alcoholic is so conflicted that effective role playing cannot take place initially. In these circumstances, we have found it helpful to first have the therapists role-play the skills in question. Following this, the significant other is paired with one therapist and the scenario is repeated, followed by feedback from group members. Next, the alcoholic will role-play with the other therapist. Finally, the alcoholic will be paired with his/her significant other. By this time, after receiving feedback on several role plays, the pair may be better equipped to engage in effective role playing together.

Although the logistics of conducting group treatment with significant others present are challenging, the effort is worthwhile because of enhanced realism and the opportunity to change clients' and significant others' behaviors simultaneously. Clients and partners can gain perspective on the skills that will prevent drinking, thus providing a bridge between treatment and the real world (generalization and maintenance).

In couples with a great deal of marital distress, it is best not to try to deal with all of the complex marital and perhaps sexual dysfunction issues in the group. It is sometimes useful to limit the skills training focus to more basic, "safe" skills (i.e., giving and receiving compliments, criticism, assertiveness, nonverbal behavior), at least early on.

A more difficult but essential next step is to explore communication concerning drinking behaviors and triggers of drinking. Such an exploration may lead to more deep-seated marital conflicts over trust, anger, intimacy, abandonment, dependency, and narcissistic needs. Sometimes these issues can be dealt with briefly in the group, but they tend to require large amounts of time, and consequently the didactic skills materials may not get covered. Therapists need to bring the focus back to the specific observable behaviors that appear to be functionally related to drinking or poor communication skills. These are the behaviors that set the stage for drinking or reinforce drinking, such as when the alcoholic comes home drunk and the spouse wraps him/her in a warm blanket, provides excessive "TLC," and offers to call work the next day to say that the client is "ill." Such spouse behavior is considered to be providing secondary gain, and in fact may be termed "enabling" because it encourages drinking (McCrady et al., 1986; O'Farrell & Cutter, 1979). If it is obvious that more severe individual deficits (e.g., narcissistic or other personality disorders) or severe marital distress exists, then the therapists should educate the clients (and the group) about the utility of other forms of psychotherapy or marital/family therapy.

## Inpatient Treatment Considerations

Treatment Goals

The primary aim of inpatient treatment is to offer the impaired alcoholic a safe haven in which to master the skills needed to maintain abstinence from alcohol and drugs, once he/she leaves the protected environment of the treatment facility. The "protection" offered by the inpatient setting allows therapists to elicit the emotions associated with clients' high-risk situations, without endangering current sobriety. Clients are taught appropriate coping skills so that they can deal effectively with these situations without drinking.

Given the frequency and intensity of treatment in an inpatient setting, therapists quickly learn the existing strengths and weaknesses of group members. This knowledge may enable therapists to accelerate the intensity of training and thus to maximize learning in a safe environment.

Menu of Topics

The topics covered in our inpatient treatment program are presented in a logical fashion. The sequence progresses from the easier and more concrete to the more difficult and complex. This sequence not only provides a logical order of presentation, but also accommodates any residual cognitive impairment from alcohol detoxification.

The following list of topics and order of sessions has been designed to follow a 3- to 5-day detoxification and orientation period. It should be noted that the majority of our alcohol detoxifications do not involve the use of medications. When medications are used during detoxification, additional time may be required before alcoholics are functioning at a cognitive level where they can incorporate even the most basic and concrete skills presented early in our program.

Our inpatient sessions are 50–60 minutes long. They can be scheduled either daily or twice daily, depending on the length of inpatient hospitalization. Since homework assignments are an important component of our treatment program, we recommend that two sessions per day be scheduled only when absolutely necessary. Therapists may decide to modify the topics or their order to make the program compatible with various inpatient programs. Finally, since 28 sessions may be too many for some inpatient programs, therapists may eliminate some sessions according to the needs of particular inpatient populations.

The recommended sequence of INPATIENT THERAPY SESSIONS is as follows:

Number                              Topic
1.   Introduction, Group Building, Problem Assessment
2.   Starting Conversations
3.   Giving and Receiving Compliments
4.   Nonverbal Communication
5.   Review and Relaxation Training: I. Deep Muscle and Imagery Techniques
6.   Feeling Talk and Listening Skills
7.   Introduction to Assertiveness
8.   Giving Criticism
9.   Receiving Criticism
10.  Review and Relaxation Training: II. Letting Go
11.  Awareness of Anger
12.  Anger Management
13.  Receiving Criticism about Drinking
14.  Managing Thoughts about Alcohol
15.  Review and Relaxation Training: III. Relaxing in Stressful Situations
16.  Problem Solving
17.  Drink Refusal Skills
18.  Refusing Requests
19.  Close and Intimate Relationships
20.  Awareness of Negative Thinking
21.  Managing Negative Thinking
22.  Review
23.  Enhancing Social Support Networks
24.  Increasing Pleasant Activities
25.  Seemingly Irrelevant Decisions
26.  Planning for Emergencies
27.  Coping with Persistent Problems
28.  Wrap-Up and Goodbyes

## Concurrent Treatments

Since our inpatient coping skills treatment program has not been designed as a "stand-alone" inpatient treatment program, it is important to consider other aspects of the inpatient treatment context. Our program was initially designed to supplement other traditional inpatient treatment components. These included alcohol education, occupational therapy, individual counseling, involvement in AA, and ongoing family groups. Since these other components are derived from different theoretical schools, it is important to begin by presenting the rationale for the coping skills approach. This inevitably prompts discussion of contrasting treatment approaches. We urge our therapists to stress the complementary aspects of coping skills training, rather than engaging in philosophical digression. We have found it helpful to be prepared to discuss such topics as how craving and relapse are linked to certain situations, moods, or thoughts; how a coping skills/social learning approach adds another dimension to understanding alcohol dependence; and how assuming responsibility for one's treatment differs from assuming the position of a helpless victim of a disease. (These topics are expanded upon in Chapter 1 and in this chapter.)

Following Marlatt (1985c), one example that we have found helpful in clarifying the issues above is the case of diabetes. Diabetes is inherited, and one is the victim of a disease. However, if one takes insulin, watches his/her diet, and exercises (i.e., assumes behavioral responsibility to manage the disease), then one can live a normal healthy life.

A related concern that can emerge in the inpatient treatment setting is the relative importance of coping skills training as a complementary treatment. Our skills training program has always earned a high degree of respect in the settings where it has been used and has been given the status of "required treatment." Clients who refuse our groups are treated much the same as those who might refuse any prescribed form of treatment: They are considered noncompliant and are subject to discharge from the program. Clients are not allowed to make conflicting appointments during group time, and lateness and absences are strongly discouraged. Thus, skills training is perceived as an important component of treatment by staff and clients alike.

Since clients enrolled in an inpatient treatment program are more likely than outpatients to be involved in more than one concurrent group experience, clarification of how skills training groups will differ from other groups can be especially important. Many clients tend to assume that all group treatments are simply forums where feelings are discussed. Although it is important that the group therapists not be perceived as uninterested in clients' needs and feelings, the quantity of material to be covered in any given group session requires that therapists "keep up the pace." A mix of supportive therapy and structured behavioral procedures is always desirable, and seasoned therapists are essential to establish the necessary balance in this regard.

## Communication with Other Staff Members

Just as it is important for therapists to be sensitive to both content and process issues if they are to be effective leaders of coping skills training groups, the therapists should also know about other aspects of each client's treatment. Our therapists have found it most helpful to read clients' charts on a routine basis and to attend the unit's clinical care-planning meetings. This enables therapists to know what is going on with clients on a day-to-day basis, as well as what shape the larger treatment plan is taking. Such information may provide therapists with case material and examples that can be used in groups. By attending these meetings, therapists can add their input into clients' treatment plans, and can better integrate this aspect of treatment into each client's overall plan.

It is also helpful if therapists make notes in the chart about clients' progress in groups at least twice weekly, as well as whenever something particularly noteworthy happens in a group session. Good communication among all involved in the treatment process fosters better client care, and skills training therapists should have the same obligation in this regard as any other member of the treatment team.

## Dealing with Psychopathology

The relationship between substance abuse and psychopathology has received a great deal of attention over the past several years. Two recent books offer excellent reviews for readers who want information on this important area (Alterman, 1985; Meyer, 1986).

In an inpatient setting, it is likely that therapists will have to deal with more psychopathology than in the outpatient setting. However, we routinely screen out of our groups those alcoholics who are either floridly psychotic or suicidal. Perhaps the most common type of psychopathology we have had to treat in inpatient alcohol treatment units is cognitive impairment secondary to either detoxification or chronic alcohol abuse.

The cognitive impairment most frequently associated with detoxification usually clears with the passage of time. We find that hospitalized alcoholics are usually able to participate productively in groups within 3–5 days after detoxification. To ensure that as little cognitive impairment as possible will interfere with our program, we have structured our inpatient program in such a way that more cognitively complex sessions come later in the series.

Organic impairment secondary to chronic alcohol abuse poses a much more difficult problem. Although organically impaired clients are capable of some learning, much repetition is essential, and progress is very slow because of poor retention. We have found that with some clients, special work outside of the group can be helpful. Periodically testing the recall of material and providing written notes in outline format have both proven helpful with our more impaired alcoholics.

Our coping skills training approach may be more appropriate than other forms of therapy for the organically impaired alcoholic. Indeed, since the core elements of our program were originally derived from our work with severe psychiatric populations (e.g., Monti et al., 1982; Monti & Kolko, 1985), modification for especially impaired clients is usually accomplished with minimum difficulty. Some of the benefits of our approach for the organic client include the use of concrete examples, role plays, small learning units, review sessions, homework assignments, and reinforcement for specific behavior change.

Severe depression is also more likely to be encountered in the inpatient setting. Motivating the depressed alcoholic is likely to present a special challenge. Once motivated, the depressed client can especially benefit from skills training (Bellack, Hersen, & Himmelhoch, 1981).

Another challenging group of alcoholics consists of those also identified as having severe personality disorders. Such clients are likely to question therapists a great deal, may be manipulative, and may be disruptive in groups. We have found such clients to be especially critical of and resistant to the idea of role playing. Firm limit setting is essential from the outset when dealing with the more characterologically disordered alcoholic. Clients who persistently attempt to sabotage their treatment, as well as that of others, should not be allowed to continue in treatment. It is of interest to note that data from a treatment-matching clinical trial at the University of Connecticut suggest that our coping skills approach is more effective than interactional group therapy for alcoholics with significant psychopathology. (See Chapter 5 for further description of this clinical trial.)

An important concern in dealing with a heterogeneous group of inpatient alcoholics is gauging how much time to spend on particularily impaired clients without boring the remainder of the group members. Often, higher-functioning clients can help with the slower learners. Indeed, working in a group with some more impaired members can be an enlightening experience for less impaired alcoholics; helping the more impaired can provide valuable review and deepen the understanding of those less impaired. If process issues emerge relevant to the theme "Am I going to wind up like him/her?", therapists must be sensitive to the concerns and needs of the higher- as well as the lower-functioning members.

## Outpatient Aftercare Considerations

### Rationale for Outpatient Treatment

We have utilized this training program in an outpatient aftercare program, following 3 weeks of inpatient treatment. We are confident that this program can also be integrated into a direct-admission outpatient treatment program (we are planning to do so) in much the same way as it has been combined with inpatient treatment, as described above. The advantages that apply to outpatient aftercare should certainly also apply to treatment offered entirely on an out-patient basis.

The primary advantages associated with outpatient aftercare treat-ment are the structured and supportive transition it provides back to daily activities and family life after an inpatient or residential experi-ence, and the considerable opportunity for interaction between the treatment program and the realities of each client's daily existence. The events of clients' daily lives can be brought into treatment ses-sions and used as the basis for problem-solving exercises, role plays, and homework assignments. As clients are confronted with the stres-ses of everyday living, particularly the inevitable drinking cues and tempting opportunities to drink, previously unsuspected triggers for drinking may be revealed that require skills training. These factors are often masked during inpatient treatment by the protected en-vironment and by the cognitive impairment that may follow soon after detoxification.

A limitation of inpatient treatment can be restricted generalization of behavior beyond the artificial, institutional treatment setting. Although several techniques that can help with this problem have been discussed (see Chapter 1 and the "General Considerations" sec-tion of this chapter), there is no doubt that outpatients have the advantage of being able to practice new skills in a variety of problem situations. Homework can be tailored to provide practice in using new coping skills in real-life situations between sessions, whether on the job, within the family, or in other interpersonal interactions. This greatly enhances generalization of new behaviors to various aspects of a client's natural environment. In addition, session-by-session monitoring of progress in applying new skills, and supervised prob-lem solving to deal with difficulties as they arise, can be provided.

The opportunity to practice skills in real situations overcomes a major obstacle associated with residential treatment.

Outpatient aftercare meets a basic need for ongoing support as clients struggle to deal with problems in their lives, with cravings, and with temptations to drink. Also, an actual relapse can be dealt with relatively soon after it occurs, allowing for early intervention in the relapse process.

Of course, some of the advantages of outpatient treatment are also limitations. Relapse is a substantial risk, because clients have considerable exposure in their natural environment to cues associated with drinking and to opportunities to drink. Greater exposure to life problems and stress in the natural environment may also trigger relapse. Finally, distractions or resistance to treatment can easily interfere with attendance at outpatient sessions. These risks must be taken into account when choosing between outpatient and inpatient initial treatment. However, regardless of which initial treatment is chosen, ambulatory aftercare makes a great deal of sense and can be quite helpful to those who stick with it (Ito & Donovan, 1986).

Treatment Goals

The primary goal of aftercare treatment is to master the skills needed to maintain abstinence from alcohol and drugs. An important element in developing the skills needed to achieve long-term abstinence is identification of high-risk situations that may increase the likelihood of renewed drinking. These high-risk situations include precipitants of drinking that are external to the individual, as well as internal events such as cognitions and emotions. Some of these elements may be easily identified early in treatment, whereas the importance of others may emerge only gradually over the course of treatment as clients leave the protection of the inpatient environment further behind and increasingly confront the problems, conflicts, and drinking opportunities of their daily lives.

Having identified situations that represent a high risk for relapse to drinking, clients must develop skills to cope with them. In our program, all clients are first taught basic skill elements for dealing with common high-risk problem areas (Marlatt & Gordon, 1980); they are then encouraged to engage in problem solving and role playing, and to design homework practice exercises that will enable each of them to apply the new skills to meet his/her own particular needs.

Although it is recognized that clients will not always remain abstinent during outpatient treatment, they are expected to accept and remain committed to the goal of abstinence, no matter how difficult they find it to comply with that goal. The focus of this program is mainly on alcohol. Nevertheless, it is recognized that increasing numbers of clients use several mood-altering substances. It has been our experience that many substance abusers have similar treatment needs, many of which are addressed by the components of this program. It is expected that clients accept the goal of abstinence from *all* mood-altering substances.

## Menu of Topics

Before we list the specific contents of our outpatient program, a word is needed about the sequence in which clients are exposed to the various topics. In an ambulatory program, there is an inherent conflict regarding the order in which skills are taught and rehearsed. Good teaching practice demands that skills be taught in a logical sequence, in which more basic topics are covered first and serve as the foundation for subsequent presentation of higher-order skills. However, there is a conflicting need to help clients deal with immediate threats to their sobriety, which may lead them to an early relapse and/or undermine their continuation in the program. Therefore, sessions such as "Managing Thoughts about Alcohol" and "Drink Refusal Skills," which might otherwise have come late in the program after more fundamental skills have been acquired, are instead presented early, to give the group members tools to cope with situations that may overwhelm them and lead them to relapse or drop out of treatment. Another session, "Problem Solving," consists of a complex set of cognitive skills that would be more appropriately taught late in the program, but is instead also presented early to provide clients and staff with a common language and framework for dealing with problems and crises in clients' lives that can lead to early relapse. Following these sessions, the related sessions on "Giving and Receiving Criticism" and "Anger Management" are presented because of the frequent involvement of these problem areas in relapse. Only after the topics that represent a potentially serious risk of relapse have been dealt with are the more basic skills of interpersonal relationships, decision making, and pleasant activities covered.

Review sessions have been scheduled every fourth or fifth session, in order to provide continued practice of skills learned earlier. A portion of each review session is also devoted to relaxation training.

Toward the end of the program, several sessions are devoted to termination issues. This includes preparing clients to cope without the support of the treatment program by developing specific plans to deal with further problems that may arise, and by enhancing their social support networks.

The following list of topics and order of sessions has been designed to follow a 3-week inpatient treatment program not based on this treatment manual. The 90-minute sessions are scheduled weekly over a 6-month period. Clinicians may decide to modify the list, the order of the topics, or the frequency of meetings, in order to make the program compatible with various inpatient programs or to meet administrative requirements (e.g., more condensed sessions for briefer aftercare treatment).

The recommended sequence of OUTPATIENT THERAPY SESSIONS is as follows:

| Number | Topic |
|---|---|
| 1. | Introduction, Group Building, Problem Assessment |
| 2. | Managing Thoughts about Alcohol |
| 3. | Problem Solving |
| 4. | Drink Refusal Skills |
| 5. | Review and Relaxation Training: I. Deep Muscle and Imagery Techniques |
| 6. | Nonverbal Communication |
| 7. | Giving Criticism |
| 8. | Receiving Criticism |
| 9. | Awareness of Anger |
| 10. | Anger Management |
| 11. | Review and Relaxation Training: II. Letting Go |
| 12. | Awareness of Negative Thinking |
| 13. | Managing Negative Thinking |
| 14. | Receiving Criticism about Drinking |
| 15. | Starting Conversations |
| 16. | Giving and Receiving Compliments |
| 17. | Review and Relaxation Training: III. Relaxing in Stressful Situations |
| 18. | Introduction to Assertiveness |
| 19. | Refusing Requests |
| 20. | Feeling Talk and Listening Skills |
| 21. | Close and Intimate Relationships |
| 22. | Seemingly Irrelevant Decisions |
| 23. | Review |
| 24. | Increasing Pleasant Activities |
| 25. | Enhancing Social Support Networks |
| 26. | Planning for Emergencies |

27. Coping with Persistent Problems
28. Wrap-Up and Goodbyes

## Structure of Sessions

Although the topics covered in each session are intended to teach skills that are highly relevant to the problems and needs of clients' daily lives, it is unlikely that the problems clients actually encounter will occur in the same sequence as our topics. Rigid adherence to an agenda of topics may lead to the perception that the skills being taught are irrelevant to clients' current needs. To help clients cope with immediate problems and to encourage them to view the group as relevant to their daily lives, a period of supportive therapy is offered at the beginning of each group meeting. Clients take turns discussing problems they are having, while the other group members offer suggestions for dealing with them. Therapists structure this opening discussion along behavioral lines, using a problem-solving strategy, engaging in functional analysis, and, whenever possible, building upon skills developed in earlier sessions.

There is frequently conflict between the desire of clients to get help with their immediate problems, and perhaps to "show and tell" to some extent about their daily lives, and the desire of the therapists to get on with the day's agenda. Good communication between the therapists (see "General Considerations" section) is essential for appropriate balance. Often the first phase of a session lasts 30–45 minutes, longer than the therapists would like but shorter than the clients desire. Clients are reminded that this time-limited group cannot always explore problems to the point of complete resolution. Where problems are persistent or seem overwhelming, recommendations for additional treatment are made (e.g., family therapy, individual counseling, etc.).

After the initial period of supportive therapy, the structured portion of the session is initiated, with a review of the skills taught in the preceding session and of the homework assignment. New material is then introduced, beginning with the "Rationale," which emphasizes the relationship of the new skills both to maintaining sobriety and to dealing with problems that are commonly faced by recovering alcoholics. The "Skill Guidelines" are presented verbally, listed on a blackboard and/or poster board, and printed in handouts for the group members to take home. Therapists model the performance of the skills, and clients are then encouraged to generate role-play scenes based on their daily experience.

As in our inpatient program, role playing is viewed as a critical part of the group experience, and at least one-third of each session is allocated to it. Nevertheless, it is sometimes even more of a struggle to engage outpatient clients than inpatients in role plays. This may be due to the fact that individuals in outpatient treatment are usually less familiar with one another than are inpatients. Although clients may participate more freely once the ice is broken, the therapists usually have to provide considerable structure and encouragement in each session to get the process underway.

At the end of each session, clients are given a review sheet that outlines all the elements of the new skills, and a homework exercise for further practice of the new skills. Clients are urged to arrange some form of self-reinforcement for working on the homework exercise. Five or ten minutes are allocated at the end of each session to review and briefly practice relaxation exercises, and to troubleshoot problems clients may have encountered in doing relaxation at home.

As noted earlier, there is a danger that, with such a full agenda and such highly structured sessions, the clients may come to feel that the therapists' agenda is more important than their own needs. Therefore, it is essential that the therapists not read from written material or be too rigid in following the set agenda, and that they strive as much as possible to provide examples from material that the clients have previously brought up. Usually this is not difficult, because the skills training sessions cover commonly encountered problems that are likely to have been raised already by the clients. Occasionally it is necessary to sharply curtail a session's agenda or abandon it altogether in order to deal with some individual crisis. When this occurs, the schedule is modified to shorten or eliminate a subsequent review session, so that all topics in the program can be covered.

## Review Sessions

Review sessions are scheduled every fourth or fifth session. The primary reason for frequent reviews is to foster retention of newly learned material, despite the cognitive impairment often found early in alcoholics' recovery. Recent group sessions are reviewed in detail, including skill guidelines and role playing. Clients are asked to discuss their experience in applying these new skills to their daily lives, and problems they may have encountered in doing so. The group brainstorms solutions to problems that have been encountered, and members try role-playing the solutions arrived at by this process. During the review sessions that occur later in the program, not only are recent sessions reviewed, but also some review of much earlier sessions is given. As noted above, review sessions also double as relaxation skills training sessions.

Review is not entirely confined to specified review sessions. During the initial portion of every session, when clients discuss problems they are encountering in their daily lives, the therapists review previously taught skills that may be applied to resolve the problems. This may involve review of specific skill guidelines as well as role playing of those skills.

## Closed versus Open Groups

One decision that must be made prior to beginning an aftercare therapy group is whether dropouts will be replaced or not. Nonreplacement enables the development of consistent working relationships and cohesiveness among group members, which clearly facilitate achievement of the group's goals. A closed group also allows for a consistent sequence of session topics, with later sessions building on material covered earlier. However, a closed group means that as time goes on, the number of group members who attend regularly will decline.

Replacement of dropouts after the first few sessions allows the group census to be maintained, but at the price of having to integrate strangers who have not been exposed to all the material that the original group members have previously learned. Since each unit in this program starts "from scratch" in developing the "Rationale" and "Skill Guidelines" components, the program can be run with rolling admissions (open groups), but new arrivals will not begin with the abstinence training sessions that the original participants have been exposed to at the beginning of the group.

The outpatient groups we have conducted using this program have been closed; we admit 11–12 clients into each new group, in anticipation of declining attendance over time. We have found that those who do not attend one of the first three sessions are very likely to be eventual dropouts, so we add an additional member to the group for each person who misses one of the first three sessions. After this point, the groups are closed to further admissions.

## Transition from Inpatient to Aftercare Treatment

Engaging alcoholics in aftercare treatment is a difficult and sometimes frustrating experience. Clients are at risk for dropping out during the transition from inpatient to aftercare treatment. This section describes several procedures aimed at increasing the rate of client engagement in aftercare treatment.

One strategy that we employ to minimize early attrition involves having clients meet with one of their aftercare therapists while they are still inpatients. The goal of this meeting is to allow clients to begin to establish rapport with the therapist, and to teach clients how the aftercare group may help them. Many of the procedures described by Orne and Wender (1968) as anticipatory socialization for psychotherapy can be utilized in this first meeting. The assumption is that clients who get to know their therapist, and who understand the process and "rules of the game," are more likely to remain and succeed in therapy.

We typically have a therapist begin this preliminary meeting by providing general information about the aftercare program, such as the day, time, and location of the meetings; the starting date for the group; the duration of treatment; the names of the therapists; and the number of clients in the group. After providing this information, the therapist begins to establish rapport by taking a very brief history. The client's major current problems associated with drinking are also assessed. The therapist may inquire about marital or family problems, employment problems, mood states associated with drinking, and social situations that promote drinking. While taking this history, the therapist has the opportunity to use empathic reflection to show understanding of the client's problems. Reassurance and support may also be offered at this time.

After briefly identifying one or more specific client problems, the therapist gives a rationale for the aftercare treatment, drawing a connection between the client's specific problems and a potential return to drinking. Clients are told that they must learn how to cope more effectively with these problems if they are to stay sober. The forthcoming aftercare meetings are designed to teach the necessary coping skills. At these meetings, clients will learn and rehearse new coping skills. They will also be asked to practice these new skills outside the group, between sessions. In explaining the concept of coping skills training, the therapist uses concrete examples, drawn from each client's stated problems. For example, if a client describes a conflicted marital relationship, the therapist may focus on the units in which communication and anger management skills are taught.

The respective roles of the client and therapist are also discussed in the anticipatory socialization meeting. The client's role is to be active in the group. He/she is expected to recognize and discuss personal strengths and weaknesses, even if it is very difficult to do so. The therapist's role is to assist the client in developing strategies to cope with his/her problems. At times the therapist will be like a teacher, explaining and demonstrating coping skills. It is the client's responsibility to try using the coping skills, both in the group meeting and between sessions. This will include practicing the skills at home and completing some brief written assignments describing his/her experience with the skills.

In the introductory meeting, it is important to anticipate potential obstacles to successful treatment, especially factors that may lead to early attrition from the group. Therefore, the therapist explores any instances in which the client previously dropped out of treatment, and advises the client that he/she should discuss with the group any thoughts of quitting treatment. Such thoughts are not uncommon, and the client may find that other group members feel the same way. Open discussion can resolve problems in the group before anyone drops out. Progress in treatment is not steady—there are ups and downs. Most clients experience hoplessness, anger, frustration, and other negative feelings about the group at times. Clients should be advised to discuss such feelings, even if they fear that it might be embarrassing to the therapists.

It is useful for the therapist to point out that terminating treatment may be one of a series of "seemingly irrelevant decisions" (SIDs) that eventually lead to a client's later drinking. For this reason, any hint that a client is considering dropping out will be taken very seriously and fully discussed.

Many clients quit treatment after their first drinking episode. Clients should be warned that, even with efforts to maintain abstinence, some of them may slip and begin drinking. As early as this introductory meeting, they are told that they should not come to group meetings intoxicated, but they are strongly encouraged to continue to attend group after a drinking episode so that they can receive help in regaining sobriety, coping with their reaction to the slip, and avoiding future lapses.

There is a delicate balance between setting the stage for clients' feeling that it is permissible to return after a lapse and actually giving them permission to drink. Therapists should take care that clients understand this distinction.

## Managing Clients on a Waiting List

An ideal arrangement is to have clients begin their aftercare treatment while they are still in the hospital or residential program. However, when outpatient groups are conducted with cohort admissions, clients often must wait for weeks after their inpatient discharge before a sufficient number of clients is recruited to begin a new group. This waiting period occurs when clients most need aftercare treatment, immediately after inpatient discharge. In our aftercare program, we have attempted to minimize the wait by holding the first group meeting before the group is completely filled. We then add new clients, as needed, in the second or third meetings. As previously mentioned, after the third meeting, groups are closed to new members. This arrangement is a compromise between a strict cohort admission policy and rolling admissions. Clients who, under this arrangement, must wait for their group to start are contacted weekly on the telephone by their group therapist for support and assistance with problem solving. They are also called on the telephone by a secretary one day before their first meeting to confirm the appointment. Using this combination of procedures (inpatient "anticipatory socialization" meeting and waiting-list telephone contacts), we have been successful at engaging clients in aftercare treatment.

## Group Ground Rules

At the first group meeting, clients are given a list of ground rules, called a "contract," which is reviewed with them and which they are asked to sign and keep. This document is intended to enhance compliance with the norms and goals of the group, and reference to it during the course of treatment is sometimes effective in modifying a group member's attitude or behavior.

### Group Member's Contract

1. I understand that this group will meet for 6 months, and I have agreed to participate for that length of time. Although I do retain the right to withdraw, I agree to attend at least the first four sessions to give the group a chance. After that, if I want to leave the group, I will discuss my reasons with the group before making my final decision.
2. I agree to attend all group meetings and to be on time for them. If some urgent circumstance forces me to be late or absent, I will call [a telephone number is given here] in advance to notify the group leaders.
3. I agree that I will not reveal the names of fellow group members or details about their personal lives. Although it is alright to talk in general terms about my experience in the group, I will protect the privacy of others in the group.
4. I accept the goal of total abstinence from alcohol and all mood-altering drugs. I promise to talk in the group about any drinking or drug use that occurs, and about any cravings or fears of relapse. I agree to give a breath or urine sample if requested by the group leaders.

What follows is a brief discussion of these ground rules and our experience in applying them.

## ATTENDANCE

Group members are asked to commit themselves to attend at least the first four sessions, in order to provide them with an adequate basis for judging the group's content, process, therapists, and members before making a decision to drop out. If they wish to withdraw after that, they are encouraged to discuss their reasons with the group before finalizing their decision. In our experience, this provision is often not honored, despite its being discussed with group members at the time they are recruited, at the beginning of group, and during the first several sessions. Most dropouts occur within the first 5 weeks, without warning.

## PROMPTNESS

Clients are asked to arrive promptly for each group session and to notify the leaders by phone if they will be absent or late for therapy. This request generally is honored by those who continue with the group.

## CONFIDENTIALITY

Participants are cautioned not to reveal the identity of group members or specifics of what is discussed. However, clients are granted permission to talk in general terms about their experiences in the group, and particularly about the personal impact of these experiences.

## ALCOHOL AND DRUG USE

Group participants are asked at the introductory session to accept the goal of total abstinence from alcohol and all nonprescribed psychoactive drugs, at least for the duration of the group. They are also asked to talk in the group about any drinking or drug use that occurs, and about any cravings or fears of relapse that they experience. It is explained that it is common for group members to have some ambivalent feelings about accepting abstinence as a goal, and they are encouraged to discuss these feelings, as well as any actual slips that might occur. Clients are allowed to attend group even after an episode of alcohol or drug use, as long as they make the commitment to work toward renewed abstinence. However, they are asked not to come to a session under the influence of alcohol or drugs, because they would not be able to concentrate on or recall the topics covered; they might be disruptive to other group members; and they might undermine others' motivation or commitment.

Breath testing for alcohol has become common in alcoholism treatment programs. However, there are different philosophies regarding the circumstances under which testing should occur. We have conducted some treatment groups with testing at the beginning of every meeting, and others with testing only at the request of the therapists. There are reasons for and against both policies. If testing occurs routinely, then unnecessary accusations and guessing can be avoided. Furthermore, therapists can avoid the awkward situation of discovering that someone has been drinking after 30 minutes into the group when the person is called on to speak. On the negative side, routine testing requires some additional time at the beginning of each group session.

The advantage of testing at the discretion of the therapists is that more trust may be conveyed to group members from the outset. Furthermore, time is not wasted unnecessarily. On the other hand, "spot" testing places the therapists in somewhat of a detective role that can be disruptive to group process. Regardless of how testing is implemented, a policy for each group should be clarified at the first group meeting, and it should be enforced throughout the entire series of meetings.

In our program, anyone found to be under the influence of alcohol or drugs is asked to leave the session. This is done in such a way that clients do not view it as a punishment; anyone asked to leave is encouraged to return to the next session sober, and to continue in the group. The remaining group members are urged to share their feelings about the incident that same session and the following week as well. Clients asked to leave are not allowed to drive themselves home. Their car keys are taken away, and they are asked to arrange safe transportation with a family member, a friend, or a group member.

If drug use is suspected but a client denies it, the therapists may request a urine sample for a toxiscreen. However, since the test results are not immediately available, therapists must make a judgment regarding possible impairment of driving ability. Clients with a history of drug abuse should be given random or weekly urine drug screens (with supervised collection of the sample). Clients are confronted in the group with any positive test results, but are discharged from the group only for repeated drug-positive urines.

When discussing episodes of drinking or drug use with the group, it is to be emphasized that they are a common occurrence, and clients are encouraged to provide personal examples of this. An atmosphere of openness about this topic is fostered. Group members are encouraged to conduct a functional analysis of their alcohol use and of urges to drink, identifying specific people, places, events, thoughts, emotions, and behaviors that preceded or followed the drinking or urges.

Clients are given specific guidelines for dealing with the immediate aftermath of a drinking episode; these include removing themselves from the situation and getting help. They are advised to get rid of the alcohol, remove themselves from the setting in which the drinking occurred, and call someone for help (their AA sponsor, a friend, their spouse, or the treatment program). They are cautioned about feelings of guilt and self-blame that often accompany a slip (Marlatt & Gordon, 1980), and are warned not to allow such reactions to prompt further drinking or drug use.

Guidelines are also given for dealing with the longer-term impact of drinking episodes. Clients are urged to examine a slip with someone, not to sweep it under the rug. They are advised to analyze possible triggers, including the "who," "when," and "where" of the situation, and anticipatory thoughts. Were there expectations that substance use would change something or meet some need? Reactions to the drinking episode should also be analyzed, including behavior, thoughts, and feelings, with special attention to feelings of guilt, depression, and self-blame. Clients are warned about catastrophizing thoughts, such as "Here I go again; I guess I'll never change" or "I'll quit again after I finish this bottle." If allowed to proceed unchecked, these common reactions can contribute to further drinking. The value of reminder cards, which list the troubles that addictive behavior has caused them and the benefits that sobriety has brought, is stressed. Group discussion of drinking episodes is designed to help clients plan more effective coping responses, renew their commitment to abstinence, and view such incidents as learning opportunities (Marlatt & Gordon, 1980).

Compliance with the requirement that drinking episodes be discussed in the group has been mixed. Some clients drop out of the group as soon as the first slip occurs; others keep it a secret; and still others use the group to help them try to recover from it. Group leaders must remain vigilant to avoid reinforcement of inappropriate behaviors that might "enable" future drinking, and to avoid allowing a lapsed client to get extra attention so frequently in the group that the client is encouraged to drink again. Specific remedial action should be suggested by the group members and leaders, and conformity with these recommendations can be made a contingency for continued participation in the group.

## Length of Program

Behavioral treatment programs are often shorter than 6 months, and there was concern when we first designed the present one that there might be a high dropout rate in an outpatient program of this length. In fact, in one of our clinical trials (see Chapter 5) there was a 40–60% dropout rate, most of which occurred within the first 6 weeks, in five different groups.

The length of the program does make clinical sense, given the considerable number of relevant topics to be covered, the need for adequate time for all clients to role-play new skills, the need to review previous material, and the pressure from clients to help them cope with ongoing problems in their daily lives. At times during the trial, in fact, it seemed that 28 sessions were insufficient. In the final analysis, the number of sessions seems about right. Perhaps the length of the program could be cut in half by conducting two sessions each week.

## Attrition

Client dropouts are a significant problem in aftercare treatment for alcoholism. As mentioned previously, when recruiting clients for the groups, we emphasize the importance of their making a commitment to attend weekly sessions for 6 months. When the group begins, the "contract" we give each client reiterates this expectation, urges clients to remain for at least 4 weeks, and requests that they discuss any thoughts of quitting with the entire group before acting upon them. At the first group meeting, clients are also given an attractive wall calendar with all scheduled session dates for the next 6 months circled in red (Ahles, Schlundt, Prue, & Rychtarik, 1983). Whenever clients miss a group session, whether they call in or not, they are contacted by one of the group therapists to determine whether there are any problems and to urge them to attend the next session. These efforts are continued until a client misses a total of ten sessions or clearly states that he/she wishes to quit the group. When a client returns to the group after an absence, he/she is urged to make future attendance a priority and to make whatever arrangements are necessary to avoid further absences.

Absences have a clear negative impact on the remaining group members. They often worry that the missing member(s) might have had a slip, and this at times causes them to worry about their own vulnerability. There is also the problem, upon the return of absent members, of their having missed prior skills training elements. No special efforts are made to recapitulate prior sessions for clients who have missed them, and so there are some group members who clearly lack certain skills. In our experience, group members rarely voice their displeasure about these problems to one another during the group.

A stronger group response is usually elicited when it becomes apparent that certain members have stopped coming to the group. At such times, displeasure is more likely to be voiced—usually about the energy that group members have invested in the dropouts, as well as feelings of abandonment and loss of a source of peer support for those remaining in the group.

In our experience, many clients do not honor their 6-month commitment, or the request that they remain in the group for the first four sessions, or the request to discuss with the group their intention of quitting prior to doing so. Most who leave do so without prior warning, and the majority of attrition occurs within the first 5 weeks.

### Concurrent Treatment

As we described earlier for the inpatient program, clients in our outpatient program may also be receiving other forms of treatment while participating in our skills training groups. Some discussion of the complementary nature of these treatments may be appropriate (see "Inpatient Treatment Considerations" section of this chapter). Clients are encouraged to become actively involved in AA and are frequently asked about meetings they are attending. AA is available for more frequent support than can be provided by our groups, and will be available long after our time-limited groups have terminated. Clients should be encouraged to view concurrent AA and aftercare group membership not as mutually exclusive, but as complementary (Vannicelli, 1982). Nevertheless, we often see clients continuing with the aftercare group but discontinuing AA involvement. For some of them, continued encouragement to go back to AA may have little effect until the completion of group treatment draws near.

Some group members require professional treatment beyond what the aftercare group can provide. Most often, this involves marital counseling. This has not been a source of conflict with clients' group involvement; often these clients have less need to report on, or receive support from the aftercare group for, problems they are having at home. Some clients receive individual psychotherapy, or see a psychiatrist for antidepressant medication or Antabuse. In general, we have not experienced any problems due to multiple therapy contacts.

## Termination

As the date for terminating the group approaches, therapists may observe varying reactions in group members, such as discouragement, pessimism, depression, and an increase in reports of problems. These can be dealt with at two levels: the practical and the exploratory. At the practical level, the therapists use the same general behavioral approach as with any other problems that have been raised throughout the course of the group. Functional analysis, problem solving, and other relevant skills are employed. At the exploratory level, the therapists help the clients to understand the functions of the problematic behavior. Difficulties in coping with emotional distress, such as terminating close relationships, may find expression in generalized negative feeling or behavior problems. If clients can be helped to understand the sources of their problems—termination— they may be able to cope with them more effectively.

The following steps are utilized to ease clients' transition out of the group: (1) The need or desire for additional treatment is considered; (2) clients are helped to develop an "emergency plan" to deal with unanticipated life crises that may arise; and (3) clients plan ways of coping with problems that they have been working on but that remain unresolved when the group ends.

### CONSIDERING THE NEED FOR MORE TREATMENT

Approximately four sessions before the end of the group, the therapists ask clients to assess their progress and remaining problems. Clients may wish to set new goals at this point. The clients' needs or desire for further treatment, and various options for treatment, are considered. The therapists can provide appropriate referrals to another group, family counseling, or individual therapy. Continued involvement in AA and other self-help groups is also encouraged.

### PLANNING FOR EMERGENCIES

Major life events and life changes can be very disruptive and can lead to drinking or drug use relapse. We devote one session late in treatment to helping clients plan ways of coping with crisis situations, such as social separations (e.g., divorce, death, child leaving home, close friend moving away), health problems, work-related changes, and financial difficulties. Life events do not necessarily have to be negative to trigger a relapse. Positive changes can also pose a risk, such as promotion, graduation, and moving. Therapists ask clients to describe life changes that they can anticipate and to consider the impact of these events.

Major life events can be considered high-risk situations that require effective coping skills to avoid relapsing in response to them. Therapists ask clients to prepare a general emergency plan for coping with a variety of possible stressful situations that may arise. Some of the skills taught in previous sessions may apply, such as problem solving, feeling talk, relaxation, and cognitive skills for controlling urges to drink; other strategies may include calling people for support, taking Antabuse, and attending AA or other self-help meetings. Clients are encouraged to provide as many specific details as possible, such as names, phone numbers, locations of meetings, and so on.

## COPING WITH PERSISTENT PROBLEMS

In spite of the fact that clients have completed 6 months of aftercare, they will certainly continue to face significant problems in daily living. We devote one session at the end of treatment to helping clients review remaining problems in their lives and develop strategies for resolving or coping with these problems.

First, common life problems are reviewed, including conflict or poor communication with family or close friends; social pressure to drink; and negative feelings such as anger, frustration, anxiety, depression, loneliness, and boredom.

Clients are then asked to describe problems that they had at the beginning of treatment, and the success they have experienced in resolving these problems. They are asked to describe the skills they have used to overcome or cope with these problems. Therapists press for specifics to enhance the opportunity for group members to learn from one another's experiences, particularly from the ways in which skills learned in the group have been applied to specific personal problems.

After recounting success experiences, each client is asked to describe the most troubling or persistent problem that remains for him/her. With help from the group, clients are encouraged to develop strategies to resolve their "worst" problems, drawing on skills taught in previous sessions. For example, a client may explain that he has become increasingly assertive with his wife and is now able to express to her that he needs to have some time to pursue a hobby, but he and his wife are still having difficulty finding mutually enjoyable activities when they do spend time together. Here, the therapists may suggest making use of the problem-solving technique as a couple, to come up with mutually acceptable activities.

In general, issues concerning termination are as important as they are in any therapeutic group. Clients need to be reassured that they have the skills to solve life's problems without having to rely on the group or the therapists for support. Clients' self-efficacy can be enhanced by reinforcing problem solving that takes place between sessions.

During the last few group sessions, therapists should begin to "fade out" of their therapeutic roles. They should encourage clients to take responsibility for solving problems on their own. Thus, clients will gain confidence in their own ability; this will facilitate termination and enhance the likelihood of generalization and maintenance of the skills acquired during treatment.

## Individual Treatment Considerations

Although initially designed for use with groups, this treatment program can be applied to individual treatment situations, for either inpatients or outpatients, with a few modifications. The program in its entirety has not been systematically tested in individual therapy settings, but many of the units have been used in this way; indeed, some of them were adapted for groups from their initial development for one-on-one treatment. When a therapist is working individually with a client, a few elements of the program that were designed or adapted for groups will have to be modified. In the following discussion of these modifications, reference is made to the materials in Chapters 2 and 3, except as otherwise noted.

In the first session, the section on introducing group members will obviously be skipped. The ground rules, contract (presented earlier in this chapter), and goals are still relevant and important, but will have to be modified somewhat to accommodate each circumstance. The group-building exercise gathers useful information but should be expanded into a more extensive collecting of client data, including assessment of coping skills, ongoing problems, and general lifestyle. On the basis of this assessment, the therapist can tailor the program to the needs of the client by placing greater emphasis on certain skills training elements; omitting some modules altogether; and adapting the examples, role playing, and practice exercises to the particulars of the client's situation.

The "Modeling" procedures that are suggested in many sessions will each have to be examined. In some instances the therapist can demonstrate the skills to be modeled, perhaps making use of an imaginary partner; in others, however, the modeling scene requires interaction between two actors and will have to be skipped. In those cases, the points that were to have been made in the modeling scene can usually be made when the therapist and client begin role-playing.

Role-playing ("Behavior Rehearsal Role Plays") is an element of most sessions. Usually, when rehearsing a skill, the therapist will play the role of other people in the client's life, and the client will play himself/herself. On some occasions, however, especially where the client is extremely reluctant to engage in role playing, it may be helpful for the therapist to assume the role of the client initially, and for the client to play the part of the other person. In general, a client should not be any more resistant to role playing with the therapist than he/she would be with members of a group, although the client may find it a little more difficult to behave naturally when the expression of strong emotions is involved. This should be discussed prior to role playing, to set the client at ease and reduce qualms about directing strong emotions toward the therapist.

Some sessions call for group members to work together to list high-risk situations, problem solutions, and so on. These exercises should still be done in individual therapy settings, but they place considerable responsibility on the client and may require extra help from the therapist if the client has difficulty getting started or providing more than just a few ideas.

As has been emphasized elsewhere in this chapter, it is critically important that therapists not spend large amounts of time lecturing to clients. This is especially true in one-on-one treatment. It is essential that the therapist solicit input and reactions from the client during the presentation of the "Rationales" and "Skill Guidelines" sections, to engage his/her interest and prevent him/her from tuning out.

Toward the end of the program, the therapist must be especially careful to shift responsibility increasingly to the client for analyzing problem situations, brainstorming, selecting appropriate coping skills, and so forth. In group settings, clients are forced to do this because not everyone can get all the individual attention he/she may desire; with individual treatment, the therapist should be careful not to allow the client to remain dependent on him/her. The process of fading out the therapist's initiative in spotting problems and suggesting solutions should begin well before the end of the program.

The final session will have to be modified considerably, since much of it deals with group termination issues. In one-on-one treatment, this session can be used to review plans and possible responses to anticipated problem situations. Of course, the process of termination with the therapist is important, and should be begun, as in group settings, several sessions prior to the end of the program.

In the next chapter, we present empirical support for coping skills acquisition and the maintenance of sobriety.

# 5

# Empirical Support, Conclusions, and Future Directions

This chapter briefly examines the conceptual approach underlying the coping skills model, describes its empirical base, and explores potential future directions. It highlights the interrelationships between and among the various components of treatment, gaps in knowledge, and possibilities for use of the core skills presented. Research on the effectiveness of the coping skills training approach to alcoholism is selectively reviewed, with emphasis on the most relevant treatment outcome studies. In addition to drinking outcomes, data are presented on program and process assessment measures suggesting patient characteristics that may be helpful for screening purposes or that are prognostic of good or poor outcomes. Where possible, the notion of matching treatment techniques to the specific characteristics of clients is addressed. Finally, suggestions for future directions are made, with emphasis on the potential for using a coping skills approach for early intervention and the prevention of alcohol abuse.

## Conceptual Issues

As is evident throughout this handbook, the treatment program has dual goals: It emphasizes coping skills to improve general psychosocial adjustment (e.g., mood management, social competence), and skills to enhance abstinence from alcohol consumption (e.g.,

**165**

drink refusal training). It is not always easy to separate these different goals, and indeed it may not even be necessary because of their interrelatedness. For example, a chain of events consisting of background life stresses (e.g., a chronically ill parent, a child with behavior problems), everyday hassles (e.g., a deadline at work, a conflict with one's spouse), and high-risk drinking situations (e.g., walking past a favorite bar, a business lunch) may all interact with one another and can accumulate over time, thereby straining both general and alcohol-specific coping skills. This strain on the client can be exacerbated or attenuated by biological/genetic predisposing factors associated with arousal and can result in a cognitive appraisal of acute distress. As outlined in more detail in Chapter 1 and elsewhere, the interaction of psychosocial and biological factors produces an acute distress response, which may be characterized by at least some of the following elements: (1) psychophysiological reactions such as tension/stress; (2) strong subjective craving; (3) severe doubts that one can cope/survive without a drink (low self-efficacy expectations); (4) minimization of the long-term negative consequences of drinking; and (5) exaggeration of the short-term "beneficial" effects (outcome expectations) of drinking (Abrams & Niaura, 1987; Marlatt & Gordon, 1985; Wilson, 1987, in press). Thus a combination of environmental demands (both chronic background stress and acute events) and other individual factors, such as predisposing biological factors, social learning history, and current cognitions/expectations, either can serve to undermine existing coping skills or can overwhelm an individual who lacks adequate coping skills in the first place. In either case, the result may well be abusive drinking.

The assumptions of the coping skills model are that drinking behavior is functionally related to problems in living and that clients have a better prognosis if they are taught specific skills to deal with their life problems. Strong emphasis is placed on the assessment of high-risk situations and individuals' cognitive, behavioral, and biological reactions to these situations. Coping with these reactions without drinking is the focus of skills training, and here the emphasis is primarily on behavioral and cognitive skills treatments.

Since biological factors will interact with behavioral and cognitive coping processes, a broader biopsychosocial conceptualization of treatment can be accommodated within a coping skills framework. First, additional treatment for underlying biological disorders can be incorporated into skills training protocols. For those clients who need additional psychiatric treatments or medication, the use of these options can become part of the clients' repertoire of problem-solving skills when they are unable to cope because of biological vulnerability. Second, coping skills training can serve to improve the clients' ability to adhere to other treatment modalities whose effectiveness depends in large part upon voluntary adherence to the prescribed regimen (e.g., Antabuse [disulfiram] or an aerobic exercise class). Improved adherence can then result in better regulation of the underlying biological factors, which in turn will reduce the risk of future alcohol abuse (e.g., Azrin, 1976). Third, coping skills training can have a direct effect on regulating the interaction between biological and psychosocial factors, as in the case of cognitive–behavioral treatment for depression or relaxation training and cognitive restructuring treatments for anxiety or psychophysiological tension (Barlow, 1985; Beck & Emery, 1985).

An important caveat about combined treatment modalities is that there are times when different conceptual models can work against each other in treatment. This possibility must be considered by the primary treatment provider on a case-by-case basis. For example, taking medication may undermine a client's self-confidence (efficacy) that he/she can cope without drugs. This may depend on the client's beliefs and expectations about the medication. However, in most cases a coping skills approach is compatible with other forms of treatment derived from different conceptual models, so that the benefits of multimodal interventions can be applied to those clients in need of them. A comprehensive integration of biological and psychosocial factors must await future developments in the field.

In the coping skills training model, a relapse is generally viewed as a sign of incomplete assessment or incomplete treatment/skills training (Abrams et al., 1986; Brownell et al., 1986). The approach also implies that the client takes an active role in both the treatment and recovery processes (Marlatt & Gordon, 1985). Although this appears reasonable in theory, one dilemma for the coping skills approach involves how best to deal with slips or relapse during the process of recovery. There is a fine line between helping clients to see relapse as a "prolapse"—a potentially positive learning opportunity along the road to recovery—and conveying the message that some drinking is acceptable (see Abrams et al., 1986; Brownell et al., 1986). By contrast, inflexible demands for total abstinence throughout treatment may set the stage for a client to avoid returning for treatment following even a minor slip, because if relapse is "taboo," then the person may feel very guilty and ashamed that he/she has totally failed. This allows for a strong "abstinence violation effect" (Marlatt & Gordon, 1985), in which the individual is so devastated by a slip (abstinence violation) that he/she goes on to heavy drinking and avoids further treatment for as long as possible.

A related problem for clinicians is determining whether the client is truly using a lapse as an opportunity for new learning and growth, or is simply stuck in a repetitive, nonproductive cycle of self-destructive behavior of repeated detoxification and relapse. Wherever possible, reasonable limits should be set, taking into account the history and current motivation of each individual client. In general, the client needs to feel that he/she is not a bad person for slipping or relapsing and that the lapse can be used as an opportunity for new learning. At the same time, the message of *total abstinence* as the only acceptable goal for treatment of alcohol dependence must also come through clearly. The whole area of how to deal with lapses (which occur in the majority of clients), what expectations about abstinence to pass on to clients, and the appropriate timing of different interventions for relapse prevention is in need of more research and clinical case study.

Another relevant conceptual issue for the coping skills approach involves the nature and severity of the skills deficits. It is possible that some clients have primary skill deficits as a result of their long-standing deficits in social learning with family and peers, whereas others have secondary skill deficits because of acute intrapersonal factors such as anxiety, irrational cognitions, or a sensitive biochemical predisposition (e.g., excessive reactivity to stressful stimuli). These intrapersonal factors can then interfere with existing interpersonal skills in a number of complex ways, such as depression or anxiety, leading to social inhibition in a usually outgoing person. An alcoholic client may be unable to perform effectively socially because of debilitating anxiety that is alleviated by alcohol consumption, rather than because of the actual absence of the social performance skills from his/her repertoire. In the case of secondary skill deficits, treatment for intrapersonal problems such as anxiety, using relaxation and cognitive restructuring techniques, may free up the previously inhibited interpersonal skills repertoire. Alternatively, the treatment of a primary social skills deficit (an interpersonal factor) with relaxation training (an intrapersonal factor) will produce nothing more than a "relaxed incompetent" (Bandura, 1977).

In similar fashion, we have found that treatment of interpersonal skills deficits can have a positive effect on intrapersonal factors. For example, social skills training (interpersonal factors) includes some elements of cognitive restructuring and behavioral skills that can directly alter negative emotional states such as anxiety or depression (intrapersonal factors). In this context, consideration of the conceptual relationship between intra- and interpersonal factors can result in more complete treatment. One must consider each factor separately, as well as the interaction between them, in a comprehensive approach to treatment.

Cognitive factors play a prominent role in the coping skills conceptual model. Although there is support for the role played by cognitive mediators in determining patterns of drinking, there is little direct evidence that modifying cognitions results in improved treatment outcome. Cognitive therapy has received some empirical and clinical support in the treatment of depression and anxiety (e.g., Beck, Rush, Shaw, & Emery, 1979; Ellis, 1975), and, to the extent that learning how to manage anxiety and depression is also important for alcoholics, the same techniques may be useful for them as well. Part of the problem with evaluation of cognitive factors in treatment is the difficulty in defining and measuring cognitive constructs (Wilson, 1987). More work needs to be done on identifying what specific maladaptive cognitions exist in alcoholics, and whether the modification of these cognitions will result in improved outcomes. Research will also be needed to establish how to provide skills training exercises to modify cognitions.

An important conceptual caveat shared by many researchers in the field is that "there are virtually no established commonalities, either of alcoholics in general or of alcoholic subtypes" (Miller, 1978, p. 659). Thus one must resist the temptation to overgeneralize research findings to all alcoholics, or to assume that there is an "alcoholic personality" with a consistent set of skill deficits. Despite the limitations on standard group treatments that are imposed by the failure to find a clear-cut alcoholic personality, there is some agreement that certain types of specific situations and coping skills deficits are likely to occur in the majority of alcoholics (Twentyman et al., 1982). Indeed, future assessment research could address this issue and collect normative descriptive data on standard high-risk situations and clients' responses to them, using large representative samples of alcoholics.

The gathering of normative data could eventually provide empirical evidence in regard to which high-risk situations or coping skills deficits occur with the highest frequency and in which alcoholics. Treatment components could then be designed to cover these most frequently cited situations, and data would be available to support their inclusion in standardized group treatment programs. This would ensure that the needs of the majority of alcoholics would be better addressed in standardized treatment programs. Despite the need for some individual tailoring of treatment and the fact that there is no alcoholic personality, many of the core skills training sessions outlined in this book were in fact derived from such data on chronic alcoholics and are likely to be helpful to many of the alcoholics in most treatment settings. The ideal balance between emphasizing standardized session content and attending to individual treatment needs is not yet clear and warrants more clinical and research attention.

Although we believe this coping skills handbook reflects the state of the science in cognitive–behavioral treatment, it has become increasingly clear that "there is no single, best, or only treatment for alcoholism" (Vaillant, 1983, p. 302). It is a complex, multidetermined disorder that requires conceptual input from several disciplines. Factors that maintain the disorder can be different from etiological or initiation factors. There is a need to bridge the gap between theory and clinical practice, as well as that between biological and psychosocial disciplines. Clinicians and researchers alike acknowledge that a more comprehensive view of the development and etiology of alcoholism is necessary, including genetic, physiological, behavioral, and sociocultural variables (Zucker & Gomberg, 1986).

## Treatment Outcome Research on Skills Training

Although several treatment outcome studies have included skills training components such as assertion training, this selective review focuses on those studies most directly relevant to the core skills training components presented in this book. Some of the studies not included here may have used some skills training components, but these techniques were part of a broad-spectrum approach whose elements cannot be isolated for evaluation (Alden, 1980; Foy, Nunn, & Rychtarik, 1984).

Chaney, O'Leary, and Marlatt (1978) used specific skills training and general problem-solving training (D'Zurilla & Goldfried, 1971). Clients were randomly assigned to one of three treatments: (1) skills training; (2) discussion control; or (3) no additional treatment beyond a regular hospital milieu program. Skills training was based on Marlatt and Gordon's (1985) analysis of specific high-risk situations that precipitate relapse, and assumed that the maintenance of abstinence depends upon the ability to analyze and cope with new problem situations. Like the core skills training in the present book, the treatment included skills for coping with interpersonal situations such as conflict and drink refusal, as well as with intrapersonal situations such as negative mood states. Results indicated that the skills training approach had an effect on posttreatment drinking behavior: At a 12-month follow-up, the skills training group and the control groups diverged significantly on measures of days drunk, amount drunk, and length of drinking episodes. The authors concluded that their findings support the clinical utility of a skills training approach to reducing problem drinking.

Of significant additional interest is the fact that Chaney et al. (1978) measured skills acquisition during audiotaped role plays of high-risk intrapersonal and interpersonal situations. The results indicated that alcoholics' responses were improved in the role plays and that two skill measures, latency and duration of responses, predicted treatment outcome. The authors did note, however, that there was some decline in the effects of skill training after 3 months following termination of treatment. They raised the issue of cognitive impairment or other factors that may impede the retention of concrete skills, especially if treatment takes place immediately after detoxification—a situation that is typical of inpatient settings.

All forms of treatment should take into account the ability of the alcoholic to use and retain the skills. Indeed, Sanchez-Craig (1976) and Sanchez-Craig and Walker (1982) also have reported that many clients could not recall cognitive or coping skills strategies 1 month following treatment. Intagliata (1978, 1979) reported that the benefits of coping skills training fell off after 3 months. There are several gaps in our knowledge about the timing of treatment, the length of treatment, and possibly the content of skills training programs with respect to the alcoholic's level of cognitive impairment and the stage of recovery. Coping behaviors may need to be taught in stages, beginning with more basic and concrete coping strategies, such as the simple avoidance of high-risk situations. Then, later in treatment, the more complex and abstract coping strategies could be introduced.

Repetition and *in vivo* practice also appear to be necessary for enhanced generalization of coping skills. For example, we have included review sessions, and it may even be necessary to consider "booster sessions" after completion of the treatment program in order to help with maintenance of sobriety. Future treatment outcome research studies could evaluate the efficacy of extending outpatient treatment or of having some form of refresher courses for a year or two following completion of the formal skills training program. It is critical to assess when the alcoholic client will be most likely to benefit from a specific learning component and what new treatment components could be designed to enhance generalization and maintenance. Research on issues of content and timing of protocols may help improve the effectiveness of skills training treatment for alcoholism.

Jones, Kanfer, and Lanyon (1982) compared the Chaney et al.

(1978) skills training package to a discussion of alternative coping strategies and to standard treatment. They replicated the effects that Chaney et al. (1978) reported for skills training, this time on measures of the amount of alcohol consumed after treatment. They also found a treatment effect of engaging alcoholics in discussions that focused their attention on how well or poorly they had been handling high-risk situations. Both of these treatments were superior to the standard treatment alone.

The Jones et al. (1982) results raise an interesting issue with respect to coping models of alcohol abuse. According to the model, successful coping requires recognition that a problem exists (appraisal), followed by use of coping skills that can solve the problem without resorting to alcohol. Given that the subjects assigned to discussion of high-risk situations did as well as the subjects assigned to skills training, questions can be raised about how much emphasis to place on coping skills training as opposed to the simple identification of high-risk situations. However, the Chaney et al. (1978) alcoholic clients were more severely impaired than the relatively high-functioning alcoholics in the Jones et al. (1982) study. Thus, one may further speculate that there is a subgroup of relatively high-functioning alcoholics who have deficits in problem identification rather than in coping responses. Since denial, minimization, and rationalization are also common in the cognitive styles of alcoholics, they may relapse because they are not fully attending to their high-risk situations, perhaps because of selective attention. It may be useful to explore the information-processing mechanisms that mediate problem recognition (appraisal), as well as to examine the relationship among appraisal, coping skills, and outcome (Lazarus & Folkman, 1985).

In another early treatment outcome study using skills training, Freedberg and Johnston (1978) found that adding assertiveness training to an inpatient program improved treatment outcome from 24% to 36% abstinence at 1 year following treatment. When they combined abstinent and improved categories of outcome, the success rates were 72% for the program plus assertiveness training and 57% for the program alone. The study suggests that assertiveness skills training enhanced treatment outcome.

In a series of treatment outcome studies, Oei and Jackson (1980) randomly assigned alcoholics to receive either social skills training or supportive psychotherapy, with half of the patients in each group in an individual format and half in a group format. On measures of alcohol consumption and social functioning during the 1-year follow-up, the social skills training conditions (regardless of group vs. individual format) showed superior results compared with the supportive therapy condition.

Oei and Jackson (1982) assigned 32 inpatient alcoholics to one of four treatment conditions: combined cognitive restructuring and social skills training; social skills training alone; cognitive restructuring alone; and supportive psychotherapy. The social skills condition employed modeling, didactic presentation, role play, videotaping, and feedback. Homework assignments were also used to teach a variety of skills. Cognitive restructuring sessions dealt with the same situations taught in the social skills sessions, but therapists led discussions about affective attitudes toward the situations and used rational persuasion to modify clients' irrational beliefs and attitudes. There was no specific social skills training provided in this condition. For all groups, behavioral interviews and paper-and-pencil questionnaires were used to assess skills acquisition. Results indicated that all three skills training groups were superior to the supportive therapy approach. Clients in the cognitive restructuring group showed better maintenance of treatment gains at the later follow-ups. The authors concluded that treatment of skills deficits by either social skills training, cognitive restructuring, or both is an effective treatment for alcoholics. It should be noted, however, that clients were preselected because of their social anxiety or assertiveness difficulties. This limits generalizability of the results to the subsample selected and may suggest a patient–treatment matching strategy that could be explored in future research.

Studies investigating intrapersonal or mood management skills training approaches have generally focused on relaxation training, based on the tension reduction hypothesis (Cappell & Greeley, 1987; Conger, 1956). Although some forms of meditation or relaxation training have shown short-term effects on reducing drinking rates — for example, among heavy-drinking college students (Marlatt & Marques, 1977)—the few controlled studies with alcoholics have found little significant treatment effect when relaxation training was added to either standard or behavioral treatment (Miller & Taylor, 1980). However, in a recent review of relaxation training, Klajner et al. (1984) concluded that there is some evidence that relaxation techniques can produce an increase in perceived sense of control and may be of benefit in coping with stressors.

Rohsenow, Smith, and Johnson (1986) examined the effects of a cognitive–affective stress management package on drinking as part of an early intervention program for heavy-drinking college students. The program included muscle relaxation, meditation training, cognitive restructuring, and coping skill rehearsal. Treated and control clients were evaluated over a 6-month period on measures of affect (anxiety, depression) and daily alcohol consumption. The treatment significantly reduced drinking at posttreatment and at a 2½ month follow-up. It also reduced anxiety at posttreatment. The cognitive restructuring component had a significant effect on measures of expectations and beliefs about where stress comes from and how to cope with it. Although the measures returned to baseline levels 6 months after treatment, there were also significant relationships between individual client characteristics and outcomes. The most anxious, heaviest drinkers showed the largest improvements and maintained these over the 6-month follow-up. This study shows some promising initial treatment effects in a high-risk population of heavy social drinkers.

In a recent analysis of irrational beliefs, using data from a treatment outcome study conducted in our laboratory with the skills approaches outlined in this book, Rohsenow, Monti, Zwick, Nirenberg, Leipman, Binkoff, and Abrams (in press) reported that a cognitive style that included blaming others for problems (external source), feeling doomed by the past, and dwelling on the past was significantly related either to cravings to drink or to actual drinking 6 months after treatment. Severity of alcohol dependence was also positively associated with problem avoidance rather than problem identification and initiation of problem-solving skills. These results lend further support to the need to examine ways to enhance problem recognition and coping skills.

In general, as previously noted, cognitive–behavioral coping skills and relaxation training designed to teach alcoholics alternatives to drinking for mood/stress management have not been adequately investigated. These strategies have been found effective with other disorders, such as depression and anxiety (e.g., Barlow, 1985; Beck & Emery, 1985; Beck et al., 1979; Ellis, 1975), and preliminary work has suggested that the approach may be useful for some alcoholics (Cummings, Gordon, & Marlatt, 1980).

In a series of studies by Azrin and colleagues, a community reinforcement approach to skills training has also been evaluated. Although this approach is much broader in scope than the skills training program described in this book, it is easy to see how the two programs complement each other. The community reinforcement approach is designed to restructure family, social, and vocational aspects of everyday living so that sobriety is selectively encouraged while drinking is discouraged. The original program included problem-solving training, behavioral family therapy, and job-finding skills training. Hunt and Azrin (1973) evaluated the effectiveness of this approach when added to a full inpatient treatment program for alcoholics. Clients were randomly assigned to receive the regular inpatient treatment alone, or the treatment with added community reinforcement training. At the 6-month follow-up, the patients receiving community reinforcement training were drinking on only 14% of the days, compared to 79% of the days for the patients receiving inpatient treatment only. Unemployed days were also 12 times higher in the control condition, and the control group spent 15 times more days in institutions.

Since the publication of the original community reinforcement studies, several others have been reported, essentially confirming the value of the approach. Azrin (1976) added an Antabuse (disulfiram) protocol, daily self-monitoring of mood states, and a "buddy" system of social support. Compared to the hospital treatment condition, the community reinforcement training condition showed superior short- and long-term follow-up results: They had more than 90% abstinent days at 12-, 18-, and 24-month follow-ups, as well as less unemployment and institutionalization. Azrin, Sisson, Meyers, and Godley (1982) and Mallams, Godley, Hall, and Meyers (1982) have also recently conducted additional research providing further support for the community skills training approach to treatment.

The community approach is consistent with the cognitive–behavioral/social learning model of treatment and illustrates how one might go about meeting the need to foster generalization and maintenance of treatment produced change. This suggests the future potential of a broadened skills approach, with family systems, work environment, and leisure-time skills training being used to enhance the transfer to the natural environment of the core skills presented in this handbook (Moos & Finney, 1983).

A recently completed study in one of our own laboratories directly evaluated many of the components of the coping skills packages presented in this book. We (Monti et al., in press) randomly assigned 73 male inpatient alcoholics to standard treatment combined with (1) cognitive–behavioral mood management, (2) individual communication skills training, or (3) communication training with a family member present. Patients participated in 12 hours of group coping skills training in addition to the usual inpatient milieu. They all received additional exposure to AA, a community meeting, and individual counseling. All patients were assessed on the Alcohol-Specific Role-Play Test (ASRPT; see Chapter 1) before and after treatment, as well as a variety of measures of drinking, such as the Time-Line Follow-Back procedure (Sobell, Brochu, Sobell, Roy, & Stevens, 1987) and the quantity–frequency index (Cahalan, Cisin, &

Crossley, 1969). Results at 6 months following treatment indicated that alcoholics who received communication skills training, with or without family involvement, consumed significantly less alcohol than alcoholics who received cognitive–behavioral mood management training. However, because it was not possible to use a fully balanced design in this study (i.e., the study lacked a no-skills-training control condition), we could not conclude whether or not the cognitive–behavioral mood management was ineffective. The inclusion of a no-skills-training control and a combination of both cognitive–behavioral mood management and communication skills training conditions would have provided additional insights into the active components of the treatment. The results obtained were generally consistent with Chaney et al.'s (1978) findings that skills training reduced the amount of drinking.

The objective evaluation of coping skills acquisition, using the 10 role-play situations in the ASRPT, demonstrated that alcoholics in all three treatment groups improved significantly in coping skills and showed reduced anxiety in both general and alcohol-specific situations. Furthermore, they showed shorter response latencies, and their skills were judged to be more effective at preventing drinking (recall that Chaney et al., 1978, reported a positive correlation between rapidity of response and successful treatment outcome). Measures of craving or urge to drink decreased for all treatment groups from pre- to posttreatment. Furthermore, measures of subjective craving (urges) to drink, taken after the role-play assessment, correlated ($r = .63$) with 6-month follow-up drinking status.

It was also interesting to note that although all three groups improved in their coping skills and mood management, those receiving interpersonal skills training improved the most in alcohol-relevant skills, and also in their relaxation and mood management skills. This once again illustrates the interaction between intrapersonal and interpersonal components. Alcoholics who were taught interpersonal social skills also showed improvement in intrapersonal skills such as ability to relax, confirming our speculation that interpersonal coping skills training may provide a more general means of coping with both interpersonal and intrapersonal high-risk situations. A 3-year follow-up of the clients treated in this study is currently underway. Since this longer-term follow-up has not been completed, the early results must be interpreted with caution. However, the data are encouraging with respect to the efficacy of the specific skills training components outlined in this book.

Another study has also recently been completed in one of our laboratories (Cooney, Kadden, Litt, Getter, & Busher, 1987), evaluating the coping skills training approach in an outpatient aftercare program. This study explored the treatment-matching hypothesis (i.e., the hypothesis that clients with severe psychological problems, neuropsychological impairment, and sociopathic traits may benefit more from coping skills training treatment than their less impaired counterparts). A total of 118 clients were assigned in cohorts to either a behavioral coping skills group or an interactional psychotherapy group. Treatment was delivered weekly in an aftercare program for the 6 months following discharge from a 3-week comprehensive in-patient treatment program. The coping skills training consisted of the sessions recommended for outpatient settings as described in Chapter 4 of this book. The interactional psychotherapy group sought to foster insight, group cohesion and support, and willingness to engage in self-disclosure and affective expression. At the time of this writing, only the posttreatment results on aftercare were available, reflecting clients' status for the 6 months during which they participated in the aftercare program. Preliminary analysis of results from 10 groups revealed that alcoholics in both coping skills training and interactional group therapy improved from pre- to posttreatment on measures of alcohol consumption. Evidence was found to support the hypothesis that the alcoholics who were more psychologically impaired and who scored higher on measures of sociopathy relapsed significantly less if they received coping skills training. By contrast, those alcoholics who were less psychologically impaired and scored lower on sociopathy measures relapsed less with interactional therapy.

It is interesting to note that both the behavioral and interactional treatments did well, but with different subtypes of alcoholics. It appears that the behavioral approach, which is characterized by formal structure and emphasis on rehearsal and repetition of skills, is of greater benefit to those who are more severely impaired. However, there is a great deal of ongoing emotional support, as well as social support and group cohesion, in both types of groups, and these common elements may be sufficient or even superior to highly structured groups for those alcoholics who are less impaired. Perhaps less impaired alcoholics are more able to use problem solving and other skills spontaneously, without the formal training and practice inherent in behavioral coping skills groups. It is necessary to wait for further follow-up data, which will provide a more stringent test of the potential for generalization and maintenance of treatment-produced change, especially once the external supports of formal group treatment have been withdrawn.

This selected review of the treatment outcome literature has been quite limited in scope. Several studies' findings support the efficacy of the skills training approach. In concluding their comprehensive review of alcohol treatment effectiveness, Miller and Heather (1986) state that current research provides sound support for at least three treatment approaches: social skills training, stress management training, and the community reinforcement approach. They note that all these approaches have a common element, in that they involve direct behavioral training of clients in specific coping skills. We believe that their conclusion is consistent with the limited review provided here and with the orientation in this book.

## Future Directions: Coping Skills Training with Cue Exposure

### Overview

Recent laboratory research, based on learning theory, has focused on the role that alcohol cues (or stimuli) play in precipitating relapse. This research has generated considerable interest, has very promising clinical implications, and, although as yet not clinically validated, could result in a major breakthrough in advancing coping skills training treatments for alcohol abusers. Clinical trials are underway in the authors' laboratories at Brown University and the University of Connecticut. In this section, we present a general overview of the clinical relevance of cue exposure, followed by a more in-depth exploration of the theory and clinical evidence available at this time.

The sight and smell of alcohol (cues) can be an important precipitant of relapse. Clients who show signs of extreme emotional reactivity in the presence of cues (perhaps also suggesting fear of loss of control) may need additional skills training and could be kept in treatment for an additional period of time until their skills and confidence are improved. Emotional reactions to cue exposure provide grist for the therapeutic mill, and additional treatment may ensure that the client is fully prepared for the unavoidable temptations that will present themselves in the natural environment. One possible result of such *in vivo* practice is that it will enhance generalization of refusal skills to highly tempting situations in the natural environment.

Training drink refusal skills in the presence of actual alcohol cues also raises questions about the appropriate timing for the introduction of this type of exposure-based skill training exercise. A decision about when a particular client is ready for an exposure-based treatment must be made with caution. There is a fine line between an "inoculation" approach, which involves building resistance to temptation by gradually exposing the client to more and more difficult tempting situations, and the possibility that such exposure will in fact undermine the client's self-control and produce a sequence of events that leads to relapse. If a client does not yet have some coping skills and a strong motivation to stay abstinent, then an exposure session can be a setup for failure or can be used as an excuse to drink. Thus, it may be safer to confine initial exposure exercises to inpatient treatment settings, where strong or "uncontrollable" urges to drink can be managed more safely. In light of the growing interest in the role of cues in relapse, the following sections present a more detailed exploration of the theoretical, clinical, and ethical issues involved in the use of cue exposure with skills training protocols.

## Theoretical Rationale for Cue Exposure Treatment

A growing body of research suggests that alcoholics respond to alcohol-related cues, such as the sight and smell of their preferred alcoholic beverage, with increased desire to drink and with cognitive and physiological changes (e.g., increased anxiety, heart rate, and salivation) (Kaplan et al., 1985; Kaplan, Meyer, & Strobel, 1983; Monti et al., 1987; Niaura et al., 1988; Pomerleau et al., 1983). These reactions might lead an individual to experience an overwhelming desire to consume alcohol to diminish the elicited craving or physiological responses. In addition, the cognitive–emotional reactions may include decreased self-confidence (self-efficacy), which may result in a failure to employ coping skills in response to the situation. It has been suggested that cue exposure methods, such as those successfully employed in reducing fear and avoidance responses in phobics and obsessive–compulsives (Foa & Kozak, 1986), may be useful in the treatment of compulsive drinking (Baker, Cooney, & Pomerleau, 1987; Cooney et al., 1983; Niaura et al., 1988; Rankin, Hodgson, & Stockwell 1983; Wilson, 1981) by reducing the intensity of the reactions to the cues and/or by enhancing the strength of coping skills and self-confidence or self-efficacy.

Several psychological processes may underlie the effects of the cue exposure procedure. In terms of learning theory, both classical and operant conditioning processes apply. Repeated presentations of the sight and smell of an alcoholic beverage, without consumption, should eventually result in a decrease in classically conditioned craving or physiological and emotional responses in the presence of alcohol (i.e., via extinction). Operant processes may also play a role in cue exposure treatments. Repeated exposure to alcohol cues, while blocking consummatory responses (reinforcing), may decrease the discriminative stimulus value (i.e., the power or reward value) of alcohol cues. If the individual does not experience the immediate reinforcing properties of alcohol (either pleasant euphoria or tension reduction), then eventually alcohol will lose its "value." Thus, the sight and smell of an alcoholic beverage, *without* consumption, would no longer signal the availability of reinforcement, thereby reducing the likelihood of subsequent operant drinking.

Another potential benefit of cue exposure is that it provides an opportunity to acquire and practice coping skills in more "realistic" situations, such as refusing a drink or engaging in relaxation in the presence of alcohol (Strickler, Bigelow, & Wells, 1976). With repeated trials and appropriate reinforcement for the performance of these skills, alcohol cues may become cues or signals for skills utilization rather than for consumption. Finally, exposure procedures may produce their effects through a process of altered cognitions. This is consistent with recent developments in cognitive–social learning theory (Abrams & Niaura, 1987; Wilson, in press). Coping with a drinking situation without consuming alcohol should increase clients' sense of self-efficacy, which may increase the likelihood that they will persist at coping in other high-risk situations without drinking. In the absence of cue exposure treatment, clients tend to think of pleasant effects of alcohol when in the presence of alcohol cues (Cooney, Gillespie, et al., 1987). Cue exposure treatment could be used to develop negative expectancies about drinking by asking clients to practice imagining the negative or aversive consequences of drinking rather than the positive or pleasant consequences. With repeated exposure and cognitive restructuring, clients' expectancies (prior to actual consumption) may come to focus on the negative rather than on the short-term positive consequences of drinking.

Indeed, in a laboratory study, Binkoff (1985) reported that the presence of drinking cues significantly interfered with drink refusal coping skills as rated by trained observers. The use of realistic "props" and beverage containers, as well as other creative methods to increase the realism of coping rehearsal, may help reduce slips or relapse after discharge from treatment; however, research has yet to evaluate the full value of such techniques with respect to their ultimate impact on relapse (Niaura et al., 1988). With repeated cue exposure treatment and practice, a variety of new behavioral and cognitive coping skills may be acquired in place of previously elicited responses.

## Clinical Trials

At this time, it would seem prudent to employ procedures that combine extinction (classical and operant processes) and coping skills training elements (cognitive–social learning theory), because initial attempts to design treatments based on extinction alone have not met with success. Meyer, Randall, Barrington, Mirin, and Greenberg (1976) used naltrexone, a narcotic antagonist, to test extinction-based treatment for heroin addicts. Clients receiving naltrexone were encouraged to go repeatedly through the ritual of herion self-administration; this provided extinction trials with exposure to drug administration cues in the absence of drug effects. Clients receiving naltrexone quickly stopped self-administering heroin on the ward, but upon return to the community, they had a relapse rate similar to that of clients who had been allowed to self-administer heroin without the narcotic blockade. Meyer et al. suggested that extinction did not occur in their protocol because consumption of the narcotic antagonist signaled the unavailability of effects from heroin. Another interpretation of the results is that the extinction-based procedure did not involve acquisition or practice of coping skills. For this to occur, cue exposure must occur in a context where drug effects are potentially available, but the client resists consumption through the use of coping skills that are incompatible with alcohol or drug consumption.

Initial applications of cue exposure treatments for reducing craving for alcohol have appeared in the literature as case studies. Blakey and Baker (1980) have reported six cases in which clients were gradually exposed to individualized cues, including watching other patrons drink at their favorite pubs. Most clients reported a decrease in craving over repeated exposure sessions, and five of the six clients reported abstinence in follow-up periods ranging from 2 to 9 months. An important feature of this work was the individualized tailoring of cue exposure situations. This was necessitated by the authors' finding that some clients expressed no desire to drink in the presence of alcohol in the hospital, but experienced intense craving in other situations, such as in a bar. Other case studies have been reported by Hodgson and Rankin (1983) and Rankin et al. (1983).

These studies of exposure procedures illustrate several different approaches to alcohol cue exposure. All three used actual alcoholic beverages. Blakey and Baker (1980) used a repeated series of *in vivo* exposure trials, taking clients through individually tailored hierarchies. These hierarchies included many situations that we believe are best avoided by alcoholic clients (e.g., bars). Our recommendation is that the stimuli utilized for cue exposure consist largely of situations that evoke craving but that cannot be easily avoided.

Hodgson and Rankin (1983) and Rankin et al. (1983) used a priming dose of alcohol, and alcohol was available for further consumption. The use of a priming alcohol dose during cue exposure treatment raises serious questions regarding treatment goals. Priming doses might be appropriate if the goal were to teach moderate drinking skills, or to teach clients how to cope with craving after a first drink. However, if cue exposure is to be employed with abstinence as the goal, then the procedure should be designed to prevent the *initiation* of drinking. We do not recommend using a priming dose of alcohol in abstinence-oriented treatment of alcohol-dependent individuals.

## Procedural Variables: Imaginal Cues, Prolonged Trials, and Attention Focusing

A controlled clinical trial of cue exposure treatment for drug abusers was conducted by McLellan, Childress, Ehrman, and O'Brien (1986). Outpatients in a methadone maintenance clinic were randomly assigned to three conditions: cognitive–behavioral psychotherapy plus 35 extinction trials; cognitive–behavioral therapy alone; or drug counseling and education. Both the psychotherapy-plus-extinction group and the psychotherapy-alone group had better 6-month outcomes than the drug counseling group. There was no evidence that the addition of the extinction procedure made a significant contribution beyond the psychotherapy. In a follow-up study, McLellan et al. (1986) adopted several new procedures for extinction-based treatment: (1) Exposure sessions were scheduled during inpatient treatment to avoid reconditioning between sessions; (2) relevant mood states were induced during cue exposure in an attempt to extinguish reactivity to such moods as well; and (3) exposure included idiosyncratic stimuli that were salient for each client. Preliminary results suggest that these procedures were effective with opiate abusers. Clients initially showed a high level of conditioned responding, followed by reductions in physiological and subjective withdrawal and craving responses with repeated exposure trials.

Blakey and Baker (1980) have noted that the sight and smell of a drink in the hospital is by no means a universal cue for craving. Some of the more salient cues may be difficult to present, and considerations may need to be given to the use of imaginal cue exposure.

Cues such as interpersonal conflict (e.g., an argument with a supervisor) may not lend themselves to repeated *in vivo* exposure, but could be presented in imagery. Another possibility is to combine alcohol cues with imaginal cues. For example, alcohol cues might be presented in the context of a client's imagining having a difficult time with the children while at home.

Borkovec and Grayson (1980) have called attention to the need for "functional exposure" to stimuli. The client is encouraged to attend to and cognitively process the emotional and behavioral memories associated with the stimulus. Several procedures may enhance functional exposure to alcohol cues. Relaxation may help clients to visualize scenes or attend to stimuli that they might otherwise avoid because of the negative feelings elicited by the sight and smell of alcohol. Prolonged trials may prove more effective than brief trials in alcohol cue exposure, as they have for exposure treatment of phobias (Foa & Kozak, 1986). Instructions and prompts that encourage clients to focus their attention on alcoholic stimuli may also enhance exposure, as has been shown in the treatment of obsessions and compulsions (Grayson, Foa, & Steketee, 1982).

Baker, Cooney, and Vinnick (1983) evaluated procedures to enhance cue exposure treatment with alcoholics. They compared the effects of interrupted versus prolonged exposure trials and distraction versus attention-focusing manipulations on 1 hour of alcohol cue exposure. These authors found the lowest posttreatment alcohol cue reactivity in clients who received prolonged stimulus exposure, with verbal instructions that focused their attention on the taste, smell, and expected positive effects of drinking alcohol. The implication of this finding is that prolonged exposure with attention-focusing instructions may enhance the efficacy of alcohol cue exposure treatment.

## Suggested Clinical Procedures

The following is a description of cue exposure treatment procedures as conceived at this time. These procedures should be considered untested, but we believe they are promising. Clinical trials are currently underway at both the University of Connecticut and Brown University.

Treatment begins with a detailed assessment of situations and mood states that represent possible high risk for relapse. In 1-hour sessions, clients are exposed to the sight and smell of their favorite alcoholic beverage with instructions to "resist consuming this drink." If a client does drink, he/she should not be scheduled for future cue exposure sessions, and alternative treatment methods should be employed. Clinically, however, this is a strong sign that the individual is having difficulty coping with temptation. To maximize between-session habituation (reduced reactivity and increased confidence in coping), exposure is continuous for 45 minutes, with repeated reminders to focus attention on the alcoholic beverage (Baker et al., 1983). In addition to using alcoholic beverages, clients are exposed to particular idiosyncratic stimuli from their prior drinking history that elicit craving responses. For example, a client who thinks about drinking when he gets paid at work would be exposed to his paycheck stub. A divorced client who craves alcohol when talking to her ex-husband about the children would recreate that situation in imagination.

Since mood states are likely to be important antecedents to craving (Childress, McLellan, Natale, & O'Brien, 1986; Litt, Cooney, Kadden, & Gaupp, in press), clients should also undergo induction of anger, depression, and anxiety, with later sessions focusing on the mood state that evokes the greatest craving response for a particular client. Mood induction involves recalling a recent event in which a particular mood was experienced, in order to recreate the mood state. Recent data (Litt et al., in press) indicate that mood induction procedures (and hypnotic techniques) are effective with alcohol clients. At the end of every cue exposure session, clients should undergo induction of relaxation to remove any discomfort associated with reactivity to alcohol cues or mood induction. The relaxation induction also provides practice with a behavioral coping skill.

Clients are instructed to practice a variety of skills for coping with the cravings that arise during cue exposure. Relevant skills include progressive muscle relaxation, calming self-statements, and recalling the negative consequences of drinking and positive consequences of sobriety. Images of mastery or control over craving may also be suggested. Thus, clients are exposed to external stimuli and internal moods that induce craving, while at the same time practicing skills to reduce the craving. (See Cooney et al., 1983, for further description of how to combine cue exposure with coping skills training.)

Our work has shown that some clients will not demonstrate an observable reaction to the alcohol-related stimuli. We anticipate that some clients may also be unresponsive to the mood induction procedures (although our work suggests that this number will be small). Through use of a combination of different alcohol-related stimuli and mood scenes, we expect that most clients will respond to at least one of them.

## Ethical Guidelines

Most alcohol treatment facilities protect their clients from exposure to alcohol-related stimuli. Alcoholic beverages are not permitted on inpatient wards, and outpatients are discouraged from entering drinking situations. Avoidance of alcohol-related stimuli is taught as a way to reduce the frequency and intensity of craving for alcohol. It is also an effective coping strategy. If a treatment program decides to expose clients to alcohol-related stimuli, particularly alcoholic beverages, care must be taken that a mixed message is not communicated. It would not be therapeutic if clients come to think that there is no harm in entering bars or attending heavy-drinking parties. This misconception can be avoided by giving the following rationale: Although most high-risk drinking situations should be avoided, one must still learn to cope with (or extinguish) craving responses to alcohol-related stimuli, because some of these stimuli will be unavoidable.

Another concern with cue exposure treatment is that it may precipitate alcohol consumption either during or immediately after treatment sessions. In our experience over 8 years with over 300 alcoholic clients in clinical research sessions, only 1 client consumed alcohol. This client, described in Pomerleau et al. (1983), had made prior statements to the effect that he *could* handle situations where alcohol was present. After the drinking session, the client became convinced of his need to learn coping skills, to attend AA meetings, and to take disulfiram. Thus, within-session drinking is extremely rare and could ultimately be used to good therapeutic advantage. However, we do not recommend that clients initiate alcohol cue exposure as outpatients. Clients may need an opportunity to discuss their experience with members of the treatment staff in a protected environment after early sessions. Also, until coping skills are thoroughly practiced in the presence of alcohol and high-risk situations, reactivity to alcohol may sensitize alcoholics to any alcohol-related stimuli. Thus, clients require the protection offered by the inpatient setting until coping skills training is well underway. Outpatient sessions may be useful only after clients have acquired basic skills for coping with their alcohol cue reactivity.

Although still in its infancy, cue exposure with coping skills training may provide an exciting breakthrough in the field of treatment and relapse prevention. The specific clients, settings, procedures, and timing of treatments (i.e., parametrics) still have to be empirically tested. Actual practice in the presence of realistic cues, or even in the natural environment, should be considered to enhance generalization and maintenance. This area of clinical research is likely to generate a good deal of interest in the coming decade.

## Other Future Directions and Challenges

Maximizing the effectiveness of treatment is especially important, in light of increased concern over the costs associated with lengthy inpatient hospitalization programs. Given the present climate of fiscal accountability, treatment programs are frequently faced with the difficult decision of whether to eliminate treatment components and, if so, what components. Therapists are under pressure to reduce clients' length of stay, and therefore must begin treatment soon after detoxification, when neuropsychological impairment is most likely to interfere with learning. Implementation of complex treatment programs too soon after detoxification may result in failure to grasp the skills being taught and increased confusion for the clients, and may exacerbate the likelihood of dropouts or lack of maintenance of skills following discharge.

The cost and practical constraints of providing highly tailored individual treatment must be weighed against the limitations of standardized groups in which individuals may either receive treatments that they do *not* need or fail to receive treatments that they *do* need. As illustrated in this chapter, certain key concepts (e.g., severity of impairment) could lead to development of better screening for individuals and improved patient–treatment matching strategies. Ultimately, it is hoped that the matching approach to treatment will enable clients to be triaged more effectively into the appropriate treatment setting and, within that setting, into the appropriate mix of individual and group treatment components. In order to accomplish these goals, more work needs to be done on identifying the specific active components of treatment and the related individual-difference variables that will lead to improved matching and presumably to better outcomes.

Related questions for future research and clinical work concern not only the content of client screening protocols, but also issues of generalization, maintenance, and timing of treatments. For example, should outpatient treatment follow inpatient programs? How long should outpatient treatment be? And should "booster sessions" be introduced to help enhance maintenance of skills beyond the end of treatment? In line with Cronkite and Moos's (1980) and Azrin's (1976) research about the importance of continuation of care in the extratreatment environment, alternative delivery systems should be considered to meet the long-term needs of alcoholics more effectively.

Chronic alcohol dependence may require some form of ongoing treatment across the remainder of the clients' lifespan. Community-based support, health maintenance organization (HMO) settings, and workplace programs could be structured so as to be better integrated with treatment programs; this would result in better coordination of all treatments, both medical and psychosocial (Nathan & Niaura, 1987). Sobell, Brochu, Sobell, Roy, and Stevens (1987) argue that at least 18 months to 2 years of follow-up should be used to evaluate treatment programs adequately.

A broader view of the process of treatment emerges from this approach. A lapse in sobriety followed by treatment should not be evaluated in isolation as if it were the only opportunity to treat a client. Chronic refractory, problems such as alcoholism may require several "cycles" of treatment, lapses, and further treatment. Each cycle can potentially build on the learning acquired during previous cycles by examining what situations have still not been mastered, and fine-tuning the assessment of deficits and the need for additional coping skills.

On the topic of inpatient versus outpatient treatment, some studies have shown that beyond the need for a medically safe detoxification, inpatient hospital settings have little advantage over day hospital treatments and are much more costly (Longabaugh et al., 1983). This finding is not without controversy, and it may be that different types of clients (e.g., younger, less dependent, more socially connected) benefit as much from day hospital treatment as from inpatient treatment, whereas older, more severely dependent alcoholics may indeed require comprehensive inpatient treatment. Inpatient settings have both advantages and disadvantages. Among the disadvantages are that clients are treated in an overly "protected" environment, so that skills training cannot be adequately tested and corrective feedback cannot be given prior to discharge. Clients may develop a false sense of mastery over drinking without having been tempted in the "real world," and this may result in early relapse. By contrast, there are also advantages for having 1–3 weeks of intensive treatment in a 24-hour monitored inpatient environment. A Veterans Administration cooperative study (McLellan, Woody, Luborsky, O'Brien, & Druley, 1983) examined alcoholism treatment outcome for veterans assigned to one of six treatment modalities. Clients having moderate psychiatric problems as well as serious family or employment problems showed significantly better outcomes in the inpatient treatment programs. An inpatient environment can help clients acquire basic coping skills; can assist therapists to evaluate the possible presence/ emergence of major psychiatric symptoms; and can allow therapists and clients enough time to begin to develop other sources of alternative support, such as links with AA, job evaluation, and alternative living arrangements. It may be helpful to combine formal treatment with self-help groups such as AA in a more coordinated fashion (Thoreson & Budd, 1987). The problem of selecting the least intensive but most appropriate treatment setting for which type of client, and the related issue of how best to use community resources in order to make the transition from inpatient to outpatient treatment, still have to be adequately addressed.

The problems of preventing relapse, achieving generalization, and maintaining treatment gains have not yet received enough attention. Several issues already discussed relate to the challenge of improving the maintenance of treatment-produced gains and preventing relapse. Among these issues are the following: timing of the introduction of different skills components; the cognitive level of the client (abstract–concrete, time since detoxification); transfer from inpatient to outpatient programs; booster sessions; length of treatment; the need to build in alternative, extratreatment supports (job skills, a social network of nonproblem drinkers, community reinforcement approaches); the importance of doing practice exercises between treatment sessions; and, finally, the possible use of realistic situations, such as including alcohol cues in skills training.

Behavioral approaches to alcoholism treatment have advocated the use of stimulus control strategies to cope with high-risk situations (Sobell & Sobell, 1973). In this case, the clients are instructed to *avoid* tempting situations and to rearrange their environment so as not to risk exposing themselves to an opportunity for relapse. They may be advised to remove all alcoholic beverages from the house, or to take a new route home from work that does not involve going past any favorite drinking place or package store. If all else fails, and the clients find themselves in a situation with an overwhelming desire to drink, then they are advised to leave the situation immediately and (if necessary) call their counselor or their AA sponsor. Thus, avoidance of alcohol cues (stimulus control) can also be an effective coping strategy under some circumstances.

At first glance, there appears to be a contradiction in treatment philosophy here, with one form of learning theory (stimulus control) advocating avoidance of cues or high-risk situations as a coping strategy, and another (social learning) advocating repeated exposure to cues with rehearsal of coping skills strategies. However, if one adopts a problem-solving approach, then both approaches can be utilized for different people or for the same person under different circumstances. Obviously, if a particular client has too strong a reaction to situational cues and/or has been unable to develop adequate coping skills to resist drinking, then removing himself/herself from the cues or avoiding certain kinds of tempting situations would appear to be a prudent coping strategy. Since individuals cannot avoid drinking cues for the rest of their lives, our treatment philosophy is that clients must *eventually* be taught the coping skills that will enable them to remain in tempting situations without drinking (perhaps through extinction of the psychological cravings and the physiological response, and/or through enhanced coping skills and increased self-efficacy expectations). Each clinician and client must be clear on the problem-solving steps involved in making the "right choice," and these should be reviewed periodically. For a more comprehensive review of the conceptual and treatment issues involved in cue exposure, see Niaura et al. (1988) and Baker et al. (1987).

Controlled or social drinking, rather than total abstinence, would be a logical extension of the coping skills approach. This might be construed as advocating the possibility of controlled or social drinking rather than total abstinence. Although it is true that the coping skills model advocated here can be used in early intervention/ prevention programs to help individuals to regulate their behavior better, we believe that the overwhelming data to date do not argue for controlled drinking as a viable treatment for individuals diagnosed with alcohol dependence (Foreyt, 1987; Nathan, 1986). Nathan states,

> [T]he consensus among informed observers is that alcoholism treatment with controlled drinking as a prime treatment goal is neither efficacious nor ethical when offered to chronic alcoholics. . . . the weight of the available data now suggests both that we have not developed treatment programs that can reliably teach chronic alcoholics to become controlled drinkers and that status as a controlled drinker is not in the best interests of most chronic alcoholics. (1986, p. 44)

For a more comprehensive review of the issues and research studies involving controlled drinking, see Heather and Robinson (1983).

A much-needed focus of coping skills training techniques should be on the potential for early identification and prevention of problem drinking in young adults, using skills training approaches. There is little research devoted to the use of skills training to help high-risk individuals (e.g., children of alcoholics) remain social drinkers instead of progressing on to alcohol abuse or alcohol dependence. This approach has been referred to as "secondary prevention"; the main objectives are to develop procedures for identifying early-stage problem drinkers, attracting them into treatment, and treating them in a cost-effective manner with self-control skills training and education (Sanchez-Craig, Wilkinson, & Walker, 1987).

Promising approaches to prevention in school-age children have been developed, especially in the area of smoking prevention. Flay (1984) has summarized three generations of research on prevention of tobacco and drug use among junior high and high school students. Many of these research protocols involve a skills training approach, with role playing of how to counter peer pressure to smoke, drink, or try drugs while retaining one's identity in a meaningful peer group. Other components of treatment include challenging advertising media portrayals of positive outcomes (adventure, success, sexual prowess) and examining peers' and parents' attitudes toward drugs. Research studies that have evaluated the approach reveal encouraging support for the notion that the total package can be used to prevent regular tobacco use, which is usually a "gateway" to abuse of alcohol, marijuana, and other drugs. Studies have been replicated in various parts of the United States and Canada, speaking to the robustness of this approach. Unfortunately, little published work has been done on alcohol prevention using the skills training approach.

There is an increasing focus on understanding the role played by spouses, significant others, or the family system in maintaining alcohol abuse or in potentially maintaining sobriety. Coping skills approaches, particularly communication skills training, have significant potential for contributing to the development of future treatments that also employ behavioral marital or family treatment approaches to alcohol abuse (McCrady et al., 1986). The coping skills of spouses may be directly related to the level of functioning of the client (McCrady, 1986). Indeed, spouse/family programs such as Al-Anon and Alateen have emerged from the self-help movement in an effort to address the important needs of these social network members in the recovery process (Thoreson & Budd, 1987). However, because members of an alcoholic's social network need help and support themselves, this may detract from their ability to assist the client with his/her sobriety. Research work and clinical case studies on the role played by significant others and the family in alcoholism have been reported for decades (e.g., Kaufman & Pattison, 1982;

Steinglass, 1979), but there is still potential for a large contribution to be made to the field in exploring this area, because of recent advances in the field of behavioral family and marital therapy.

In a three-condition randomized study, McCrady et al. (1986) reported little effect (at 6 months posttreatment) of spouse training or spouse plus behavioral marital therapy training, compared to a control condition of individual treatment with spouses present but without spouse training. However, at an 18-month follow-up, there was a differential and beneficial effect of spouse plus behavioral marital communication training. The marital system may have been gradually changing over the longer time period as a result of the combined marital and alcohol treatment program. Future research is needed to examine the potential for including spouse skills training and/or family treatments, not only to enhance treatment but especially to ensure generalization and maintenance of change following treatment termination. As in the McCrady et al. (1986) study, results may not be evident until 1–2 years later, but over this time period a treatment that can achieve maintenance is clearly worth exploring, even if it requires a greater initial investment.

Preliminary results of a recently completed treatment outcome study lend further support to the coping skills model, the importance of the extratreatment environment (family and occupational), and the notion of matching treatment components to client characteristics (Longabaugh, Beattie, Stout, Malloy, & Noel, 1988). These authors have developed a prognostic model—a theoretical formulation for making prognoses concerning outcome. Five variables are identified: alcohol involvement, psychological health, social investment, social environmental support for alcohol health, and social environmental support for psychological health. The theory includes hypotheses concerning the set of conditions under which specific treatment interventions will be differentially effective. Three outpatient treatment interventions are defined: (1) individual focus, a social learning/coping skills approach to helping alcohol abusers learn how to achieve and maintain abstinence; (2) enhancement of social support, an intervention that includes incorporation of significant others into the patients' treatment programs; and (3) enhancement of occupational role, an intervention that is added to individual focus and enhancement of social support.

To test the theory and the differential effectiveness of the interventions, clients were randomly assigned to one of the three treatment conditions and treated for up to 20 outpatient sessions over the course of a year. They were followed as research subjects for 18 months after treatment initiation. Interviews and comprehensive measurements were made of their alcohol, physical, psychological, social, and vocational health. Treatment and changes in prognostic variables were also measured, in order to test the goodness of fit of the theoretical formulation.

Tests of the validity of the prognostic model have been conducted. Preliminary results showed a strong relationship between increased social environmental support for alcohol health and the proportion of days abstinent in the year following treatment initiation. This relationship was moderated by social investment: For persons highly invested in their social environment, the relationship was strong, but for those with low investment there was no relationship. Furthermore, among those highly invested, the correlation was strongest for those who received treatment focusing on their social environment. It appears that this form of treatment has long-term benefits. Although those receiving relational enhancement initially reported fewer abstinent days than those in individually focused treatment, they reported a higher proportion of days abstinent by the 15th month following treatment initiation. This time × treatment crossover effect replicates a similar finding from a study of outpatient treatment with alcoholic couples (McCrady et al., 1986) reported earlier in this chapter. This confirms that social environmental coping skills treatment results in slow but gradual improvement, but over a longer follow-up time period than previously thought.

The evolving cognitive–social learning skills training approach to the treatment of alcohol abuse is gaining increasing interest and acceptance in the field (Abrams & Niaura, 1987; Marlatt & Gordon, 1985; Mendelson & Mello, 1985; Miller & Heather, 1986; Nathan & Lipscomb, 1985; Nathan & Niaura, 1987; Wilson, 1987, in press). The focus on situation specificity; concrete skills training; direct behavioral practice; and program, process, and outcome evaluation research has begun to show promise. There are signs of an increasingly fertile cross-collaboration between scientists and practitioners, although the field could benefit greatly from more interaction between clinicians and researchers. The possibility of combining coping skills training approaches with other forms of treatment (medical, self-help) has not been adequately explored. Although many conceptual and pragmatic challenges remain, one can be cautiously optimistic about the efficacy of the coping skills approach to the treatment of alcohol dependence. The potential of using a coping skills model for prevention, early intervention, treatment, and relapse prevention has yet to be fully explored or evaluated. Initial results are encouraging, and more clinical research is warranted.

# Reminder Sheets and
# Practice Exercises

## Session: Introduction, Group Building, Problem Assessment

### Practice Exercise: Problem List

You will be able to stay sober if you can develop better ways to handle problems that could lead you back to drinking. The first step is to become aware of what those problems might be. In each section below, briefly describe one or more problems that you think you may have trouble with. Things that happen between now and our next session may give you ideas for this list.

Problems with my family or close friends: _____

_____

_____

_____

Loneliness: _____

_____

_____

_____

Feeling angry: _____

_____

_____

_____

Anxiety or tension: _____

_____

_____

_____

Social pressure to drink: _____

_____

_____

_____

Other problems: _____

_____

_____

_____

## Session: Starting Conversations

## Reminder Sheet

These pointers should make it easier for you to start a conversation.

- It's OK to:
    - Start with simple topics.
    - Talk about yourself.
- Remember to:
    - Listen and observe.
    - Speak up.
    - Use open-ended questions to prompt a response.
    - Check your reception.
    - End the conversation gracefully.

## Practice Exercise: Conversation Skills

Start a conversation with someone you don't know very well or with someone you'd like to practice having more comfortable conversations with.

Where did the conversation take place? _____

_____

_____

_____

What was the conversation about? _____

_____

_____

_____

What were the results of the conversation? _____

_____

_____

_____

*Communication Checklist:*

|  | Yes | No |
|---|---|---|
| 1. Did you listen and observe prior to speaking? | ____ | ____ |
| 2. Did you start with small talk? | ____ | ____ |
| 3. Did you ask open-ended questions? | ____ | ____ |
| 4. Did you share any of your own ideas, opinions, information? | ____ | ____ |
| 5. Did you end gracefully? | ____ | ____ |

## Session: Giving and Receiving Compliments

### Reminder Sheet

Keep the following points regarding compliments in mind.

- Giving Compliments: .
    State the compliment in terms of your own *feelings,* not in terms of absolutes or facts.
    Compliment something *specific* that the person does, that you like.
- Receiving compliments:
    Don't turn down a compliment that is given to you.
    Show that you appreciate it.

### Practice Exercise

*Exercise 1*

Approach someone and find something about that person to compliment. This can be done in the context of a conversation, or you can approach him/her specifically to provide a compliment. Afterwards, write the compliment in the space below:

_____

_____

_____

*Communication Checklist:*

|  | Yes | No |
|---|---|---|
| 1. I stated the compliment in terms of my own feelings. | ___ | ___ |
| 2. I made the compliment specific. | ___ | ___ |

*Exercise 2*

Stay alert until our next session for any compliments you may receive. Try to respond according to the guidelines discussed in today's session. For one compliment that you receive, record the following:

Describe situation:_____

_____

_____

What was your response?_____

_____

_____

*Communication Checklist:*

|  | Yes | No |
|---|---|---|
| 1. Did you accept the compliment? | ___ | ___ |
| 2. Did you turn down or differ with the compliment given to you? | ___ | ___ |
| 3. Did you show your appreciation? | ___ | ___ |

## Session: Nonverbal Communication

### Reminder Sheet

"Body language" can be very useful in helping you to get your point across.

- Posture
- Eye contact
- Facial expression
- Tone of voice
- Head nods
- Hand movements and gestures
- Personal space

### Practice Exercise

*Exercise 1*

Between now and the next session, notice what you like about the nonverbal behavior of some of the people you see. List some of the positive things you observe. Briefly describe how those things may have had a positive effect on the communication process. _____

_____

_____

_____

_____

_____

*Exercise 2*

Start a conversation with someone. As you are talking, try to notice some of your nonverbal behaviors. Then, after the conversation is over, jot down those nonverbal behaviors that you thought you did well, and some that you'd like to improve on.

Person you talked with:_____

I did these nonverbal behaviors pretty well: _____

_____

_____

_____

I could use some improvement on these nonverbal behaviors: _____

_____

_____

_____

## Session: Feeling Talk and Listening Skills

### Reminder Sheet

- Sharing your feelings with other people:

  *It's OK* to talk about your feelings (both positive and negative ones).
  Choose an appropriate amount of *self-disclosure.* You'll share more with
  people you feel (or want to feel) closer to than with new people you meet.

- Listening to other people:

  Use "body language" to show that you are listening to the other person
  (leaning forward, eye contact, head nods, etc.).
  Pay attention to the tone of voice, facial expression, and body language of the
  other person, to help you "tune in to" his/her feelings.
  Listen for an appropriate time to talk.
  Show interest and understanding by asking questions about feelings, rephras-
  ing what was said, or adding comments of your own.
  Share similar experiences or feelings that you have had.

### Practice Exercise

Practice expressing your feelings and listening to the feelings of others. Describe the
situations below.

*Exercise 1: Practice Expressing Feelings*

Start a conversation with someone and share a feeling during the conversation.

1. Whom did you talk with? _____

2. What feeling did you share? _____

   _____

   _____

   _____

3. How did he/she respond? _____

   _____

   _____

   _____

*continued*

*Exercise 2: Practice Listening to Feelings*

During an interaction you have with someone, notice a feeling that he/she is expressing both verbally and nonverbally.

1. What feeling did he/she express verbally? _____

_____

_____

_____

2. What nonverbal behaviors did you notice? _____

_____

_____

_____

3. What feeling was he/she expressing nonverbally? _____

_____

_____

_____

4. How did you show you were listening? _____

_____

_____

_____

## Session: Introduction to Assertiveness

### Reminder Sheet

Remember the following points in practicing assertiveness:

- Take a moment to think before you speak.
- Be specific and direct in what you say.
- Pay attention to your body language.
- Be willing to compromise.
- Restate your assertion if you feel that you're not being heard.

### Practice Exercise

This exercise is to help you become aware of your style of handling various social situations. The four common response styles are passive, aggressive, passive–aggressive, and assertive.

Pick three different social situations prior to the next session. Write brief descriptions of them and of your response to them. Then decide which of the four common response styles best describes your response.

*Situation 1:* _____

_____

Your response: _____

_____

_____

Circle response style: passive, aggressive, passive–aggressive, assertive

*Situation 2:* _____

_____

Your response: _____

_____

_____

Circle response style: passive, aggressive, passive–aggressive, assertive

*Situation 3:* _____

_____

Your response: _____

_____

_____

Circle response style: passive, aggressive, passive–aggressive, assertive

## Session: Giving Criticism

### Reminder Sheet

Here are some suggestions for giving constructive, assertive criticism:

- Calm down first.
- State the criticism in terms of your own feelings, not in terms of absolute facts.
- Criticize the behavior, not the person.
- Request a *specific* behavior change.
- Be willing to negotiate a compromise.
- Start and finish on a positive note.
- Tone of voice: clear and firm, not angry.

### Practice Exercise

Approach a person to whom you have been meaning to tell something negative. Provide that person with some constructive criticism. Try to follow the guidelines that were outlined in the session.

*Before Leaving Today's Group Session:*

Identify the problem: _____

_____

_____

_____

Your goals: _____

_____

_____

_____

*After Speaking to the Person, Describe What Happened:*

What did you say to him/her? _____

_____

_____

_____

How did he/she respond? _____

_____

_____

_____

## Session: Receiving Criticism

### Reminder Sheet

When you receive criticism, remember the following:

- Don't get defensive, don't debate, don't counterattack.
- Find something to agree with in the criticism.
- Ask questions for clarification.
- Propose a workable compromise.

### Practice Exercise

Stay alert until our next session for any criticism you may receive. Try to respond according to the guidelines outlined in today's session. For one criticism that you receive, record the following:

Describe the situation: _____

_____

_____

_____

_____

_____

Describe your response: _____

_____

_____

_____

_____

_____

*Communication Checklist:*

|  | Yes | No |
|---|---|---|
| 1. Did you behave as if the criticism was nothing to get upset about? | ___ | ___ |
| 2. Did you find something to agree with in the criticism? | ___ | ___ |
| 3. Did you ask questions to clarify the criticism? | ___ | ___ |
| 4. Did you propose a workable compromise? | ___ | ___ |

## Session: Receiving Criticism about Drinking

### Reminder Sheet

When you receive criticism about drinking, remember the following:
- Don't get defensive, don't debate, don't counterattack.
- Find something to agree with in the criticism.
- Ask questions for clarification.
- Propose a workable compromise:
    Ask the criticizer to calmly express his/her concerns.
    Agree to keep the criticizer better informed about your feelings and moods, your activities, and any slips you may have.

### Practice Exercise

Imagine the following situation: You come home from work after a long hard day. You've been sober for about 3 months and have had nothing to drink today. However, your eyes are red, and you're feeling somewhat "down" and irritable. Your spouse (or someone you live with) approaches you, smells your breath, and says, "You've been drinking again, haven't you?"

In the space below, write an assertive response: _____

_____

_____

_____

_____

_____

_____

_____

## Session: Drink Refusal Skills

### Reminder Sheet

When you are urged to drink, keep the following in mind:

- Say "no" first.
- Voice should be clear, firm, and unhesitating.
- Make direct eye contact.
- Suggest an alternative:
    Something else to do.
    Something else to eat or drink.
- Ask the person to stop offering you a drink and not to do so again.
- Change the subject.
- Avoid the use of vague answers.
- Don't feel guilty about refusing to drink.

### Practice Exercise

Listed below are some people who might offer you a drink in the future. Give some thought to how you will respond to them, and write your responses under each item.

Someone close to you who knows about your drinking problem: _____

_____

_____

Coworker: _____

_____

_____

Boss: _____

_____

_____

New acquaintance: _____

_____

_____

Waitress/waiter with others present: _____

_____

_____

Relative at a family gathering: _____

_____

_____

## Session: Refusing Requests

### Reminder Sheet

When someone makes a request of you, remember the following:

- Review your priorities.
- If you decide to refuse, restate the request in your own words, so the other person will know that you understood him/her.
- Be firm, clear, and brief in your refusal, and pay attention to body language.
- Consider negotiating a compromise.
- If the requester persists, calmly repeat your refusal.

### Practice Exercise

*Exercise 1*

To help you decide how to respond to requests, it is helpful to have a good idea of what your priorities are at this time in your life. Your priorities might include spending more time with family or friends, activities you consider important, goals you are working toward, and so on. Make a list of what you consider to be your most important priorities right now: _____

_____

_____

_____

Now, list them in their order of importance to you. _____

_____

*Exercise 2*

Think of a request that has been made of you, or that might be made of you, that you would like to be able to refuse. The request might be made by someone at home, at work, or by a friend. Write down the circumstances, and the words you might use to refuse it:

The situation: _____

_____

The request: _____

_____

Your reason for refusing: _____

_____

State your refusal: _____

_____

## Session: Close and Intimate Relationships

### Reminder Sheet

The following points can be of assistance to you within a close relationship:

- Don't expect your partner to read your mind.
- Don't let things build up: Give constructive criticism at an early point.
    Calm down.
    State the criticism in terms of your own feelings.
    Criticize specific behavior, not the person.
    Request specific behavior change.
    Offer to compromise.
- Use your skills in receiving criticism.
    Don't get defensive.
    Find something to agree with.
    Ask questions for clarification.
    Offer to compromise.
- Be an active listener.
    Pay attention to the other person's feelings.
    Ask questions.
    Add comments of your own.
    Share similar experiences.
- Express your positive feelings.
    State the compliment in terms of your own feelings.
    Compliment specific behavior.

### Practice Exercise: Communication Skills in Close Relationships

Think about a current situation that is bothering you with your spouse or other close person. Choose a situation that matters to you and that is important to try to change, but one that is not extremely difficult. You may want to look over the list of topics on the "Reminder Sheet" to help you think about situations in your relationship that you'd like to improve on. After you think of the situation, answer the following questions:

1. Describe the situation. (For example, "We sit at the dinner table and ignore each other.") _____

_____

_____

_____

_____

*continued*

2. Describe what you usually do or fail to do in the situation. (For example, "I usually read the paper and ignore my spouse while eating dinner.")

_____

_____

_____

_____

_____

3. What specifically would you like to try to do differently in this situation? (For example, "I'd like to ask my spouse about how his/her day was and to listen actively to what he/she has to say.") _____

_____

_____

_____

_____

_____

4. Now, choose the right time and place, and try out your new behavior or skill in the problem situation. In the space below, describe the results of the interaction and how your partner responded: _____

_____

_____

_____

_____

_____

## Session: Enhancing Social Support Networks

## Reminder Sheet

- WHO might be able to support you? Consider which people have in the past been:
    Usually supportive
    Usually neutral (friends or relatives who don't know about your problems)
    Usually hindering (they may become supportive with some effort on your part)
- WHAT types of support will be most helpful?
    Help with problem solving
    Moral support
    Someone to share the load
    Information and resources
    Emergency help
- HOW can you get the support or help you need?
    Ask for what you need. Be specific and direct.
    Add new supporters (people who can help you with current problems).
    Lend your support to others; it helps you strengthen your own skills.
    Be an active listener when giving or receiving support.
    Give feedback about what was or wasn't helpful; thank the person for his/her support.

## Practice Exercise

*Exercise 1*

Think of a current problem that you would like help with.

Describe the problem: _____

_____

_____

_____

Who might be helpful to you with this problem?_____

What might he/she do to lend you the support you'd like? _____

_____

_____

_____

*continued*

How can you try to get this support from him/her? _____

_____

_____

_____

Now, choose the right time and situation, and try to get this person to support you.

Describe what happened: _____

_____

_____

_____

*Exercise 2*

Name a friend or family member who is currently having a problem, and who could use some more support from you. _____

Describe what you could do to lend him/her some support: _____

_____

_____

_____

Now, choose an appropriate time and setting, and give support to this person. Describe what happened: _____

_____

_____

_____

## Session: Managing Thoughts about Alcohol

## Reminder Sheet

Here are several ways of managing thoughts about alcohol:

- Challenge your thought: Do you really *need* a drink? Will you really not have fun without a drink?
- Think of the benefits of not drinking (read list on card).
- Remember unpleasant drinking experiences and aftereffects (read list on card).
- Distraction: Think of something unrelated to drinking.
- Positive thinking: Remind yourself of your successes so far.
- Use images of riding out the craving until it passes.
- Use images or photographs of loved ones who would be disappointed if you drank.
- Decision delay technique: If nothing else is working, then look at your watch and put off decision to drink for 15 minutes or more. (Use images to tough it out until the urge passes.)
- Leave or change the situation.
- Call someone and try to talk it out.

## Practice Exercise

One way to cope with thoughts about drinking is to remind yourself of the benefits of not drinking, and of the unpleasant effects of drinking. Use this sheet to make a list of these reminders, then transfer this list onto a pocket-sized index card. Read this card whenever you start to have thoughts about drinking or using drugs.

Benefits of not drinking: ———————————————————————

———————————————————————————————

———————————————————————————————

———————————————————————————————

———————————————————————————————

———————————————————————————————

Unpleasant effects of drinking: —————————————————————

———————————————————————————————

———————————————————————————————

———————————————————————————————

———————————————————————————————

## Session: Problem Solving

## Reminder Sheet

These, in brief, are the steps of the problem-solving process:

- *Recognize that a problem exists.* "Is there a problem?" We get clues from our bodies, our thoughts and feelings, our behavior, our reactions to other people, and the ways that other people react to us.
- *Identify the problem.* "What is the problem?" Describe the problem as accurately as you can. Break it down into manageable parts.
- *Consider various approaches to solving the problem.* "What can I do?" Brainstorm to think of as many solutions as you can. Try taking a different point of view, try to think of solutions that worked before, and ask other people what worked for them in similar situations.
- *Select the most promising approach.* "What will happen if . . . ?" Consider all the positive and negative aspects of each possible approach, and select the one likely to solve the problem with the least hassle.
- *Assess the effectiveness of the selected approach.* "How did it work?" After you have given the approach a fair trial, does it seem to be working out? If not, consider what you can do to beef up the plan, or give it up and try one of the other possible approaches.

## Practice Exercise

Select a problem you expect to have difficulty coping with. Describe it accurately. Brainstorm a list of possible solutions. Evaluate the possibilities, and number them in the order of your preference.

Identify the problem: _____

_____

_____

_____

_____

Brainstorm list: _____

_____

_____

_____

## Session: Increasing Pleasant Activities

### Reminder Sheet

- Develop a list of pleasant activities.
- "Positive addictions" are activities that are noncompetitive; do not depend on others; and have some physical, mental, or spiritual value for you. You can improve your performance with practice, and you can accept your level of performance without criticizing yourself.
- Plan 30–60 minutes of "personal time" each day.
- The goal is to achieve some balance between the things that you should do and the things that you want to do, so that you feel satisfied with your daily life.
- The more fun things you have to do, the less you will miss alcohol, and the less likely you will be to use alcohol to create fun in your life.

### Practice Exercise

First, review the Pleasant Events Schedule and write down your own personal "menu" of pleasant activities. _____

_____

_____

_____

_____

_____

Now schedule 30–60 minutes of "personal time" every day to engage in these activities. Set aside the time, but do not decide on the activity until the time comes. Select the activity from the menu above.

|  | *Appointments for personal time* | *After your personal time, record the activity you decided to do* |
|---|---|---|
| Monday_____ | | |
| Tuesday_____ | | |
| Wednesday_____ | | |
| Thursday_____ | | |
| Friday_____ | | |
| Saturday_____ | | |
| Sunday_____ | | |

## Session: Relaxation Training: I. Deep Muscle and Imagery Techniques

### Practice Exercise

Arrange a quiet time in a room where you will not be interrupted. Practice at least three times during the next week.

Relaxation appointments: Day _____     Time _____

Day _____     Time _____

Day _____     Time _____

Proceed through the eight groups of muscles in this list, first tensing each for 5 seconds and then relaxing each for 15–20 seconds.

Settle back as comfortably as you can, take a deep breath, and exhale very slowly. You may feel most comfortable if you allow your eyes to close. Notice the sensations in your body; you will soon be able to control those sensations. First, focus your attention on your hands and forearms. . . .

- Squeeze both hands into fists, with arms straight.
- Flex both arms at the elbows; push upper arms into the floor.
- Shrug shoulders toward head. Tilt chin toward chest.
- Clench jaw, gritting your teeth together.
- Close your eyes tightly.
- Wrinkle up your forehead and brow.
- Harden your stomach muscles, as if expecting someone to punch you there (continue to breathe slowly as you tense your stomach).
- Stretch out both legs, point your toes toward your head, and press your legs together.

Actual practice:

|       |       | Self-rating (0–100) | |
|-------|-------|---------------------|--------|
| Day   | Time  | Before              | After  |
|       |       |                     |        |
|       |       |                     |        |
|       |       |                     |        |
|       |       |                     |        |

# Session: Relaxation Training II. Letting Go

## Practice Exercise

Recall the sensation of muscle release from your tension–relaxation practice. Then let go of tension in all eight muscle groups:

- Hands and forearms
- Upper arms and biceps
- Shoulders and neck
- Forehead and brow
- Eyes
- Jaw
- Stomach
- Legs

Begin to apply your relaxation skills in daily living. Start relaxing during slow, nonstressful activities. From time to time, stop what you are doing and identify which muscles are unnecessarily tense. Then relax those muscles by using the "letting go" technique. Use steady, slow breathing, and think the word "Relax" (or other relaxing word) as you exhale.

Pay special attention to your "trouble spots." These are muscles that tend to get particularly tense when you are feeling stress (jaw, shoulders, etc.).

Try practicing in situations such as these:

- Reading
- Watching TV or a movie
- Playing cards or table games
- Sitting and talking with others
- Waiting in line
- Riding a bus
- Driving

Since this relaxation technique takes little time, you can practice several times a day.

## Session: Relaxation Training III. Relaxing in Stressful Situations

### Practice Exercise

Choose a situation that is moderately stressful for you. Before, during, or after the situation, practice using the brief relaxation procedures that you have learned in group (letting go, steady breathing, softly saying a word such as "Relax" to yourself).

Describe the situation in which you practiced the relaxation procedure. Who was there, where was it, and what was happening? _____

_____

_____

_____

_____

Which relaxation procedure(s) did you practice? _____

_____

_____

_____

_____

How did it work? _____

_____

_____

_____

## Session: Awareness of Anger

Reminder Sheet

Anger is a normal human emotion. Increased awareness of angry feelings will make it possible for you to cope with them so that they don't get out of hand. Increase your awareness of the following:

- Events that trigger anger:

    Direct attack on you
    Inability to reach a goal
    Unfair treatment
    Seeing an attack on someone else
    Excessive demands on you

- Internal reactions that signal anger:

    Feelings: frustration, annoyance, irritation, feeling on edge or wound up
    Physical reactions: muscle tension, headache, sweating, rapid breathing
    Difficulty falling asleep
    Depression or feelings of helplessness

Practice Exercise

Pay attention to your negative feelings. For one situation involving anger or its predecessors (e.g., frustration, annoyance, or irritation), record the following:

When and where? _____

_____

Who else was involved? _____

_____

What happened that provoked your reaction? _____

_____

_____

_____

_____

*continued*

Any physical sensations? _____

_____

_____

_____

Thoughts and feelings? _____

_____

_____

_____

Anger rating:

```
 1              2              3              4              5
 |              |              |              |              |
```

Not at all                                              Burning
  angry                                                   mad

## Session: Anger Management

### Reminder Sheet

Anger can result from the way we think about things:

$$\text{Events} \rightarrow \text{Thoughts} \rightarrow \text{Anger}$$

- Use phrases like these to help you calm down in a crisis:

| | |
|---|---|
| Slow down. | Chill out. |
| Take it easy. | Deep-freeze. |
| Take a deep breath. | Relax. |
| Cool it. | Count to 10. |
| Easy does it. | |

- Next, think about what's getting you so angry. Review the situation point by point.

    What's getting me angry?
    Is this a personal attack or insult?
    Am I angry because I'm expecting too much of myself or someone else?
    What are the positives here?

- Then think about your options:

    What can I do?
    What is in my best interests here?
    Anger should be a signal to start problem-solving.
    Relaxation skills, communication skills, or other coping skills may be helpful
       here.

- If the problem won't go away:

    Remember that you can't fix everything.
    Try to shake it off.
    Don't let it interfere with your life.
    Use relaxation exercises.

- If you resolve the conflict, congratulate yourself:

    I handled that pretty well.
    I'm doing better at this all the time.
    I didn't blow my cool.

## Practice Exercise

Until the next session, pay attention to your response to anger-provoking situations. Try to identify and change your thoughts in those situations. Pick one occasion before the next session involving angry feelings (or feelings of annoyance, frustration, irritation) and record the following:

Trigger situation: _____

_____

_____

_____

_____

Calm-down phrases used: _____

_____

_____

_____

_____

Anger-increasing thoughts: _____

_____

_____

_____

_____

Anger-reducing thoughts: _____

_____

_____

_____

_____

What other thoughts might have helped you to cope with this situation? _____

_____

_____

_____

## Session: Awareness of Negative Thinking

### Reminder Sheet

We don't just get upset, depressed, or tense. It's what we think or say to ourselves ("self-talk") about events, that causes us to get upset. Self-talk (B) comes in between events (A) and feelings or behavior (C). This ABC model helps us become *aware* of our negative thoughts. If we can catch our negative thoughts and then change them into positive thoughts, we will feel better about ourselves; be less moody, upset, tense, angry, or depressed; and be less likely to have cravings to drink as a way to get rid of our upset feelings.

We must catch our negative self-talk, even though it is hard to do and seems to happen "in a flash." We must learn how to *slow down the action* and become more aware of our negative self-talk by talking out loud what we think or say to ourselves. Sometimes we have to work backwards from our feelings or cravings to drink, in order to figure out what thoughts and situations set us off in the first place. Once we are able to catch our negative thoughts, we can learn to change them.

We must learn to identify unrealistic expectations (in words such as "should," "never," "always," etc.) and types of negative self-talk (perfectionism, catastrophizing, overgeneralizing, expecting the worst, self-putdowns, and black-and-white thinking).

### Practice Exercise

*Remember:* (A) Event → (B) Thinking, self-talk → (C) Feelings/behavior

Briefly describe an event or situation (A) that seemed to make you feel upset or want to drink. _____

_____

Now write down all the things you might have been thinking to yourself or saying to yourself (B) that could explain why the event made you upset. Write as many as you can. _____

_____

_____

Now write down all the bad or upset feelings (C) that you had about the event or situation. _____

_____

*Note:* Sometimes you first notice that you are upset (C), and only then think backwards to the situation (A). It feels like it happens so fast—in a flash. It's OK to fill out the C part on this form first, and then go back to the A and B parts. You should be able to fill out the B part even if you can't remember your thoughts exactly. You can usually take a good stab at coming up with at least two or three negative self-statements (self-talk) that must have occurred in a flash between A and C.

## Session: Managing Negative Thinking

### Reminder Sheet

- Catch negative self-talk whenever you feel upset by an event or crave a drink.
- Shout "STOP!" to yourself quietly in your head.
- Challenge your negative self-talk and substitute positive self-talk.
- Relabel your upset feelings, or cravings, as signals to cope.
- Remind yourself of good things you have done.
- Notice how you feel better (even if only slightly at first—it gets better with practice). Pat yourself on the back for having stopped your upset feelings.
- You really must *believe in* the positive things you are saying to yourself. You deserve to feel good about yourself, even when things are going badly.

### Practice Exercise: Positive Thinking Worksheet

Use this worksheet to write down one or two events that occur before the next session, your negative thoughts or self-talk, and then your positive thoughts or constructive challenge to the self-talk.

| (A)<br>Event or<br>situation | (B)<br>Thoughts/self-talk | | |
|---|---|---|---|
| | Negative<br>thoughts | → STOP! → | *Substitute* positive thoughts or<br>*challenge* the negative<br>thoughts |
| _____ | _____ | STOP! | _____ |
| _____ | _____ | | _____ |
| _____ | _____ | | _____ |
| _____ | _____ | | _____ |
| _____ | _____ | | _____ |
| _____ | _____ | | _____ |
| _____ | _____ | STOP! | _____ |
| _____ | _____ | | _____ |
| _____ | _____ | | _____ |
| _____ | _____ | | _____ |
| _____ | _____ | | _____ |
| _____ | _____ | | _____ |

## Session: Seemingly Irrelevant Decisions

### Reminder Sheet

When making any decision, whether large or small, do the following:

- Consider what options you may have.
- Think ahead to the possible outcomes of each option. What positive or negative consequences can you anticipate, and what are the risks of relapse?
- Select one of the options:
  Choose one that will minimize your relapse risk.
  If you decide to choose a risky option, plan how to protect yourself while in the high-risk situation.

### Practice Exercise

Think about a decision you have made recently or are about to make. The decision could involve any aspect of your life, such as your job, recreational activities, friends, or family. Identify "safe" choices and choices that might increase your odds of relapsing.

Decision to be made: _____

_____

_____

_____

_____

_____

Safe alternatives: _____

_____

_____

_____

_____

Risky alternatives: _____

_____

_____

_____

## Session: Planning for Emergencies

Practice Exercise

Write a detailed emergency plan for coping with high-risk relapse situations.

1. _____

_____

_____

2. _____

_____

_____

3. _____

_____

_____

4. _____

_____

_____

5. _____

_____

_____

# References

Abrams, D. B. (1983). Psycho-social assessment of alcohol and stress interactions: Bridging the gap between laboratory and treatment outcome research. In L. A. Pohorecky & J. Brick (Eds.), *Stress and alcohol use* (pp. 61–86). New York: Elsevier Biomedical.

Abrams, D. B., Binkoff, J. A., Zwick, W. R., Liepman, M. L., Nirenberg, T. D., Munroe, S. M., & Monti, P. M. (in press). Alcohol abusers' and social drinkers' responses to alcohol-relevant and general situations. *Journal of Studies on Alcohol.*

Abrams, D. B., Monti, P. M., Carey, K. B., Pinto, R. P., & Jacobus, S. I. (1988). Reactivity to smoking cues and relapse: Two studies of discriminant validity. *Behaviour Research and Therapy, 26,* 225–233.

Abrams, D. B., Monti, P. M., Pinto, R., Elder, J. P., Brown, R. A., & Jacobus, S. I. (1987). Psychosocial stress and coping in smokers who relapse or quit. *Health Psychology, 6,* 289–303.

Abrams, D. B., & Niaura, R. S. (1987). Social learning theory of alcohol use and abuse. In H. Blane & K. Leonard (Eds.), *Psychological theories of drinking and alcoholism* (pp. 131–180). New York: Guilford Press.

Abrams, D. B., Niaura, R. S., Carey, K. B., Monti, P. M., & Binkoff, J. A. (1986). Understanding relapse and recovery in alcohol abuse. *Annals of Behavioral Medicine, 8*(2–3), 27–32.

Abrams, D. B., & Wilson, G. T. (1986). Habit disorders: Alcohol and tobacco dependence. In A. J. Frances & R. E. Hales (Eds.), *American Psychiatric Association annual review* (Vol. 5, pp. 606–626). Washington, DC: American Psychiatric Press.

Ahles, T. A., Schlundt, D. G., Prue, D. M., & Rychtarik, R. G. (1983). Impact of aftercare arrangements on the maintenance of treatment success in abusive drinkers. *Addictive Behaviors, 8,* 53–58.

Alden, L. (1980). Preventive strategies in the treatment of alcohol abuse: A review and proposal. In P.O. Davidson & S. M. Davidson (Eds.), *Behavioral medicine: Changing health lifestyles* (pp. 256–278). New York: Brunner/Mazel.

Alexander, B. K., & Hadaway, P. F. (1982). Opiate addiction: The case for adaptive orientation. *Psychological Bulletin, 92,* 367–381.

Alterman, A. (Ed.). (1985). *Substance abuse and psychopathology.* New York: Plenum.

American Psychiatric Association. (1987). *Diagnostic and statistical manual of mental disorders* (3rd ed., rev.). Washington, DC: Author.

Asher, S., & Renshaw, P. D. (1984). Children without friends: Social knowledge and social skills training. In S. Asher & J. Gottman (Eds.), *The development of children's friendships* (pp. 273–296). New York: Cambridge University Press.

Azrin, N. H. (1976). Improvements in the community-reinforcement approach to alcoholism. *Behaviour Research and Therapy, 14,* 339–348.

Azrin, N. H., Sisson, R. W., Meyers, R., & Godley, M. (1982). Alcoholism treatment by disulfiram and community reinforcement therapy. *Journal of Behavior Therapy and Experimental Psychiatry, 13*, 105–112.

Baker, L. H., Cooney, N. L., & Pomerleau, O. F. (1987). Craving for alcohol: Theoretical processes and therapeutic procedures. In W. M. Cox (Ed.), *Treatment and prevention of alcohol problems: A resource manual* (pp. 183–202). New York: Academic Press.

Baker, L. H., Cooney, N. L., & Vinnick, D. M. (1983). *Cue exposure in alcoholism treatment.* Paper presented at the Third International Conference on Treatment of Addictive Behaviors, North Berwick, Scotland.

Bandura, A. (1969). *Principles of behavior modification.* New York: Holt, Rinehart & Winston.

Bandura, A. (1977). *Social learning theory.* Englewood Cliffs, NJ: Prentice-Hall.

Barlow, D. H. (1985). *Clinical handbook of psychological disorders: A step-by-step treatment manual.* New York: Guilford Press.

Barnes, G. M. (1977). The development of adolescent drinking behavior: An evaluative review of the impact of the socialization process within the family. *Adolescence, 12*, 571–591.

Beck, A. T., & Emery, G. (1985). *Anxiety disorders and phobias.* New York: Basic Books.

Beck, A. T., Rush, A. J., Shaw, B. F., & Emery, G. (1979). *Cognitive therapy of depression.* New York: Guilford Press.

Bedell, J. R., Archer, R. P., & Marlowe, H. A. (1980). A description and evaluation of a problem solving skills training program. In D. Upper & S. M. Ross (Eds.), *Behavioral group therapy: An annual review.* Champaign, IL: Research Press.

Bellack, A. S., Hersen, M., & Himmelhoch, J. (1981). Social skills training compared with pharmacotherapy and psychotherapy in the treatment of unipolar depression. *American Journal of Psychiatry, 138*, 1562–1567.

Benson, H. (1975). *The relaxation response.* New York: Morrow.

Biddle, B. J., Bank, B. J., & Marlin, M. M. (1980). Social determinants of adolescent drinking: What they think, what they do and what I think they do. *Journal of Studies on Alcohol, 41*, 215–241.

Binkoff, J. A. (1985). *Cue exposure and drink refusal.* Unpublished doctoral dissertation, State University of New York at Stony Brook.

Binkoff, J. A., Monti, P. M., Abrams, D. B., Zwick, W. R., Collins, L., Nirenberg, T. D., & Liepman, M. (1988). *Exposure and reactivity to alcohol cues: Impact on drink refusal skills of alcoholics.* Unpublished manuscript, Brown University/Veterans Administration Medical Center, Davis Park, Providence, RI.

Blake, W. (1969). The poison tree. In G. Keynes (Ed.), *The complete writings of William Blake* (p. 218). London: Oxford University Press.

Blakey, R., & Baker, R. (1980). An exposure approach to alcohol abuse. *Behaviour Research and Therapy, 84*, 319–325.

Borkovec, T. D., & Grayson, J. B. (1980). Consequences of increasing the functional impact of internal emotional stimuli. In K. R. Blankstein, P. Pliner, & J. Polivy (Eds.), *Advances in the study of communication and affect* (Vol. 6, pp. 117–137). New York: Plenum.

Braucht, G. N., Brakarsh, D., Follingstad, D., & Berry, K. L. (1973). Deviant drug use in adolescence. *Psychological Bulletin, 79*, 92–106.

Brickman, P., Rabinowitz, V. C., Karuza, J., Coates, D., Cohn, E., & Kidder, L. (1982). Models of helping and coping. *American Psychologist, 37*, 368–384.

Brown, R., & Lichtenstein, E. (1979). *Relapse prevention: A non-smoking maintenance program.* Unpublished treatment manual. University of Oregon.

Brown, S. A. (1985). Reinforcement expectancies and alcoholism treatment outcome after a one-year follow-up. *Journal of Studies on Alcohol, 46,* 304–308.

Brown, S. A., Goldman, M. S., Inn, A., & Anderson, L. R. (1980). Expectations of reinforcement from alcohol: Their domain and relation to drinking patterns. *Journal of Consulting and Clinical Psychology, 48,* 419–426.

Brownell, K. D., Marlatt, G. A., Lichtenstein, E., & Wilson, G. T. (1986). Understanding and preventing relapse. *American Psychologist, 41,* 765–782.

Cadoret, R. J., O'Gorman, T. W., Troughton, E., & Heywood, E. (1985). Alcoholism and antisocial personality: Interrelationships, genetic, and environmental factors. *Archives of General Psychiatry, 42,* 161–167.

Cahalan, D., Cisin, I. H., & Crossley, H. M. (1969). *American drinking practices: A national study of drinking behavior and patterns* (Monograph No. 6). New Brunswick, NJ: Rutgers Center for Alcohol Studies.

Cappell, H., & Greeley, J. (1987). Alcohol and tension reduction: An update on research and theory. In H. T. Blane & K. E. Leonard (Eds.), *Psychological theories of drinking and alcoholism* (pp. 15–54). New York: Guilford Press.

Caudill, B. D., & Marlatt, G. A. (1975). Modeling influences in social drinking: An experimental analogue. *Journal of Consulting and Clinical Psychology, 43,* 405–415.

Chaney, E. F., O'Leary, M. R., & Marlatt, G. A. (1978). Skill training with alcoholics. *Journal of Consulting and Clinical Psychology, 46,* 1092–1104.

Childress, A. R., McLellan, A. T., Natale, M., & O'Brien, C. P. (1986). *Mood states can elicit conditioned withdrawal and craving in opiate abuse patients.* Unpublished manuscript, University of Pennsylvania.

Christiansen, B. A., & Brown, S. A. (1985, August). *Adolescent alcohol expectancies: Further evidence of their robust nature.* Paper presented at the annual meeting of the American Psychological Association, Los Angeles.

Collins, R., Parks, G., & Marlatt, G. (1985). Social determinants of alcohol consumption: The effects of social interaction and model status on the self-administration of alcohol. *Journal of Consulting and Clinical Psychology, 53,* 189–200.

Conger, J. J. (1956). Alcoholism: Theory, problem and challenge. II. Reinforcement theory and the dynamics of alcoholism. *Quarterly Journal of Studies on Alcohol, 13,* 296–305.

Cooney, N. L., Baker, L., & Pomerleau, O. F. (1983). Cue exposure for relapse prevention in alcohol treatment. In R. J. McMahon & K. D. Craig (Eds.), *Advances in clinical behavior therapy* (pp. 174–210). New York: Brunner/Mazel.

Cooney, N. L., Baker, L., Pomerleau, O. F., & Josephy, B. (1984). Salivation to drinking cues in alcohol abusers: Toward the validation of a physiological measure of craving. *Addictive Behaviors, 9,* 91–94.

Cooney, N. L., Gillespie, R. A., Baker, L. H., & Kaplan, R. F. (1987). Cognitive changes after alcohol cue exposure. *Journal of Consulting and Clinical Psychology, 2,* 150–155.

Cooney, N. L., Kadden, R. M., Litt, M. D., Getter, H., & Busher, D. A. (1987, August). *Alcoholism aftercare treatment matching: Post-treatment results.* Paper presented at the Fourth International Conference on Treatment of Addictive Behaviors, Os (Bergen), Norway.

Cronkite, R., & Moos, R. (1980). The determinants of post-treatment functioning of alcoholic patients: A conceptual framework. *Journal of Consulting and Clinical Psychology, 48,* 305–316.

Cummings, C., Gordon, J., & Marlatt, G. A. (1980). Relapse: Strategies of prevention and prediction. In W. R. Miller (Ed.), *The addictive behaviors* (pp. 291–321). Oxford: Pergamon Press.

Curran, J. P., & Monti, P. M. (Eds.). (1982). *Social skills training: A practical handbook for assessment and treatment.* New York: Guilford Press.

Dean, L., Dubreuil, E., McCrady, B. S., Paul, C. P., & Swanson, S. (1983). *Problem drinkers project manual.* Unpublished manuscript, Butler Hospital, Providence, RI.

Depue, J. (1982). Getting a little help from your friends. In J. Depue (Ed.), *Managing stress* (Pawtucket Heart Health Program treatment manual) (pp. 1–9). Pawtucket, RI: The Memorial Hospital.

D'Zurilla, T. J., & Goldfried, M. R. (1971). Problem solving and behavior modification. *Journal of Abnormal Psychology, 78*, 107–126.

Ellis, A. (1975). *The new guide to rational living.* New York: Harper & Row.

Erickson, E. (1963). *Childhood and society.* New York: Norton.

Fensterheim, H., & Baer, J. (1975). *Don't say yes when you want to say no.* New York: Dell.

Flay, B. R. (1984). What do we know about the social influence approach to smoking prevention? Review and recommendations. In C.S. Bell & R.J. Battjes (Eds.), *Prevention research: Determining drug abuse among children and adolescents* (Research Monograph No. 63, pp. 67–112). Rockville, MD: National Institute on Drug Abuse.

Foa, E. B., & Kozak, M. J. (1986). Emotional processing of fear: Exposure to corrective information. *Psychological Bulletin, 99*, 20–35.

Foreyt, J. P. (1987). The addictive disorders. In G. T. Wilson, C. M. Franks, P. C. Kendall & J. P. Foreyt (Eds.), *Review of behavior therapy: Theory and practice* (Vol. 11, pp. 187–233). New York: Guilford Press.

Foy, D. W., Nunn, L. B., & Rychtarik, R. G. (1984). Broad-spectrum behavioural treatment for chronic alcoholics: Effects of training controlled drinking skills. *Journal of Consulting and Clinical Psychology, 52*, 218–230.

Freedberg, E. J., & Johnston, W. E. (1978). *The effects of assertion training within the context of a multi-modal alcoholism treatment program for employed alcoholics.* Toronto: Alcoholism and Drug Addiction Research Foundation.

Glasser, W. (1976). *Positive addiction.* New York: Harper & Row.

Goodwin, D. (1977). *Is alcoholism hereditary?* New York: Oxford University Press.

Grayson, J. B., Foa, E. B., & Steketee, G. (1982). Habituation during exposure treatment: Distraction vs. attention-focusing. *Behaviour Research and Therapy, 20*, 323–328.

Grunberg, N., & Baum, A. (1985). Biological commonalities of stress and substance abuse. In S. Shiffman & T. A. Wills (Eds.), *Coping and substance use* (pp. 25–65). New York: Academic Press.

Hamilton, F., & Maisto, S. A. (1979). Assertive behavior and perceived discomfort of alcoholics in assertion-required situations. *Journal of Consulting and Clinical Psychology, 47*, 196–197.

Heather, N., & Robinson, I. (1983). *Controlled drinking.* New York: Methuen.

Higgins, R. L., & Marlatt, G. A. (1975). Fear of interpersonal evaluation as a determinant of alcohol consumption in male drinkers. *Journal of Abnormal Psychology, 84*, 644–651.

Hodgson, R. J., & Rankin, H. J. (1983). Cue exposure and relapse prevention. In W. M. Hay & P. E. Nathan (Eds.), *Clinical case studies in the behavioral treatment of alcoholism* (pp. 207–226). New York: Plenum.

Hunt, G. M., & Azrin, N. H. (1973). A community-reinforcement approach to alcoholism. *Behaviour Research and Therapy, 11*, 91–104.

Intagliata, J. C. (1978). Increasing the interpersonal problem-solving skills of an alcoholic population. *Journal of Consulting and Clinical Psychology, 46*, 489–498.

Intagliata, J. C. (1979). Increasing the responsiveness of alcoholics to group therapy: An interpersonal problem-solving approach. *Group, 3*, 106–120.

Ito, J. R., & Donovan, D. M. (1986). Aftercare in alcoholism treatment: A review. In W. R. Miller & N. Heather (Eds.), *Treating addictive behaviors: Processes of change* (pp. 435–456). New York: Plenum.

Jackson, J. K., & Connor, R. (1953). Attitudes of the parents of alcoholics, moderate drinkers, and nondrinkers toward drinking. *Quarterly Journal of Studies on Alcohol, 14*, 596–613.

Jellinek, E. M. (1960). *The disease concept in alcoholism.* New Brunswick, NJ: Hill House Press.

Jessor, R. (1984, November). *Adolescent problem drinking: Psychosocial aspects and developmental outcomes.* Paper presented at the Carnegie Conference on Unhealthful Risk-Taking Behavior among Adolescents, Stanford, CA.

Jones, M. C. (1968). Personality correlates and antecedents of drinking patterns in adult males. *Journal of Consulting and Clinical Psychology, 32*, 2–12.

Jones, S. L., Kanfer, R., & Lanyon, R. I. (1982). Skill training with alcoholics: A clinical extension. *Addictive Behaviors, 7*, 285–290.

Jones, S. L., & Lanyon, R. I. (1981). Relationship between adaptive skills and outcome of alcoholism treatment. *Journal of Studies on Alcohol, 42*, 521–525.

Kadden, R. M., Pomerleau, O. F., & Meyer, R. E. (1984). On the stimulus control of drinking in alcoholics. In L. S. Harris (Ed.), *Problems of drug dependence, 1983* (Research Monograph No. 49). Rockville, MD: National Institute on Drug Abuse.

Kalin, R. (1972). Self-descriptions of college problem drinkers. In D. C. McClelland, W. N. Davis, R. Kalin, & E. Warner (Eds.), *The drinking man* (pp. 21–44). New York: Free Press.

Kaplan, R. F., Cooney, N. L., Baker, L. H., Gillespie, R. A., Meyer, R. E., & Pomerleau, O. F. (1985). Reactivity to alcohol-related cues: Physiological and subjective responses in alcoholics and non-problem drinkers. *Journal of Studies on Alcohol, 46*, 267–272.

Kaplan, R. F., Meyer, R. E., & Stroebel, C. F. (1983). Alcohol dependence and responsivity to an ethanol stimulus as predictors of alcohol consumption. *British Journal of Addiction, 78*, 256–267.

Kaufman, E., & Pattison, E. M. (1982). The family and alcoholism. In E. M. Pattison & E. Kaufman (Eds.), *Encyclopedic handbook of alcoholism* (pp. 663–672). New York: Gardner Press.

Klajner, F., Hartman, L. M., & Sobell, M. B. (1984). Treatment of substance abuse by relaxation training: A review of its rationale, efficacy and mechanisms. *Addictive Behaviors, 9*, 41–54.

Kolko, D. J., Sirota, A. D., Monti, P. M., & Paolino, R. (1985). Peer identification and empirical validation of problematic interpersonal situations of male drug addicts. *Journal of Psychopathology and Behavioral Assessment, 7*(2), 135–144.

Koller, K. M., & Castanos, T. N. (1969). Family background and life situation in alcoholics. *Archives of General Psychiatry, 21*, 602–610.

Lazarus, A. A. (1965). Towards the understanding and effective treatment of alcoholism. *South African Medical Journal, 39*, 736–741.

Lazarus, A. A. (1984). *In the mind's eye.* New York: Guilford Press.

Lazarus, R., & Folkman, S. (1985). *Stress, appraisal and coping.* New York: Springer.

Lentz, T. F. (1941). Personality correlates of alcohol beverage consumption. *Psychological Bulletin, 38,* 600.

Levine, J., & Zigler, E. (1973). The essential–reactive distinction in alcoholism: A developmental approach. *Journal of Abnormal Psychology, 81,* 242–249.

Lewinsohn, P. M., Antonuccio, D. O., Steinmetz, J. L., & Teri, L. (1984). *The coping with depression course: A psychoeducational intervention for unipolar depression.* Eugene, OR: Castalia.

Lied, E. R., & Marlatt, G. A. (1979). Modeling as a determinant of alcohol consumption: Effect of subject sex and prior drinking history. *Addictive Behaviors, 4,* 47–54.

Litman, G. K., Eiser, J. R., Rawson, N. S. B., & Oppenheim, A. N. (1979). Differences in relapse precipitants and coping behaviours between alcohol relapsers and survivors. *Behaviour Research and Therapy, 17,* 89–94.

Litman, G. K., Stapleton, J., Oppenheim, A. N., Peleg, M., & Jackson, P. (1983). Situations related to alcoholism relapse. *British Journal of Addiction, 78,* 381–389.

Litt, M. D., Cooney, N. L., Kadden, R. M., & Gaupp, L. (in press). Eliciting "craving" in alcoholics: The role of alcohol cues and induced moods. *Addictive Behaviors.*

Longabaugh, R., Beattie, M., Stout, R., Malloy, P., & Noel, N. (1988, February). *Environmental treatment of alcohol abusers.* Paper presented at Evaluating Recovery Outcomes, University of California at San Diego.

Longabaugh, R., McCrady, B., Fink, E., Stout, R., McAuley, T., Doyle, C., & McNeil, D. (1983). Cost-effectiveness of alcoholism treatment in partial vs. inpatient settings at six-month outcomes. *Journal of Studies on Alcohol, 44,* 1049–1071.

MacAndrew, C., & Edgerton, R. B. (1969). *Drunken comportment.* Chicago: Aldine.

MacPhillarny, D. J., & Lewinsohn, P. M. (1971). *A scale for the measurement of positive reinforcement.* Unpublished manuscript, University of Oregon.

Mallams, J. H., Godley, M. G., Hall, G. M., & Meyers, R. J. (1982). A social-systems approach to resocializing alcoholics in the community. *Journal of Studies on Alcohol, 43,* 115–123.

Marlatt, G. A. (1985a). Cognitive assessment and intervention procedures for relapse prevention. In G. A. Marlatt & J.R. Gordon (Eds.), *Relapse prevention: Maintenance strategies in the treatment of addictive behaviors* (pp. 201–279). New York: Guilford Press.

Marlatt, G. A. (1985b). Coping and substance abuse: Implications for research, prevention, and treatment. In S. Shiffman & T. A. Wills (Eds.), *Coping and substance use* (pp. 367–386). New York: Academic Press.

Marlatt, G. A. (1985c). Relapse prevention: Theoretical rationale and overview of the model. In G. A. Marlatt & J. R. Gordon (Eds.), *Relapse prevention: Maintenance strategies in the treatment of addictive behaviors* (pp. 3–70). New York: Guilford Press.

Marlatt, G. A., & Gordon, J. R. (1980). Determinants of relapse: Implications for the maintenance of behavior change. In P. O. Davidson & S. M. Davidson (Eds.), *Behavioral medicine: Changing health lifestyles* (pp. 410–452). New York: Brunner/Mazel.

Marlatt, G. A., & Gordon, J. R. (Eds.). (1985). *Relapse prevention: Maintenance strategies in the treatment of additive behaviors.* New York: Guilford Press.

Marlatt, G. A., Kosturn, C. F., & Lang, A. R. (1975). Provocation to anger and opportunity for retaliation as determinants of alcohol consumption in social drinkers. *Journal of Abnormal Psychology, 84,* 652–659.

Marlatt, G. A., & Marques, J. K. (1977). Meditation, self-control and alcohol use. In R.

B. Stuart (Ed.), *Behavioral self-management: Strategies, techniques, and outcomes* (pp. 117–153). New York: Brunner/Mazel.

Marlatt, G. A., & Rohsenow, D. J. (1980). Cognitive process in alcohol use: Expectancy and the balanced placebo design. In N. K. Mello (Ed.), *Advances in substance abuse* (Vol. 1, pp. 159–199). Greenwich, CT: JAI Press.

McAlister, A. L., Perry, C., & Maccoby, N. (1979). Adolescent smoking: Onset and prevention. *Pediatrics, 63,* 650–658.

McCrady, B. S. (1986). The family in the change process. In W. E. Miller & N. Heather (Eds.), *Treating addictive behaviors: Processes of change* (pp. 305–318). New York: Plenum.

McCrady, B. S., Dean, L., Dubreuil, E., & Swanson, S. (1985). The problem drinkers project: A programmatic application of social-learning-based treatment. In G. A. Marlatt & J. R. Gordon (Eds.), *Relapse prevention: Maintenance strategies in the treatment of addictive behaviors* (pp. 417–471). New York: Guilford Press.

McCrady, B. S., & Irvine, S. (in press). Self-help groups in the treatment of alcoholism. In R. Hester & W. R. Miller (Eds.), *Comprehensive handbook of alcoholism treatment approaches.* New York: Pergamon Press.

McCrady, B. S., Noel, N. E., Abrams, D. B., Stout, R. L., Nelson, H. F., & Hay, W. M. (1986). Comparative effectiveness of three types of spouse involvement in out-patient behavioral alcoholism treatment. *Journal of Studies on Alcohol, 47,* 459–467.

McLellan, A. T., Childress, A. R., Ehrman, R., & O'Brien, C. P. (1986). Extinguishing conditioned responses during opiate dependence treatment: Turning laboratory findings into clinical procedures. *Journal of Substance Abuse Treatment, 3,* 33–40.

McLellan, A. T., Woody, G. E., Luborsky, L., O'Brien, C. P., & Druley, K. A. (1983). Increased effectiveness of substance abuse treatment: A protective study of patient–treatment "matching." *Journal of Nervous and Mental Disease, 171,* 597–605.

Meichenbaum, D. (1977). *Cognitive-behavior modification: An integrative approach.* New York: Plenum.

Meichenbaum, D., Butler, L., & Gruson, L. (1981). Toward a conceptual model of social competence. In J. D. Wine & M. D. Smye (Eds.), *Social competence* (pp. 36–60). New York: Guilford Press.

Mendelson, J. H., & Mello, N. K. (Eds.). (1985). *The diagnosis and treatment of alcoholism* (2nd ed.). New York: McGraw-Hill.

Meyer, R. E. (1986). How to understand the relationship between psychopathology and addictive disorders: Another example of the chicken and the egg. In R. E. Meyer (Ed.), *Psychopathology and addictive disorders* (pp. 3–16). New York: Guilford Press.

Meyer, R. E., Randall, M., Barrington, C., Mirin, S., & Greenberg, I. (1976). Limitations of an extinction approach to narcotic antagonist treatment. In O. Julius & P. Ranault (Eds.), *Narcotic antagonists: Naltrexone progress reports* (Research Monograph No. 9, pp. 123–135). Rockville, MD: National Institute on Drug Abuse.

Miller, P. M. (1978). Alternative skills training in alcoholism treatment. In P. E. Nathan, G. A. Marlatt, & T. Loberg (Eds.), *Alcoholism: New directions in behavioral research and treatment* (pp. 657–677). New York: Plenum.

Miller, P. M., & Eisler, R. M. (1977). Assertive behavior of alcoholics: A descriptive analysis. *Behavior Therapy, 8,* 146–149.

Miller, P. M., Hersen, M., Eisler, R. M., & Hilsman, G. (1974). Effects of social stress on operant drinking of alcoholics and social drinkers. *Behaviour Research and Therapy, 12,* 67–72.

Miller, P. M., & Mastria, M. A.. (1977). *Alternatives to alcohol abuse: A social learning model.* Champaign, IL: Research Press.

Miller, W. E., & Heather, N. (Eds.). (1986). *Treating addictive behaviors: Processes of change.* New York: Plenum.

Miller, W. R., & Taylor, C. A. (1980). Relative effectiveness of bibliotherapy, individual and group self-control training in the treatment of problem drinking. *Addictive Behaviors, 5,* 13–24.

Monti, P. M., Abrams, D. B., Binkoff, J. A., & Zwick, W. R. (1986). Social skills training and substance abuse. In C. R. Hollin & P. Trower (Eds.). *Handbook of social skills training* (pp. 111–142). Oxford: Pergamon Press.

Monti, P. M., Abrams, D. B., Binkoff, J. A., Zwick, W. R., Liepman, M. R., Nirenberg, T. D., & Rohsenow, D. J. (in press). Communication skills training, communication skills training with family, and cognitive behavioral mood management training for alcoholics. *Journal of Studies on Alcohol.*

Monti, P. M., Binkoff, J. A., Abrams, D. B., Zwick, W. R., Nirenberg, T. D., & Liepman, M. R. (1987). Reactivity of alcoholics and nonalcoholics to drinking cues. *Journal of Abnormal Psychology, 96,* 122–126.

Monti, P. M., Corriveau, D. P., & Curran, J. P. (1982). Social skills training for psychiatric patients: Treatment and outcome. In J. P. Curran & P. M. Monti (Eds.), *Social skills training: A practical handbook for assessment and treatment* (pp. 185–223). New York: Guilford Press.

Monti, P. M., Corriveau, D. P., & Zwick, W. R. (1981). Assessment of social skills among alcoholics versus other psychiatric patients. *Journal of Studies on Alcohol, 42,* 526–529.

Monti, P. M., Curran, J. P., Corriveau, D. P., DeLancey, A., & Hagerman, S. (1980). Effects of social skills training groups and sensitivity training groups with psychiatric patients. *Journal of Consulting and Clinical Psychology, 48,* 241–248.

Monti, P. M., & Kolko, D. (1985). A review and programmatic model of group social skills training for psychiatric patients. In D. Upper & S. M. Ross (Eds.), *Handbook of behavioral group therapy* (pp. 25–62). New York: Plenum.

Monti, P. M., Rohsenow, D. J., Abrams, D. B., & Binkoff, J. A. (1988). Social learning approaches to alcohol relapse: Selected illustrations and implications. In B. A. Ray (Ed.), *Learning factors in substance abuse* (Research Monograph No. 84, pp. 141–160). Rockville, MD: National Institute on Drug Abuse.

Monti, P. M., Wallander, J. L., Ahern, D. K., Abrams, D. B., & Munroe, S. M. (1983). Multimodal measurement of anxiety and social skills in a behavioral role-play test: Generalizability and discriminant validity. *Behavioral Assessment, 6,* 15–26.

Monti, P. M., Zwick, W. R., Binkoff, J. A., Abrams, D. B., & Nirenberg, T. (1984, March). *The development of behavior-analytically derived categories and role play situations for alcoholics.* Paper presented at the 5th annual meeting of the Society of Behavioral Medicine, Philadelphia.

Moos, R. (1985). Foreword. In S. Shiffman & T. A. Wills (Eds.), *Coping and substance use* (pp. xiii–xix). New York: Academic Press.

Moos, R., & Finney, J. (1983). The expanding scope of alcoholism treatment evaluation. *American Psychologist, 38,* 1036–1044.

Nathan, P. E. (1986). Outcomes of treatment for alcoholism: Current data. *Annals of Behavioral Medicine, 8,* 40–46.

Nathan, P. E., & Lipscomb, T. R. (1985). Behavioral assessment and treatment of alcoholism. In J. H. Mendelson & N. K. Mello (Eds.), *The diagnosis and treatment of alcoholism* (2nd ed., pp. 305–358). New York: McGraw-Hill.

Nathan, P. E., & Niaura, R. S. (1987). Prevention of alcohol problems. In M. Cox (Ed.), *Treatment and prevention of alcohol problems: A resource manual* (pp. 332–355). New York: Academic Press.

National Institute on Alcohol Abuse and Alcoholism. (1983, December). *Fifth special report to the U.S. Congress on alcohol and health*. Rockville, MD: Author.

Niaura, R., Rohsenow, D., Binkoff, J., Monti, P., Pedraza, M., & Abrams, D. B. (1988). The relevance of cue reactivity to understanding alcohol and smoking relapse. *Journal of Abnormal Psychology, 2*, 133–152.

Oei, T. P. S., & Jackson, P. (1980). Long-term effects of group and individual social skills training with alcoholics. *Addictive Behaviors, 5*, 129–136.

Oei, T. P. S., & Jackson, P. R. (1982). Social skills and cognitive behavioural approaches to the treatment of problem drinking. *Journal of Studies on Alcohol, 43*, 532–546.

O'Farrell, T. J., & Cutter, H. S. G. (1979). A proposed behavioral couples group for male alcoholics and their wives. In D. Upper & S. M. Ross (Eds.), *Behavioral group therapy: An annual review* (pp. 277–298). Champaign, IL: Research Press.

O'Leary, D. E., O'Leary, M. R., & Donovan, D. M. (1976). Social skill acquisition and psychosocial development of alcoholics: A review. *Addictive Behaviors, 1*, 111–120.

O'Leary, K. D., & Wilson, G. T. (1975). *Behavior therapy: Application and outcome.* Englewood Cliffs, NJ: Prentice-Hall.

Orne, M. T., & Wender, P. J. (1968). Anticipatory socialization for psychotherapy: Method and rationale. *American Journal of Psychiatry, 124*, 1202–1212.

Paolino, T. J., Jr., & McCrady, B. S. (1977). *The alcoholic marriage: Alternative perspectives.* New York: Grune & Stratton.

Pentz, M. A. (1985). Social competence and self-efficacy as determinants of substance use in adolescence. In S. Shiffman & T. A. Wills (Eds.), *Coping and substance use* (pp. 117–139). New York: Academic Press.

Pomerleau, O. F., Fertig, J., Baker, L., & Cooney, N. L. (1983). Reactivity to alcohol cues in alcoholics and non-alcoholics: Implications for a stimulus control analysis of drinking. *Addictive Behavior, 8*, 1–10.

Rankin, H., Hodgson, R., & Stockwell, T. (1983). Cue exposure and response prevention with alcoholics: A controlled trial. *Behaviour Research and Therapy, 21*, 435–446.

Rist, F., & Watzl, H. (1983). Self-assessment of social competence in situations with and without alcohol by female alcoholics in treatment. *Drug and Alcohol Dependence, 11*, 367–371.

Robins, L. N., Bates, W. M., & O'Neal, P. (1962). Adult drinking patterns of former problem children. In D. J. Pittman & C. R. Snyder (Eds.), *Society, culture, and drinking patterns* (pp. 395–412). New York: Wiley.

Rohsenow, D. J. (1983). Drinking habits and expectancies about alcohol's effects for self versus others. *Journal of Consulting and Clinical Psychology, 51*, 752–756.

Rohsenow, D., Monti, P. M., Binkoff, J. A., Zwick, W. R., & Abrams, D. B. (1988). *Alcohol expectancies and alcohol dependence, urge to drink, and drinking among alcoholics.* Manuscript submitted for publication.

Rohsenow, D., Monti, P. M., Zwick, W. R., Nirenberg, T. D., Liepman, M. L., Binkoff, J. A., & Abrams, D. B. (in press). Irrational beliefs: Urges to drink, and drinking among alcoholics. *Journal of Studies on Alcohol.*

Rohsenow, D. J., Smith, R. E., & Johnson, J. (1986). Stress management as a prevention program for heavy social drinkers: Cognitions, affect, drinking and individual differences. *Addictive Behaviors, 10,* 45–54.

Rosenberg, C. M. (1969). Determinants of psychiatric illness in young people. *British Journal of Psychiatry, 115,* 907–915.

Rosenberg, H. (1983). Relapsed versus non-relapsed alcohol abusers: Coping skills, life events, and social support. *Addictive Behaviors, 8,* 183–186.

Sanchez-Craig, M. (1976). Cognitive and behavioral coping strategies in reappraisal of stressful social situations. *Journal of Counseling Psychology, 23,* 7–12.

Sanchez-Craig, M., & Walker, K. (1982). Teaching coping skills to chronic alcoholics in a coeducational halfway house: 1. Assessment of programme effects. *British Journal of Addiction, 77,* 35–50.

Sanchez-Craig, M., Wilkinson, A., & Walker, K. (1987). Theory and methods for secondary prevention of alcohol problems: A cognitively-based approach. In M. Cox (Ed.), *Treatment and prevention of alcohol problems: A resource manual* (pp. 286–328). New York: Academic Press.

Sank, L. I., & Shaffer, C. S. (1984). *A therapist's manual for cognitive behavior therapy in groups.* New York: Plenum.

Schuckit, M. A., Goodwin, D., & Winokur, G. (1972). A study of alcoholism in half-siblings. *American Journal of Psychiatry, 128,* 1132–1136.

Sher, K. J. (1987). Stress response dampening. In H. Blane & K. Leonard (Eds.), *Psychological theories of drinking and alcoholism* (pp. 227–271). New York: Guilford Press.

Sher, K. J., & Levenson, R. W. (1982). Risk for alcoholism and individual differences in the stress-response-dampening effect of alcohol. *Journal of Abnormal Psychology, 91,* 350–368.

Shiffman, S., & Wills, T. A. (Eds.). (1985). *Coping and substance abuse.* New York: Academic Press.

Sobell, M. B., Brochu, S., Sobell, L. C., Roy, J., & Stevens, J. A. (1987). Alcohol treatment outcome evaluation methodology: State of the art 1980–1984. *Addictive Behaviors, 12,* 113–128.

Sobell, M. B., & Sobell, L. C. (1973). Individualized behavior therapy for alcoholics. *Behavior Therapy, 4,* 49–72.

Sontag, S. (1978). *Illness as metaphor.* New York: Farrar, Straus & Giroux.

Steinglass, P. (1979). An experimental treatment program for alcoholic couples. *Journal of Studies on Alcohol, 40,* 159–182.

Strickler, D. P., Bigelow, G., & Wells, D. (1976). *Electromyograph responses of abstinent alcoholics to drinking related stimuli: Effects of relaxation instructions.* Paper presented at the annual meeting of the Association for Advancement of Behavior Therapy, New York.

Strickler, D. P., Dobbs, S. O., & Maxwell, W. A. (1979). The influence of setting on drinking behavior: The laboratory versus the barroom. *Addictive Behaviors, 4,* 339–344.

Sturgis, E. T., Best, C. L., & Calhoun, K. S. (1977). The relationship of self-reported assertive behavior to alcoholism. *Scandinavian Journal of Behavior Therapy, 6*(4), 126.

Sturgis, E. T., Calhoun, K. S., & Best, C. L. (1979). Correlates of assertive behavior in alcoholics. *Addictive Behaviors, 4,* 193–197.

Suinn, R. M. (1977). *Manual: Anxiety management training.* Unpublished manuscript. (Available from Rocky Mountain Behavioral Science Institute, P.O. Box 1066, Fort Collins, CO 80522)

Tarter, R., Alterman, A., & Edwards, K. (1985). Vulnerability to alcoholism in men: A behavior–genetic perspective. *Journal of Studies on Alcohol, 46*, 329–356.

Tarter, R., & Edwards, K. (1986). Antecedents to alcoholism: Implications for prevention and treatment. *Behavior Therapy, 17*, 346–361.

Thoreson, R. W., & Budd, F. C. (1987). Self-help groups and other group procedures for treating alcohol problems. In M. Cox (Ed.), *Treatment and prevention of alcohol problems: A resource manual* (pp. 157–180). New York: Academic Press.

Trower, P., Yardley, K., Bryant, B. M., & Shaw, P. (1978). The treatment of social failure. *Behavior Modification, 2*, 41–60.

Twentyman, G. T., Greenwald, D. P., Greenwald, M. A., Kloss, J. D., Kovaleski, M. E., & Zibung-Hoffman, P. (1982). An assessment of social skill deficits in alcoholics. *Behavioral Assessment, 4*, 317–326.

Upper, D., & Ross, S. M. (Eds.). (1985). *Handbook of behavioral group therapy.* New York: Plenum.

Vaillant, G. (1983). *The natural history of alcoholism: Causes, patterns, and paths to recovery.* Cambridge, MA: Harvard University Press.

Vannicelli, M. (1982). Group psychotherapy with alcoholics. *Journal of Studies on Alcohol, 43*, 17–39.

Wills, T. A., & Shiffman, S. (1985). Coping and substance use: A conceptual framework. In S. Shiffman & T. A. Wills (Eds.), *Coping and substance use* (pp. 3–24). New York: Academic Press.

Wilson, G. T. (1978). Booze, beliefs and behavior: Cognitive factors in alcohol use and abuse. In P. Nathan, G. Marlatt, & T. Loberg (Eds.), *Alcoholism: New directions in behavioral research and treatment* (pp. 315–339). New York: Plenum.

Wilson, G. T. (1981). Expectations and substance abuse: Does basic research benefit clinical assessment and therapy? *Addictive Behaviors, 6*, 221–231.

Wilson, G. T. (1987). Cognitive processes in addiction. *British Journal of Addiction, 82*, 343–353.

Wilson, G. T. (in press). Alcohol use and abuse: A social learning analysis. In A. Wilkinson & D. Chaudron (Eds.), *Theories of alcoholism.* Toronto: Addiction Research Foundation.

Wilson, G. T., & O'Leary, K. D. (1980). *Principles of behavior therapy.* Englewood Cliffs, NJ: Prentice-Hall.

Wilson, G. T., Perold, E., & Abrams, D. (1981). The influence of attribution of alcohol intoxication on interpersonal interaction patterns. *Cognitive Therapy and Research, 5*, 251–264.

Wittman, M. P. (1939). Developmental characteristics and personalities of chronic alcoholics. *Journal of Abnormal Psychology, 34*, 361–377.

Yalom, I. D. (1974). Group therapy and alcoholism. *Annals of the New York Academy of Sciences, 233*, 85–103.

Yalom, I. D., Block, S., Bond, G., Zimmerman, E., & Qualls, B. (1978). Alcoholics in interactional group therapy. *Archives of General Psychiatry, 35*, 419–425.

Zucker, R. A., & Gomberg, E. S. L. (1986). Etiology of alcoholism reconsidered: The case of a biopsychosocial process. *American Psychologist, 41*, 783–793.

# Index